ANATOMY OF A REGIMENT

Also by Trevor Royle

WE'LL SUPPORT YOU EVER MORE
THE IMPERTINENT SAGA OF SCOTTISH FITBA (with Ian Archer)

JOCK TAMSON'S BAIRNS (ed.)

PRECIPITOUS CITY
The Story of Literary Edinburgh

A DIARY OF EDINBURGH (with Richard Demarco)

EDINBURGH

DEATH BEFORE DISHONOUR:
The True Story of Fighting Mac

THE MACMILLAN COMPANION TO SCOTTISH LITERATURE

JAMES AND JIM: THE BIOGRAPHY OF JAMES KENNAWAY

THE KITCHENER ENIGMA

THE BEST YEARS OF THEIR LIVES

WAR REPORT:
THE WAR CORRESPONDENT'S VIEW OF BATTLE FROM THE
CRIMEA TO THE FALKLANDS

THE LAST DAYS OF THE RAJ

A DICTIONARY OF MILITARY QUOTATIONS

ANATOMY OF A REGIMENT

Trevor Royle

MICHAEL JOSEPH
LONDON

MICHAEL JOSEPH

Published by the Penguin Group
27 Wrights Lane, London W8 5TZ, England
Viking Penguin Inc., 40 West 23rd Street, New York, New York 10010, USA
Penguin Books Australia Ltd, Ringwood, Victoria, Australia
Penguin Books Canada Ltd, 2801 John Street, Markham, Ontario, Canada L3R 1B4
Penguin Books (NZ) Ltd, 182–190 Wairau Road, Auckland 10, New Zealand

Penguin Books Ltd, Registered Offices: Harmondsworth, Middlesex, England

First published 1990

Copyright © Trevor Royle 1990

A CIP catalogue record for this book is available
from the British Library.

Typeset in Monophoto Ehrhardt $11\frac{1}{2}/13\frac{1}{2}$ pt
Printed and bound in Great Britain by
Richard Clay Ltd, Bungay, Suffolk

ISBN 0 7181 3306 4

To the Welsh Guards
1915–1990

Contents

List of Illustrations

23. Jungle communications. Radio operators provide the vital links with patrols dispersed in the Belizean jungle. (*Soldier Magazine*)
24. A patrol carrying the new SA–80 personal weapon. (*Soldier Magazine*)
25. 'We produce a marvellous product . . .' A squad of Scots, Irish and Welsh Guards recruits marches off the square at the Guards Depot, Pirbright.
26. 'Stevo'. W. Stevenson was the first Regimental Sergeant-Major of the Welsh Guards.

Unless otherwise indicated, copyright for illustrations is held by the Welsh Guards.

Foreword

THE WELSH GUARDS celebrate their seventy-fifth anniversary this year. This lively account, by Trevor Royle, of the Regiment since their formation in 1915 illuminates the very full life they have achieved since then. It spans their history from the First World War to the present day and is a fascinating insight into the contemporary life of a Guards Regiment.

The Welsh Guards have never consisted of more than three service Battalions. As they are recruited largely from Wales, there has always been a very strong family feeling in the Regiment which exists to the present day. This is a thread which runs throughout the book and illustrates to anyone the strength of the Regimental System. There is no doubt that the Welsh Guards can be proud of their first seventy-five years. They are very much part of the Household Division and truly reflect and match the standards and ethos of all the other Foot Guards regiments.

As Colonel of the Welsh Guards, I commend this book to anyone with an interest in the Army and anyone who wishes to focus in on the varied life of this, the youngest, Regiment in the Household Division.

Acknowledgements

No book of this kind could have been written without the help and co-operation of the officers, warrant officers, non-commissioned officers and men of the 1st Battalion Welsh Guards. That it was readily and cheerfully given speaks volumes for their professional candour on the one hand, and their very human kindness on the other. They welcomed me into their midst and during the course of several invigorating visits, both in this country and abroad, I was offered nothing but helpfulness and good fellowship. They all have my thanks, and although few have been named I hope that they will recognize in the book's pages the private nature of the debt I owe them.

Most of the interviews were taped and then, with some modest editing, transcribed for use in the book. Many more were the result of private conversations for it was not always practical, or indeed suitable, to tape record every discussion. At all times, though, the interviews were conducted in private and it is to the regiment's great credit that no attempt was made to oversee or to censor my research in any way. In the case of serving members of the battalion no names have been named. This has nothing to do with a wish for anonymity; rather, it is a practical solution to the question of rank. The army never stands still and in the period between my researches and the book's publication many men will have been promoted or will have left the regiment. In the case of retired Welsh Guardsmen, they have been named, although I have respected requests for anonymity.

My first debt is to Lieutenant-Colonel Charles Dawnay who first set the project running as one of the ways in which the Welsh Guards would celebrate their seventy-fifth anniversary in 1990. He was succeeded as Regimental Lieutenant-Colonel by Brigadier Johnny Rickett who proved to be no less enthusiastic and involved. At Headquarters I received kindly advice in arranging interviews and locating photographs and papers from Major Julian Sayers, Major Ken Lewis and WO1 (SC) Peter Richardson. They all gave me such help and encouragement as I shall not readily forget.

If I were to thank individually every serving Welsh Guardsman who helped me with the book the result would be a list of names several hundred long. However, I should be indeed blameworthy if I did not offer a special word of thanks to the battalion's Commanding Officer in 1988 and 1989 Lieutenant-Colonel Paul Belcher and to his Adjutant Captain Hugh Bodington both for their expert guidance and also for their kindness and consideration while I was in their care. I am also grateful to Lieutenant-Colonel Guy

Sayle for his frank comments on the role played by the Welsh Guards during the Falklands War.

I was fortunate in having an army of helpers both within and without the regiment. Of those who have retired from the army but who still think of themselves as Welsh Guardsmen, the following make up my roll-call: Meirion Ellis, G. E. Griffin, J. H. Hughes, Major-General Peter Leuchars, Major Arthur Rees, James Richards, Elwyn Roberts, Major Ivor Roberts, Brigadier Sir Alexander Stanier Bt., Simon Weston. Others who helped with the loan of manuscripts and photographs or who offered advice are: Dr Christopher Dowling, Imperial War Museum; Sir Charles Fraser; Nigel de Lee, Royal Military Academy Sandhurst; S. W. Murray-Threipland; Lieutenant-Colonel Trevor Morris, HQ London District; Meic Stephens, Welsh Arts Council. I also wish to thank the Commandant and his staff at the Guards Depot, Pirbright.

Through the good offices of the Ministry of Defence I received much practical help from the staff of the Directorate of Public Relations (Army) whose head, Brigadier Christopher Wallace, was kind enough to take a personal interest in the project.

I acknowledge with thanks the gracious permission of Her Majesty the Queen to make use of material from the Royal Archives relating to the formation of the Welsh Guards in 1915.

I also acknowledge with thanks permission to include in this volume quotations from Simon Weston, *Walking Tall* (Bloomsbury, 1989).

In such a book a formal bibliography is unnecessary although readers who are interested in the war histories of the Welsh Guards should read the admirable *History of the Welsh Guards* by C. H. Dudley Ward (John Murray, 1920) and *Welsh Guards at War* by L. F. Ellis (Gale and Polden, 1946). Also to be recommended is John Retallack's concise history of the regiment which was published by Leo Cooper in 1981. The written archives of the regiment are held at Regimental Headquarters, Wellington Barracks and special mention should be made of the pioneering work undertaken by Meirion Ellis to collate the most important items. His own privately printed account of his wartime service with the 1st battalion is a model of its kind.

Finally, a word of thanks to '23' who looked after me from the fields of Norfolk to the jungles of Belize and who, in turn, offered me his own views of a remarkable family organization, the Welsh Guards.

Trevor Royle
October 1989

Chapter One

START LINE

THE ROAD FROM Norwich to Thetford drives through the flat part of England. There are few features to tantalize the eye and the surrounding landscape has all the presence of an empty Monopoly board. Among the hidden lanes away from the hustle and bustle of the convoys of heavy traffic things may be different, but, here, on the busy A11 trunk route, Norfolk is no-man's-land. On both sides of the road huge featureless fields stretch into the far distance, grim monuments to the efficient brutality of modern industrialized farming. It's not a pretty sight.

Beside me in the black staff car the young Welsh Guards lance-sergeant softly curses the traffic. 'You know, sir,' he says, 'I once had to drive the CO to a meeting in London. It took one and a half hours to cover twelve miles. The south? It's madness, I tell you.' At the airport he had introduced himself by his surname together with the last two digits of his army number – the usual way of identifying a man in a regiment which contains so many Joneses, Reeses, Williamses and Evanses. He was, he explained, a sarn't by rank. In a Scottish regiment he would have been a sar-junt, in an English regiment a sergeant but the Welsh Guards prefer an abbreviation so softly spoken that it scarcely sounded like a rank at all. Sarn't. He came from Aberystwyth and had been in the regiment for nine years – old enough to have been in the Falklands.

East of Attleborough, a small undistinguished village which straddles the main thoroughfare, the driver pulls off on to a minor road. We have the right of way but ahead of us a truck carrying logs continues its unhurried progress towards us. Politely, but firmly, the sergeant tells the driver to pull over while he passes on the verge. A stream of abuse comes from the cab, although whether this is directed at the soldier's sensible suggestion or at the general presence of the military in the area, it is difficult to say. Eventually the manoeuvre is completed. 'Bloody civilians,' sighs the sergeant as we pull away. 'Never can make up their minds about anything.' Such a failing, he hints, would be impossible in his regiment.

Within a mile or so everything starts to change. The lane – for it deserves no other accolade – is taking us into a landscape that is altogether different from the regimentation imposed on the nearby countryside. This is Ministry of Defence territory, the huge Thetford training area that has been in their hands since the years before the Second World War. It's like taking a journey back in time. The fields are smaller and wilder and are bounded by hedgerows instead of wire fences. Trees – huge elms and stately oaks – grow in the ordered profusion planned for them by their eighteenth-century planters. Ancient farm buildings dot the landscape – all are deserted, though well maintained. The routes through the estate – it is difficult to think of it as a military training area – are trim and well kept, the railings smartly painted, the hedgerows tended by expert hands. This is what the English countryside looked like sixty years ago – long before the men who now use it had been born.

The first blot on this enlightened landscape comes at West Tofts, an unlovely collection of Nissen huts which forms the transit camp for the main training area. 'Those are ours,' says the sergeant as we round a corner and at first the direction of his glance escapes me for he's not referring to the barracks. Then I see them. In the near distance a group of soldiers are walking cautiously through the woodlands. They are all wearing the familiar disruptive pattern combat dress and the newish grp helmet of the British infantryman. On their backs they carry packs and in their hands they carry the SA80, the army's new individual combat weapon. At this distance they could come from any infantry regiment in the British Army.

It's only a few minutes later, at battalion headquarters, that the distinctive gold leek cap badge worn on the khaki berets of a handful of officers reveals the troops' identity as the 1st Battalion of the Welsh Regiment of Foot Guards. A Land Rover draws up in the area which is enclosed under giant elms, and the Commanding Officer jumps out. 'How nice of you to come down here to be with us,' he greets me. 'I do hope you'll enjoy your stay. Now, where would you like to begin?'

Like his men he wears the same distinctive combat dress but his is covered by a slightly superior looking waterproof smock – as happens in all formations of the army, it seems, officers and men like to introduce small details of dress and uniform which they guard fiercely as their own. Succinctly and courteously he provides a brief introduction to the exercise. The battalion has been training in the Thetford area since the previous week. Having disposed of the Leuchars Cup, the annual inter-company march and shoot competition, they are training for real in a home defence exercise against a common enemy; already ten nights have been spent in the open and, as he admits, some of his guardsmen are beginning to look the worst for wear.

'We're not like the Paras or the Gunners, you know,' a disgruntled guardsman tells me before I set off. 'They always get the best stuff as it becomes available, but we're left with the dross.' Morosely he points to his boots, the new issue which came into use after the Falklands War when their predecessors had been found wanting. With the uppers coming away from the moulded soles, they look more like refugees from a Charlie Chaplin movie than a serious piece of military equipment.

A quick walk through the trees leads to the forward positions occupied by The Prince of Wales's Company. Shortly after the regiment's formation the battalion's leading company was named after the King's eldest son; in June 1980 Prince Charles made a further change when he ordered that it should be known as his own company, The Prince of Wales's Company. By tradition it contains the tallest men in the battalion but curiously at Thetford the company commander is towered over by his men – the Welsh Guards do not have a height requirement for officers. He tells me with a smile that by rights he should command 3 Company as they have the shortest men in the battalion and are known, somewhat self-consciously as the 'little iron men'. It comes as no surprise later in the day to find that their company commander is a rangy six-footer. Like most army officers the company commander of Prince of Wales's Company is on his guard in the presence of an outsider. Soldiers tend to be wary of anyone who might represent the 'media' and ever since the Falklands, when the regiment had more than its fair share of hostile criticism, the Welsh Guards have shied away from any form of publicity – or so I had been warned. But any aloofness gives way to polite curiosity as he leads me to the positions occupied by his men – the first, a massive trench dug into the soft loam and chalky Norfolk subsoil. At our approach a sergeant and four men scamper out of the safety of their underground hiding place.

Usually men in forward positions who experience the sharp end of battle form a club which strangers may not join. Their sense of separateness tends to be a mixture of cynical fatalism and an intense pride in their capabilities. Amongst Scots the mood expresses itself as self-conscious aggression, the English are bored or bland or both, but these Welshmen want to talk. I'm probably the first outsider they've seen for days. Taking his cue, the officer excuses himself and moves off but is replaced, disconcertingly, by a tall guardsman with a south London accent. 'We call him the Grenadier,' explains the sergeant. 'But he'll do – his father was in the regiment, you see.' Over ninety per cent of the men in the Welsh Guards come from Wales, the rest from Liverpool or London, but being Welsh, it seems, can also be a state of mind.

In front of their sergeant the platoon are reserved, even taciturn and well they might be for the man who commands them is every inch the image of a Guards' non-commissioned officer, tall, well-built and confident. Behind him are fourteen years of service and he exudes the kind of authority that must terrify the raw recruit – later the Commanding Officer acknowledges that the sergeant is perhaps the hardest man in the regiment. He is a Welsh Guardsman – and proud of it:

> The Paras say they're the best infantry regiment. Well, that's what we say too, but we don't argue about who's second best. The thing is, we're different. We have to do this kind of infanteering but we also have to do public duties. Next week it's back to London to do Queen's Guard. God knows what the other 'chippy' regiments do with their time.

Like all soldiers he believes that his regiment is second to none, but there is another basis for his reasoning – the superior discipline and training of a Guards regiment:

> Of course we have to be better. If we have two roles then it stands to reason that we have to be that much smarter. We're in the public eye and we have to look the part. All the time. It just comes with the job.

His men nod in agreement. Probably they have to, but the subject of public duties has struck an unexpected chord. The Welsh Guards are based at Pirbright, having just spent four years with the British Army of the Rhine in Hohne on the Lüneberg Plain. In London they regularly provide men for ceremonial duties where to most people they are the red-tunicked guardsmen who wear five buttons in two rows, a white-green-white plume in their bearskins and who stand on guard outside the Royal palaces. On a warm October morning in the Norfolk countryside the mention of public duties is an unwelcome reminder of that more familiar role. 'Once you've done one, you've done the lot,' is the consensus view but when I mention this to the company commander later in the day he retorts that his men thought somewhat differently three nights previously when it was raining heavily. 'I never thought I'd see the day when a guardsman would sigh for the pleasures of Queen's Guards!'

Without the subject ever being raised, the topic of discipline is never far away from the conversation. Once upon a time, says the sergeant, a guardsman never thought twice if he was clipped over the ear for doing something wrong. Nowadays, he thinks that the most recent recruits have been mollycoddled at the Guards Depot and are the worse for it. During basic training, for instance, they now wear trainers – horror of horrors – instead of boots and the senior NCOs are frightened to shout at their young charges in case they write to their MPs or take up the complaint with the tabloid press. When he was a young guardsman, he tells me, the common form of punishment in the field was a swift blow to the head with a steel helmet. Just as there are some old boys who like to claim that a beating at school never did *them* any harm, the sergeant feels that short sharp shocks are invaluable aids to maintaining discipline and morale. We're supposed to be soldiers, he says, not schoolgirls.

To clinch his argument he points to four young guardsmen, all new to the battalion, who turned up in the pouring rain without their protective clothing. He shudders at the memory: such a lapse would have been unthinkable a few years ago. And if it had happened in action, in the Falklands, say, they would have been guilty of not only letting themselves down but also the rest of the platoon. Once more the shadow of that conflict flits briefly across the conversation.

Lunch interrupts further talk. This is an agreeable affair which is served inside a largish tent in the battalion headquarters area. Next door, so to speak, the men are queuing up, half-section by half-section, for their hot midday meal. For the officers, it's rather different. Before lunch, drinks are offered outside the tent where a Land Rover armed with wooden mess boxes does duty for a bar. Most of the officers choose soft drinks or squash, drinking tactically for the duration of the exercise. The lunch is melon, beef stroganoff and rice followed by cheese, all served on trestle tables with Windsor Palace place mats and there is wine for the Commanding Officer and his two guests, myself and a visiting Welsh Guards officer from Headquarters London District.

For a fleeting moment the image that comes into focus is from the scene in *Journey's End* when the officers eat fresh chicken and get drunk on champagne after 'Uncle's' death during a trench raid. Outside in the trenches the men eat their bread and cheese and brace themselves for the coming German attack, listening wonderingly to the noise and laughter from the company mess. But then, didn't Sherriff's company commander, Stanhope, chide the young subaltern, Raleigh, for refusing to eat with his brother officers, reminding him that he had to keep aloof from his men in order to command their respect?

Yes, there is something in that conceit, one of the younger captains confides over his orange juice. Still, it does seem to be rather incongruous to be eating such a pleasant meal in the middle of a woodland setting while a training exercise is in full swing, but if it is, then the officers around the table betray no surprise. Sitting next to me is a young officer who discusses the regiment with an aplomb that would seem to be more at home in the mess at Pirbright. He has a degree in history and seems to be faintly surprised by the suggestion that he might be Welsh or have some connection with Wales. Like many of the other officers he joined the regiment by choice, in his case a master at school had the right connections and he had the right stuff to be accepted. Wales could be a foreign country, but, of course, he reassures me, it really is a beautiful place.

'I hope you're not just going to concentrate on us,' he tells me, 'because if you are, then that would give a very false picture of the regiment. The men are the different parts which help to make up the whole picture.' What sort of soldiers are they? And does he know them well? 'They've got a tremendous sense of humour, some wonderful one-liners which really make you laugh. And, yes, I do recognize their national characteristics. When the going is good, there's no better soldier than the Welsh Guardsman. They're tough and tenacious and can overcome adversity. If they have any faults, their heads tend to go down when the weather's bad and they're tired and cold. Then you have to give them a lot of encouragement. But speak to the men. There are things I can't discuss with them because, to a certain extent, I have to stand apart from them and their lives.'

After lunch his remark is given some weight when the Adjutant calls over the company commander of 3 Company and tells him that one of his officers has gone over his limit for guests – next week he will be on Queen's Guard and one of the privileges is to invite guests, close friends or family, to dine in the officers mess at St James's Palace. The young man concerned – a ridiculously young second-lieutenant with a face like a faun and the manner of a much older man – blushes violently and immediately promises 'to do the necessary' when he gets back to Pirbright. All this is conducted in front of the men and it is an object lesson to observe the relationship between them, their company commander and the three platoon commanders, all young second-lieutenants: it is much more relaxed than many other management situations. Afterwards one of the guardsmen chaffs the by now embarrassed second-lieutenant about his rugby playing exploits in a manner that might seem impertinent in the office or on the shop floor.

The real business after lunch, though, is the Commanding Officer's afternoon briefing which takes place under one of the huge elm trees which give cover to the battalion headquarters area. The setting might be sylvan but the atmosphere is redolent of the boardroom or the committee meeting. The exercise has been going well, the colonel reports, but as the weather is good, now is the time to keep the men on their toes. Then follows a detailed change to the general game plan which necessitates the withdrawal of the rifle companies from their forward positions in the early hours of the morning. It is all very business-like and the meeting ends with a flurry of questions: afterwards one of the officers reminds me that these have only been asked because they already knew the answers.

Later in the afternoon, before taking my leave, I take tea with the Commanding Officer in his tent. There is one brief shock of recognition when we realize that we are the same age: sitting in his chair surrounded by his senior officers at the briefing he had seemed much older and wiser. 'It's been a time of great privilege,' he admits cheerfully. 'Somebody once told me that if one is ever made commanding officer one must never consider that one owns the battalion but that it has been entrusted into one's care for a period of two and a half to three years.' How this works out, he says, is a simple matter of understanding that there cannot be privilege without responsibility. 'Providing one truly cares for the people one commands and one truly thinks about the decisions and rulings one makes and one takes careful soundings one is amazed at the support and the backing which one gets from the officers and non-commissioned officers – and support from the guardsmen, too.'

The problems will come when he has to relinquish command in a year or so's time; then the decision will have to be taken – or made for him – to stay in the army or to look elsewhere. The army is changing, he admits, and so, too, is the complexion of his regiment:

> The battalion is full of rather more intelligent people than perhaps would have been the case, ten, fifteen or twenty years ago. To take anybody for granted is to be a fool and the only occasion when I've become angry is when external forces attempt to treat the battalion in an off-hand or thoughtless fashion. Because the British Army today is full of very talented, dedicated and infinitely more intelligent and versatile people than I think was probably the case before, to treat them as they might have been treated during the days of National Service would be the views of a fool.

For the Commanding Officer the most refreshing shift in that wind of change has been the introduction of a more liberal process of officer selection. Gone are the artificial criteria, he says, the emphasis on wealth and breeding: the Welsh Guards now cast their net very widely indeed. 'We're rather more enlightened now and we're certainly tackling it in a more intelligent fashion – we will basically take any young man as an officer if we feel we would like him to work with us or, as important, if he feels happy with us.'

Such a sensible point of view might appear to be at odds with the fun of military myth-making. By tradition the Guards regiments have always taken their officers from a narrow selection of men – an upper-class elite who come from similar backgrounds and who have been educated at the country's leading public schools. Guards officers are supposed to be gentlemen, whatever the circumstances, to be slightly eccentric and they know that they should never take their work too seriously. They are also supposed to govern their lives by a code of behaviour that might seem slightly odd to the outsider. For example, the blushing young second-lieutenant solemnly informed me that whilst in London he was forbidden to travel on public transport or to carry a package from a shop. When he carried an umbrella it was to remain unfurled whatever the weather and off duty he was not to wear casual clothes in public, quite a drawback for a young man looking for fun and a good time in the capital. Not only that, he added mournfully, but baked beans were never served at breakfast.

How wonderful it would be if that were all true and if myth and reality could become one! The young man stood in grave danger of creating a Guards officer who was more stock caricature than genuinely rounded character with all the virtues and failings of common humanity. Later his company commander was to be quite cross when he heard about this harmless piece of wishful thinking. 'I think there is a rule about when you wear your Brigade tie, but nobody ever seems to know what it is. Certainly all the rules about going on the underground and things went out ages ago. I don't think that people would stick to such blimpish rules nowadays – everyone I know in the Welsh Guards leads a life very similar to their civilian counterparts.'

Having taken the precaution of discussing the Welsh Guards with officers and men in other regiments of the British Army I found that while they might be occasionally exasperated by the Brigade's aloofness they were not unamused by the guardsmen's different behaviour and outlook. Regimental spirit is extremely strong in the infantry, they warned, and the individual Guards regiments are all very different from each other. Just as a Lowland Scottish regiment like the Royal Scots hates to be confused with a Highland kilted regiment like the Gordons, so too do the Guards have their own characteristics. The Grenadier and Coldstream Guards are thought to be so grand that they can hardly bring themselves to talk to other people, let alone to each other. The Scots Guards are held to be aloof and lacking in humour while the Irish Guards are hopelessly reckless and daft. By common consent, though, the Welsh Guards are regarded as being quite charming and much less rigid in their ways than their seniors. First impressions confirmed that the officers and men came up to that mark for they were indeed courteous and charming to a fault, with an unstated politeness that seems almost oriental.

But here, seemingly, is a conundrum. When performing ceremonial duties in London the red-tunicked Welsh Guardsman in the sentry box is as familiar a symbol as roast beef or the Tower of London. To people the world over he, and the guardsmen of the other regiments of the Guards Division, says 'Britain' in a way that few other advertising symbols can and if he did not exist then the British Tourist Authority would be hard-pressed to find a substitute. Yet the Welsh Guards are also an elite regiment, a highly motivated and cohesive fighting unit whose emphasis is on physical fitness and mental toughness. Once trained, the officers and men – all from different backgrounds – consider themselves to be not only different from, but superior to, other formations of the British Army. The Parachute Regiment would dispute the claim but the tough sergeant in The Prince of Wales's Company had expressed it in so many words: even if it were not true, the Welsh Guards certainly seem to regard themselves as a different species of soldier. The link between the ceremonial duties, therefore, and the battalion's operational role was obviously going to be one key to understanding what made the regiment tick.

A first clue, by no means complete, but a realistic observation, was provided by a platoon commander who took me to one side to point out his wireless operator asleep in a trench. 'Things haven't changed that much as far as the infantry is concerned. Take away the modern gear and that could be a scene straight from the Western Front during the First World War.' In fact, it could have been a scene from any war in which infantrymen have fought.

Even during an exercise, when conditions are bound to be easier than those experienced in actual warfare, sustained operations take their toll on the men. Some of the guardsmen complain that the equipment issued to them is second-rate but the real answers begin and end with the men themselves. In the field they are far from the familiar environment of London or Pirbright, living in conditions which civilians might find difficult to tolerate – sleeping rough, existing on compo rations and among the unavoidable intimacies of army life. Here, on exercise, the gulf between the red tunics and burnished boots of Horse Guards Parade and the dirt and squalor of trench life must be difficult to bridge. But as the Welsh Guards constantly remind themselves, they are first and foremost operational soldiers, in this case a Type B infantry battalion which is employed primarily for home defence. They might have trucks and Land Rovers at their disposal but, generally in this role, they march into action.

As the young officer reminded me, his position in the field could have been a scene from the Somme and his guardsmen were proving their worth as footsloggers and diggers. In short, they are traditional infantrymen whose behaviour at Thetford would be recognized by any old soldier who has served in the British Army since 1914.

From the mock battlefields of Norfolk the shift to the elegant confines of Wellington Barracks is not just a matter of miles. The leap has to be made in the mind too for this is an imposing place. From Birdcage Walk the buildings shelter behind discreet lime trees and iron railings but they still manage to present a noble façade to the rest of the world. A parade ground stands in front where guardsmen – incongruous in drab barrack dress and bearskins – are put through their paces and the sound of military music is never far away but it is the grandeur of the buildings themselves which holds the imagination. They were first built as barracks for the Guards in 1834 and since that date they have been through many changes. During the Second World War, on 18 June 1944, the nearby Guards Chapel was hit by a flying bomb which killed 121 people during morning service; it was rebuilt in 1963 and its modern design became a template for the reconstruction of the whole area. By the 1980s Wellington Barracks had been completely rebuilt to a modern design which in many respects looks more like an international hotel than a military establishment. However, the façade of the old barracks was retained while behind stands the ultra-modern barrack blocks which jut out on to Petty France. It is here that the Welsh Guards, in common with the other regiments of the Guards Division, have their regimental headquarters.

The offices of the Welsh Guards stand at the west end of the block, the last in line, thus reflecting their order of precedence within the Guards Division. It is manned by a small but efficient staff headed by an impressive gentleman who is known as the Regimental Lieutenant-Colonel, a serving officer of the regiment who is responsible for the general administration of the Welsh

Guards. (Until 1989 this was a full-time appointment, as it had been since 1915; cutbacks in defence expenditure have since reduced this to a serving senior officer with a full-time job elsewhere in the army who now comes in from time to time and directs regimental policy from afar.) His number two is another serving officer, the Regimental Adjutant and the other senior post is the Superintending Clerk, held by a warrant officer. They are backed up by a retired officer as Assistant Regimental Adjutant and a team of clerks and secretaries. Headquarters also houses the regiment's Director of Music and the Band Sergeant Major and his assistant.

Inside the headquarters building the ambience is a curious mixture of gentlemen's club and Ministry of Defence austerity. No doubt it is meant to be for here are brought together the different roles which the Welsh Guards are expected to play within the British Army. The office used by the Regimental Lieutenant-Colonel looks out on to the parade ground and Birdcage Walk; it is comfortably furnished, all leather armchairs and polished woodwork with a decanter of sherry on the sidetable, while next door the main office rings to the sound of metal cupboards and vinyl floors. For the potential officer this might be his first encounter with the Welsh Guards. It is in this office, with its paintings of former glories, that he will be interviewed for the first time, probably while he is still a schoolboy, and if he is accepted it is here that the progress of his career will be recorded. Should he wish to marry while still a serving officer in the regiment he will have to make a formal request to the Regimental Lieutenant-Colonel and it is in this office that he will be interviewed before permission is given. The days are long past when a fiancée had to be vetted by the officers mess but in the Welsh Guards the courtesies are still observed.

In the early days of the regiment's existence a strong Regimental Headquarters was essential to the Welsh Guards' well-being and future prosperity. As was the case with the other regiments of Foot Guards it provided a solid foundation for the regiment's administration and a nerve centre for its recorded history. It was once possible, for example, to read the records of everyone who had served in the Welsh Guards or who was currently serving in the regular battalion. This was a tradition closely guarded by the Welsh Guards for it was one of the props which kept them separate from the rest of the army. Like any other elite force the Welsh Guards have tried to keep many of their peculiarities intact but in recent years the growing professionalism within the army has meant that many of their privileges have been whittled away. Although Regimental Headquarters still has a large say in planning the careers of Welsh Guardsmen its records have been removed to the infantry manning centre at York. Nevertheless, as the Regimental Lieutenant-Colonel was at pains to explain, Regimental Headquarters still preserves many of the usages that make the Welsh Guards different from other infantry regiments in the British Army:

> Regimental Headquarters is responsible for running the regiment and is the back-up for everything which goes on outside command of the 1st Battalion. It is particularly responsible for the career planning of all officers and all warrant officers and senior NCOs; it is responsible for people moving outside the battalion and coming back again; it is responsible for all regimental property, recruiting, and the Association, and all Welsh Guards regimental matters.

Given the responsibilities which fall upon him, the role of the Regimental Lieutenant-Colonel is crucial. During the seventy-five years of its existence not a period of Welsh Guards history has passed without reference being made to the importance of having a secure base at Regimental Headquarters. During the Second World War, for example, the Regimental Lieutenant-Colonel, Colonel R. E. K. 'Chicot' Leatham, demonstrated a masterly ability to place officers in the battalion which best suited them, the 2nd Welsh Guards having started training as an armoured reconnaissance battalion. Why the Regimental Lieutenant-Colonel should occupy such a powerful position is largely a matter of tradition:

> Historically the Regimental Lieutenant-Colonel runs the regiment on behalf of the Colonel. In the old days the Colonel raised the regiment and ran it, but over the years that's ceased to be the case and the Regimental Lieutenant-Colonel is a professional soldier who's responsible for the day-to-day running of the regiment. He's the link with the Colonel and as such he deals with the Prince of Wales's office and asks whether he can become involved in various aspects at occasions which we think would be suitable.

In other words, this imposing gentleman represents the Colonel who is at present Prince Charles, the Prince of Wales. Previous

Royal Colonels have been the Duke of Edinburgh and Edward VIII when he, too, was the Prince of Wales. The regiment's Colonels-in-Chief have always been the sovereign of the day. All around the Regimental Headquarters there are reminders of the Royal connection, reinforcing the concept that this is a Household regiment with a close connection to the Royal Family. A signed photograph of King Edward VIII while the Prince of Wales, looking somewhat wistful and forlorn, the Duke of Edinburgh purposeful in ceremonial dress and a fine portrait of the present Prince of Wales shortly after his appointment as Colonel in 1975.

The Prince of Wales takes a great deal of interest in his regiment of Foot Guards, not as much perhaps as his great-uncle who, I was told, used to wander into Wellington Barracks looking for company, but enough to make his more than an honorary appointment. When the battalion was in Germany he made a point of visiting them, he involved himself in the care of Falklands wounded and recently, marrying his architectural interests to his formal position as Colonel of the Welsh Guards, he inspected the married quarters at Pirbright which were showing signs of deterioration and disrepair. Most spectacularly of all, perhaps, he walked to the top of Snowdon with the badly wounded Welsh Guards survivors of the Caterham pub blast of 1975. One of their number, Guardsman Thomas, had lost both legs and an arm yet with their Colonel each man struggled for the last two hundred yards to the summit unaided. He is also known to be keen to use the regimental connection to promote good works. Should a commercial concern, for example, wish to sponsor a polo match involving the Welsh Guards and the Prince of Wales he will ask for a substantial 'appearance' sum to be donated to the charity of his choice. For the Regimental Lieutenant-Colonel this is a matter of ensuring that the right sponsor is matched with the right occasion and in a world which is becoming increasingly alive to the mutual benefits of sponsorship the Welsh Guards have had to enter the field just like any other organization.

The closeness of Regimental Headquarters to Buckingham Palace, the regular mounting of the Queen's Guard, the bright ceremonial uniforms and the hint of martial music are all very potent reminders of the Welsh Guards' Royal connections. Their long established function as the sovereign's personal Welsh escorts might have been overtaken by circumstances but it is still cherished by tradition. (The actual task of providing security to the Royal

Family has passed to the police.) It would be impossible, though, to visit Regimental Headquartes and not to be reminded that the Welsh Guards are Household troops. They do of course have an operational role – I had seen them being put through their paces at Thetford – but when stationed in London District their main purpose is ceremonial, albeit they take their turn on Spearhead (operational standby for duty anywhere in the world) and other operational tasks required of them. Make no mistake, a major had remarked in his dug-out in the Norfolk countryside, these ceremonial duties are important, both as a point of pride for the British people and as a spectacle for the tourists. And yes, he continued, he has never hesitated to allow himself to be photographed with a Japanese family while wearing tunic and bearskin. Indeed, it has been suggested, jokingly of course, that the Welsh Guards would be much better off if their public duties were privatized with tourists paying for the privilege of watching them.

And yet, for all that a sense of timelessness pervades the headquarters at Wellington Barracks, the Welsh Guards have had to move with the times – even if the general forward progression has not always been to their liking. The Regimental Lieutenant-Colonel can promise all Welsh Guardsmen that they will remain in the regiment, come what may, but in today's cost-conscious army this well tried custom is now being put under some pressure. When the Welsh Guards came back from Hohne they left behind in Germany thirty-four of their number with the Scots Guards, a regiment which faces perennial difficulties with recruiting. True, they will continue to wear the leek cap badge but for the Superintending Clerk, it could be the thin end of the wedge:

> I believe in regimental integrity and loyalty to the regiment and to the family values of the regiment. The Welshness of the Welsh Guards is of paramount importance; though some, perhaps, might disagree. For the last couple of years I've seen the Superintending Clerk's post – which is the pinnacle of the clerical career in the regiment – lose its importance. I've seen untouchable areas being nibbled away by the Ministry of Defence. I never thought I'd see a part-time Regimental Lieutenant-Colonel and I never thought I'd see Welsh Guards serving in the Scots Guards.

This is a true son of the regiment speaking. His father was a well respected warrant officer in the Welsh Guards and although he tried a civilian job after leaving school the pull of the 'family' proved to be too strong. He joined the Welsh Guards when he was in his early twenties, never an easy route for an intelligent young man to take because many of the training routines may seem over rigorous or just plain silly. There were times, he admits, when he felt like throwing in the towel but the NCOs who had known his father, far from giving him a harder time in time-honoured fashion, encouraged him to stick with it. He also found himself digging deep into the lore, learnt from childhood, that this is a family regiment which not only helps and encourages its sons but draws them into its fold. His career took him into clerking and his ambition to the post of Superintending Clerk, which gives him an important over-view of the NCOs and warrant officers who make up the battalion's middle management:

> I suppose you could equate me in an outside organization with the company secretary. I run our regimental accounts which consists of a central fund and an investment pool and trustees set-up. I'm also the general secretary of our Association and in an advisory capacity I look after the careers of the warrant officers, company sergeant-majors and clerks.

Now at the top of his career the next stage is a commission – a prospect he views with equanimity. Go down to the Sergeants' Mess at Pirbright, he recommends, and you will see some of the biggest changes that have taken place in the Welsh Guards in recent years. Not so long ago the senior sergeants were much older than they are now and they were probably much more forbidding – and less professional. Ten pints of beer a man was not uncommon at lunch time and CSMs were rarely seen in the afternoon; now they dig in on exercises and keep as fit as their men. They have to if they want to make any progress in today's army. 'A marked change is the professionalism in everybody in the battalion and it's a younger outfit than when I first joined it. People are more ambitious than they used to be and there's more cut and thrust. They're much more aware of where they're going and if they don't get it they're not as contented as they would have been in the past.'

With more officers leaving the army at the rank of captain – the Welsh Guards like many other infantry regiments lost many of its younger men to the city in the aftermath of 'Big Bang' – not a few

NCOs see more possibilities for their promotion to commissioned rank. After all, they say, they have the experience: just because they lacked the ambition or the education to apply for a commission in their younger days is no reason to prevent them from making the transition later. As the Superintending Clerk's leather-bound book of promotions shows, very few Welsh Guardsmen have been commissioned from the ranks but things may have to change if the regiment is to remain the same. (This radical view is not shared by everyone in the Welsh Guards, certainly not by one of the captains I had met at Thetford. 'Some of the less mature ones at times think that they can do it all but actually it's amazing – even with the older ones – when something serious happens you suddenly find that all eyes are pointing inwards.')

To be sure, says the Superintending Clerk, there is a certain dichotomy at work here. On the one hand many people regret that the regiment is changing, that its jealously guarded privileges are being whittled away, and they fear that the Welsh Guards might just become like any other infantry regiment in the British Army. On the other hand some of the changes are only signs of the times. As the army has become more professional so too have the Welsh Guards and the Commanding Officer's ideals of no privilege without responsibility could become its watchword as the regiment approaches the last decade of the twentieth century. In such a brave new world, I was told many times, there is no room for Colonel Blimp or for the twits who would follow him to hell and back.

'Oh yes, it's changed – and for the better.' The Regimental Sergeant-Major eyes the Saturday afternoon bar in the Sergeants' Mess with a fair degree of satisfaction. The air is thick with Welsh voices, soon they will be singing he says, as all Welshmen will do when they are maudlin, and their voices will be joined by the handful of members from the Welsh Guards Association who are visiting the battalion for the weekend. 'When I joined up you did a lot of public duties, a lot of guards, and we used to go on exercises only occasionally, three weeks in Wales or Otterburn or wherever. But there wasn't so much happening. There wasn't so much commitment as a regiment to the military system. Now it's all about fitness and technical skills and officers going for runs with their men.'

His company sergeant-majors agree. Look, they say, there's the mortar platoon just back from Cyprus and people are always going off on courses or schemes. 'We're a far more professional army than we were when I first joined,' agrees one. 'There's a hell of a lot more commitment, so more work has to be done out of hours. And in that respect I suppose some of the fun has gone out of the army.'

Maybe. There is certainly less drinking in the army than there was twenty years ago – the drink-drive laws and a new emphasis on healthy living have seen to that – but the Welsh Guards' Sergeants' Mess is still a lively enough place on a winter's afternoon. The members of the mess have gathered together to honour the regiment's first holder of the Victoria Cross. Sergeant Robert Bye, who won the nation's highest honour for valour during the Battle of Passchendaele (Third Ypres) in the summer of 1917. Born in Pontypridd in 1889 Bye enlisted in the Welsh Guards in April 1915; he was promoted lance-corporal in March 1916, corporal six months later and sergeant in April 1917. In the first stages of the battle, following a tremendous artillery attack on the German lines, the Welsh Guards led the 3rd Guards Brigade's attack on the left of the divisional front. (The assault itself was made to the north of the Ypres salient.) The early advance was soon halted by heavy machine-gun fire from a hidden wooded position and from a blockhouse which had escaped unhurt the allied barrage – the *London Gazette* of 6 September 1917 takes up the story:

On 31st July 1917 Sergeant Robert Bye displayed the utmost courage and devotion to duty during an attack on the enemy's position. Seeing that the leading waves were being troubled by two enemy blockhouses, he, on his own initiative, rushed at one of them and put the Garrison out of action. He then rejoined his Company and went forward to the assault of the second objective.

When the troops had gone forward to the attack on the third objective, a party was detailed to clear up the line of blockhouses which had been passed.

Sergeant Bye volunteered to take charge of this party and took many prisoners. He subsequently returned to the third objective, capturing a number of prisoners, thus rendering invaluable assistance to the assaulting Companies.

He displayed throughout the most remarkable initiative.

To honour him seventy years later the Sergeants' Mess has commissioned a painting of Bye in action, throwing a bomb at the first blockhouse amidst the mud of the Ypres salient. It was unveiled by the sergeant's granddaughter in front of the mess members and many other members of the Bye family who had driven down from the Midlands for the occasion – after the war Bye had been forced to find work as a collier in the Nottinghamshire coalfields. Also present is a Bye of a younger generation – a great-grandson who joined the Welsh Guards six weeks earlier. Still a recruit at the Guards Depot, he is shyly aware of the honour that is being bestowed on his family by the regiment – and of the privilege which allows him to enter the hallowed ground of the Sergeants' Mess.

The Regimental Sergeant-Major looks on approvingly. The mess is his domain, he makes the rules, he gives it its character, in all matters governing its welfare he makes the final decision. That is as it should be:

> I'm President of the Sergeants' Mess, I'm responsible for people's behaviour here but really I'm only a figurehead. The mess technically runs itself and it's run democratically. Provided there's a proposer and a seconder and it's not an impractible proposition I'll try to abide with what everybody else wants. But I sort the place out, as I said, I'm the figurehead here.

The atmosphere might smack of a social club in a South Wales village or in one corner, among the younger lance-sergeants, of a boisterous rugby club bar but there is one big difference. Whereas unruly behaviour in a 'social' or in the rugby club after a match might be forgiven as a necessary evil, here in the Sergeants' Mess of the Welsh Guards it would be a cardinal sin. Because the mess is open to lance-sergeants – who would be corporals in any other regiment – senior sergeants cannot afford to drop their guard in front of men they might have to command the following day. 'The standards of behaviour must be impeccable and, of course, you must have standards of dress,' he warns. 'I might relax the rules slightly on a Friday night and allow them to wear casual wear, but basically this is a collar and tie estabishment – and there's no getting away from that.'

The sad thing about it all, admits the RSM, is that occasions like the Bye reception are fast becoming the exception at weekends. Nowadays few sergeants live in the mess and, indeed, many of his colleagues have bought houses in Wales. This is something of an innovation for most of his predecessors, all Welshmen and proud of it, have settled in the London area after leaving the army. Not now though. It is the done thing to own your home in Wales: some commute to Pirbright from the valleys on a weekly basis, others let them and keep them as a bulwark against retirement. All this is quite a change from the old days when a young lad from Wales joined the regiment, lived with the regiment and when he went home on leave wore his red-tunicked uniform:

> We always had two tunics, you see, best number one and number two tunic. You wore your number two tunic for walking out and kept the other for parades and ceremonial duties. And in those days you used to carry a short cane as well, a swagger cane, and it was great to see the Welsh Guardsmen walking out in pairs, carrying themselves smartly and showing themselves off in their red tunics.

It was the Welsh Guards uniform worn by an older man in the same village that had prompted this former RSM to join the regiment in 1933 – that, and the fact that his father only received 2s. a week dole as an unemployed miner. In the Welsh Guards the pay was 2s. a day (less stoppages) and within a year he had doubled it to 3s. 3d. a day by being promoted lance-corporal. Much has happened in the intervening years to alter the character of the average Welsh Guardsman and he cites the litany of change: the ending of church parades, permission to walk out in civilian clothes, the introduction of stay-bright buttons and the abolition of unnecessary bull, better pay and prospects for promotion, better food and living conditions like those expected in civilian life. Some things, though, remain as strong as they were in his day when he joined the Welsh Guards over fifty years ago:

> Oh, there was a wonderful spirit. One thing I'd say about the regiment – and this goes back from the early days to today – it's more of a family group. Although we had – and still have, I see – strict discipline, there's always the feeling that if a chap was down then someone would always go and help him. Also, if it were necessary the regiment would go and help his family – I know a number of people, wives who lost their husbands, and the regiment took care of them at all times.

Family. Again and again the conversation drifted back to the idea of family, of belonging to an organization which provides young men with a sense of pride and security, a Welsh regiment for Welshmen. Between them the two RSMs covered almost half a century of service and over the years it was the sense of family which provided the point of connection between two very different military careers. People outside the army might smile at the idea of group loyalties and team spirit but have they evolved an alternative which can help a group of men through good times and bad? The Welsh Guardsman of today may take only a passing interest in the exploits of Sergeant Bye, but who is to say that the perpetuation of his military reputation does not act as a spur when things get tough or if he is in a tight corner? It's not a particularly logical idea but, tried and tested over the years, it would be difficult to gainsay it.

'You see, it's the way we feel about the regiment that counts,' claimed the retired RSM. 'The other day somebody said to me, "Oh, you were in the Welsh Guards, then?" I just said, "I am a Welsh Guardsman." Just like that, automatically. You're a Welsh Guardsman whether you're serving or retired. You always feel part of the Welsh Guards.'

Understand that, they told me, and you will have gone a long way to understand us.

Chapter Two

THE LIFE OF A REGIMENT

ON 29 MAY 1660 King Charles II returned to London to be restored to the throne of Great Britain. Among the excited spectators who watched the King's triumphant procession through the streets of the capital was the diarist John Evelyn. 'I stood in the Strand and beheld it and blessed God,' he noted. 'And all this was done without one drop of blood shed, and by that very army which had rebelled against him.' Evelyn was referring to the fact that the instrument of Charles' return had been the troops commanded by General George Monck, a former Commonwealth commander who had decided to declare his hand for the authority vested in the Crown.

The soldiers he commanded – the Coldstream Regiment, formed out of elements of Fenwick's and Heslrige's regiments – were the last formations of the New Model Army, a standing professional force which had been created and kept in being by a military junta. As such the Army had been feared and resented for it lacked constitutional authority and owed its allegiance solely to the Commonwealth leaders. Once Charles had returned to the throne the Convention Parliament resolved to disband the New Model Army by passing the Act for Speedy Disbanding. The cost to the Exchequer was £858,818.8s.10d. but as the Secretary of State observed it was well worth it: 'so long as the soldiery continued there would be a perpetual trembling in the nation, for they are inconsistent with the Happiness of any Kingdom'.

As events were to prove, though, the complete disbandment of the nation's armed forces was not to be such a simple task. It had been agreed that Charles should have a personal bodyguard, formed perhaps out of those members of his entourage who had kept him company in exile, but when a minor insurrection led by a lunatic called Venner took place in January 1661, the dispersement of the armed forces was halted. The revolt was suppressed by Monck's Coldstream Regiment which was ordered to be kept in being and immediate steps were taken to regularize the King's guard. It is from this period that the British Regular Army traces its origins.

The first stage was the reorganization of the household troops who had returned to London with the King: by Royal proclamation on 26 January 1661 two troops of horse guards and two regiments of foot guards were brought into being – the King's Own Troop of Lifeguards, the Duke of York's Troop of Lifeguards and two Royal Regiments of Foot Guards. Four years later the foot guards amalgamated to become the regiment known as the First, or Grenadier, Guards. Today, the horse guards are known as the Life Guards.

From the very outset these household troops were regarded as personal guards to the King and his family; in peace they would act as a police force in London and in time of war they would be the nucleus of an expanded army. In that way parliament hoped to check the growth of a standing army and to protect the civil liberties which had been infringed by Cromwell and his major-generals. In a symbolic gesture, Monck's men laid down their arms on Tower Hill on 14 February 1661 and then picked them up again in the service of the King, thus reinforcing the idea that they were the sovereign's personal escort and bodyguards. They became the Lord General's Regiment of Foot Guards, once the pride of the New Model Army but from that moment onwards, the King's loyal servants. Today they are known as the Coldstream Guards. At the same time a further horse guards regiment, the Royal Regiment of Horse, was formed out of the Earl of Oxford's Regiment of Horse: in time it came to be known as the Royal Horse Guards which amalgamated with the 1st Dragoons in 1969 to become the Blues and Royals.

Of the regiments of foot guards, the Grenadier Guards claim precedence over the Coldstream Guards because they were originally a Royal regiment. The Scots Regiment of Foot Guards was also formed in 1661, its task being to guard the royal castles of Edinburgh, Stirling and Dumbarton. It was brought on to the English establishment in 1685 and is third in order of precedence, even though the regiment dates its formation to 1642 when King Charles I raised a regiment for service in Ireland. By the end of the seventeenth century the five regiments of Household troops had become a caste apart, mainly because of their Royal duties, but also because they were quite separate from the growing number of line infantry regiments such as the Royal Regiment of Foot (The Royal Scots), the Queen's Regiment or Prince George of Denmark's Regiment (The Buffs).

In time of war the foot guards were brigaded together and often companies of the regiments formed composite battalions, particularly of flank or grenadier companies. At home in London they shared Royal ceremonial duties and helped with the policing of the capital. In 1780, for example, the Guards regiments were called upon to fulfill their ordained function as Household troops when they guarded the Royal palaces during the Gordon Riots which began after Lord George Gorden presented a petition to parliament against the Roman Catholic Relief Act of 1778. Gradually a pattern had begun to emerge, one which is recognizable today: the Household troops retained the particular privilege of guarding the Royal family while in time of war they were given an operational role, often at the head of the army's order of battle. They were regarded – and in turn regarded themselves – as an elite formation which demanded standards of dress, discipline and behaviour which were second to none. Their officers generally came from the country's leading aristocratic and landed families and the men tended to be taller than the soldiers of other regiments. By the middle of the nineteenth century the foot guards regiments had begun to wear the red tunics and bearskins (a reminder of the defeat of the French Old Guard in 1815) which they still don today on ceremonial duties. The Trooping of the Colour, which has its origins in a ceremony of 1749, had become an established part of the London season.

During the Napoleonic wars the Guards regiments had distinguished themselves in the Peninsula and at Waterloo, the closing of the doors at Hougoumont being a particularly gallant action; the Brigade of Guards fought in the Crimea and, later, in the Boer War. Unlike the line infantry regiments, though, which had two battalions each, one to serve abroad and the other to form a depot at home, no Guards regiment ever served in India or the Far East and the only overseas posting available to them was Egypt.

Shortly after the outbreak of the Boer War the first new foot guards regiment to be formed in 240 years came into being when Queen Victoria gave permission for an Irish Regiment of Foot Guards to be raised in 1900 'to commemorate the bravery shown by the Irish regiments in the recent operations in South Africa.' At the time it was suggested that, to complete the national picture, there should also be a Welsh Regiment of Foot Guards. If Ireland and Scotland (with three battalions) could have their own guards regiments, it was argued, then Wales, too, should be equally honoured. The clamour came mainly from the Welsh landed gentry and from a clutch of historians and antiquarians who pointed to the well-known fact that both King Edward I and his son King Edward II had praised the bravery of the Welsh people and that the King's Bodyguard of the Yeomen of the Guard in the time of King Henry VII was composed mainly of Welshmen who were close to the crown. The members of the distinguished Cymmrodorion Society, responsible for forming the National Eisteddfod Society and protecting other Welsh cultural matters, added their voice to the argument and petitioned the Secretary of War, W. St John Brodrick, who viewed the proposal indifferently because he doubted that Wales would be able to supply sufficient recruits. Their actions stimulated the press into joining the campaign and both the *Western Mail* and the *Daily News* published leading articles suggesting that a Welsh Regiment of Foot Guards be formed because if 'acted upon, it would be an incentive (if any such were needed) to the patriotic ardour of Welshmen'. The proposal was even given an airing in the *Household Brigade Magazine* in 1903:

> The Principality at present furnishes a good proportion of stalwart men to the Grenadier Guards, and although it might be necessary to lower the standard of height measurement in comparison with that observed in the other Regiments, it is certain that a Corps of Welsh Guards would attract a large number of suitable recruits. Ireland was given a Corps of Guards in part recognition of the bravery of her troops in South Africa and in this one regard at least, Wales is entitled to similar recognition.

Aware that Welsh pride was at stake the Army Council made discreet enquiries of the Royal Welch Fusiliers (23rd Foot) to ask if they might consider transferring to the Brigade of Guards to form a Welsh Regiment of Foot Guards. The proposal was politely declined by this distinguished Welsh line infantry regiment and although the subject continued to be raised at regular intervals in the press, the matter was quietly dropped by the War Office. Indeed, as happens after any war, contraction of the army became the order of the day and the Scots Guards lost their 3rd Battalion in 1906.

With the outbreak of the First World War in August 1914 the opportunity again presented itself to press for the establishment of a Welsh Regiment of Foot Guards. Once more the Welsh gentry was in the vanguard of the movement which began firstly as a series of agitated letters to the Welsh press and then to *The Times* in London. The leading light in the campaign was Captain Henry Erasmus Edward Philipps Bart., of Picton Castle, Haverfordwest. An officer in the Carmarthenshire militia, and a noted landowner who took his civic responsibilities seriously – he was both a JP and a county councillor –Philipps set the hare running with a series of well argued letters to the *Western Mail* and the *South Wales Daily News*. Enlisting the support of other patriotic Welshmen, the leading light being Lord Dynevor, he also corresponded with the War Office and Horse Guards and canvassed the support of Welsh MPs. For his pains he was kept at bay with the dusty response that 'the matter was under the consideration of the Army Council'.

At the time the War Office was learning how to cope with the massive response to Lord Kitchener's appeal for volunteers to join the country's armed forces. Alone among his Cabinet colleagues, Kitchener had predicted that the war would last at least three years and that Britain would require one million men to win it. The result was a professionally organized campaign to raise recruits for the new armies which Kitchener prompted into being: on one day in late August 1914 35,000 men joined up – as many as had been recruited for the whole of 1913 – and by the year's end 1,186,000 men had volunteered from all parts of Britain. Fifty-eight thousand of that number had come from Wales, a part of Britain not normally associated with high levels of recruitment.

Traditionally, Welsh people looked askance at the armed forces as a means of making a living. Quite apart from the abhorrence most Britons entertained for the army, nineteenth-century Nonconformist preachers had taught their congregations to condemn militarism, and in the South Wales mining communities there was active prejudice against the army following intervention by soldiers in miners' strikes before the war. Recruiting in Wales could have presented a problem to the government and the question of forming new and distinguishable Welsh formations might not have become an issue had it not been for the intervention of David Lloyd

George. In the Queen's Hall in London on 19 September 1914 he addressed the newly raised London Welsh battalion, praised their enthusiasm and broached the idea of establishing a separate Welsh Army Corps. His suggestion, together with a demand for the provision of Nonconformist chaplains for the Welsh troops, caused what Asquith called 'a royal row' when the Cabinet met on 28 October. Kitchener angrily told his colleagues that he would resign rather than sanction such a move. Privately he told the Prime Minster that he was not being xenophobic in reaching such a conclusion; rather he was prompted by his own military experience which told him that 'no purely Welsh regiment is to be trusted: they are always wild and insubordinate and ought to be stiffened by a strong infusion of English and Scotch.'

Having been so long out of the country Kitchener failed to understand either the strength of Lloyd George's position or his passionate mixture of Welsh nationalism and religious non-conformism. He could not see any reason why Welshmen should be treated separately. Asquith managed to curb Kitchener's temper and to placate Lloyd George, but it was only a temporary truce. Two days later the row erupted again when it was revealed to the Cabinet that Welsh soldiers had been forbidden to speak Welsh, even in private. Once again Kitchener failed to recognize the powerful emotions involved: he repeated to Asquith his estimation of Welsh military worth and warned that it could be a matter for resigning. At the Cabinet meeting, though, he decided to back down in the face of Lloyd George's arguments, a tactical retreat that temporarily patched up the quarrel. Three days later he appointed a Welsh protégé, Colonel Owen Thomas, to be the general commanding in North Wales, thus moving his opponent to admit that 'he [Kitchener] is a big man & what is more does things in a big way'. It was also agreed that the 38th Division was to be designated a Welsh division and that a Welsh Liberal MP Ivor Phipps would be given command. This gave Lloyd George especial satisfaction as one of his sons was appointed Phipps' ADC.

Kitchener had been forced to back down over the Welsh recruiting issue largely because he faced a powerful and persuasive political opponent in Lloyd George. After the Cabinet meeting of 28 October he also decided that it was too slight a matter to warrant so much of his time and energy. When he came to deal with the subsidiary matter of the proposals for the Welsh Guards Kitchener was to take a more reasonable attitude mainly because by the end of 1914 King George V had taken a direct interest in the idea. Throughout his period as Secretary of State for War, which lasted until his untimely death in June 1916, Kitchener enjoyed a particularly close relationship with the King. There were weekly audiences to discuss the war's progress and through the King's private secretary Lord Stamfordham Kitchener had open access to the Crown; in turn King George V had always taken an active interest in Kitchener's career and when the occasion demanded was able to offer him Royal protection – as he did in 1915 during a crisis in ammunition production when there were calls for Kitchener's resignation.

The exact moment when the idea of forming a Welsh Regiment of Foot Guards was discussed by the two men must remain a matter for conjecture as neither the King nor Kitchener left a written record. However, given the timing of events at the beginning of 1915 it would seem that the subject might have been raised at one of the four weekly meetings held in January. On 4 February 1915 King George V noted in his diary after a visit by train to Salisbury Plain to inspect the Canadian Division that he had used the opportunity to have 'a talk with Lord K';* this followed 'a long talk' after tea at Buckingham Palace on 23 January when one of the subjects must have been the formation of the Welsh Guards. During the course of the 'talk' the King seems to have suggested that the raising of a Welsh Regiment of Foot Guards would be 'a good thing': characteristically, Kitchener seems to have taken the suggestion as an order to proceed, for according to the evidence of Major-General Sir Francis Lloyd, commanding the London Division, the following exchange took place in Kitchener's office on 6 February:

> LORD KITCHENER, very abruptly: 'You have got to raise a regiment of Welsh Guards.'
> SIR FRANCIS LLOYD: 'Sir, there are a great many difficulties in the way which I should like to point out first.'
> LORD KITCHENER, very rudely: 'If you do not like to do it someone else will.'
> SIR FRANCIS LLOYD: 'Sir, when do you want them?'
> LORD KITCHENER: 'Immediately.'
> SIR FRANCIS LLOYD: 'Very well, sir; they shall go on guard on St David's Day.'

* RA King George V's Diary 4 February, 23 January 1915.

As an experienced Guards officer – and a well-known Welshman – Lloyd probably realized that he could raise a regiment by St David's Day from Welsh soldiers already serving in the Brigade of Guards and from the growing number of recruits in Wales. It might be a time-consuming exercise but he himself had allowed a decent period – six weeks – to accomplish his promise. The meeting probably did take place just as Lloyd recorded it for Kitchener was famous for the abruptness of his decision making. When General Sir Ian Hamilton was given command of the Gallipoli expedition a month later Kitchener summoned him into his room and said in a matter of fact way, 'We are sending a military force to support the fleet now at the Dardanelles and you are to have command.' Hamilton had served on Kitchener's staff during the Boer War and as he admitted later his boss expected him to carry out the order without further ado as if he had been given it on the veldt and not in Whitehall.

Lloyd's first task was to appoint a suitable officer to command both the battalion and regimental headquarters and his choice fell on an officer whom Kitchener had already recommended – William Murray-Threipland, Grenadier Guards. There were two good reasons for choosing him: he was an experienced officer who knew the ways of the Brigade of Guards, and, secondly, he had served under Kitchener in the Sudan campaign of 1898 and later during the Boer War. Like all successful generals Kitchener took a particular interest in the officers who had served him loyally while he was making his name.

It would be unfair, though, to place the whole credit for Murray-Threipland's preferment on his professional relationship with Kitchener. He was an able officer, well respected by his colleagues and he had the temperament and the energy to set about the difficult task of raising a new regiment from scratch. Before the appointment of Lord Harlech as Regimental Lieutenant-Colonel in June, Murray-Threipland was charged with the administration of the regiment and the command of the battalion, no mean task. One of his first appointments, Lieutenant J. A. D. Perrins, recalled that Murray-Threipland, a Scot from the Borders, was well equipped, both mentally and physically, to cope with the difficulties that, inevitably, would lie ahead. Whenever eyebrows were raised about the wisdom of appointing a Scot and a Grenadier to command a Welsh Foot Guards regiment Murray-Threipland would retort that his connections were strong – his wife was Welsh and a Welsh speaker and, besides, he felt that there were natural links between the people of Wales and the people of Scotland, particularly those from the Borders. In any case, as Perrins noted, Murray-Threipland proved time after time that he had the Scottish thrawnness of character to see any task through to the end: 'He was a truly great man, a wonderful organizer and a born trainer of men. From the time he took over the command, the Welsh Guards became the ruling passion of his life. His one thought was how to make the battalion excel, and he expected, and insisted that every officer should be of the same way of thinking.'

Perrins also believed that Murray-Threipland's abilities stemmed from his Scottish ancestry and education, that although he had 'a dour exterior' he was a hard-headed and straightforward soldier who brooked no nonsense in his determination to get things done. His family name was Scott-Kerr of Chatto, Roxburghshire in the Scottish Borders but he changed his name when he succeeded to the estates of Dale and Toftingall in Caithness from his cousin-german Sir Patrick Murray-Threipland of Fingask and Kinnaird. A professional soldier, he had served originally with the 3rd (Militia) battalion of the Black Watch before being commissioned into the Grenadier Guards in 1887. After the Boer War he retired with the rank of captain in 1902 and then held the appointment of commanding officer, 4th (Border) battalion, King's Own Scottish Borderers which was part of the Territorial Force. With the outbreak of war he rejoined the Regular Army and was promoted major with the 4th (Reserve) battalion, Grenadier Guards. At the time of his summons from General Lloyd he was employed in the 'unpleasant duty' of a court martial involving suspected German spies in London.

Having appointed the man he wanted to command the Welsh Guards Kitchener telephoned Stamfordham on 11 February requesting that Murray-Threipland's name be put before the King for his approval. The news started alarm bells ringing at Buckingham Palace, not because King George disapproved of the appointment but because he was astonished that Kitchener had moved so quickly. After discussing the problem with Stamfordham he instructed his private secretary to write to the War Office expressing grave doubts about the wisdom of rushing a new Guards regiment into being:

In continuation of our conversation by telephone, the King did not realize that the somewhat academic discussion as to the possibility of forming a Welsh Regiment of Guards had so rapidly developed into un fait accompli.

On further consideration His Majesty had appreciated the difficulties which he foresees are likely to arise in obtaining the necessary Officers, whether Welshmen or otherwise, in time of peace.*

The King obviously feared that not only would it be difficult to raise a new regiment but that there would also be problems in maintaining its strength in the years to come. From the tone of Stamfordham's letter there is also some polite consternation at the haste with which Kitchener had proceeded, but the King's over-riding concern was that one of his Guards regiments might have problems in attracting suitable recruits. As he pointed out, Colonel Nugent of the Irish Guards had warned in 1912 that his regiment was experiencing grave difficulties in appointing suitable officers because 'it is an unfortunate fact that most Irish gentlemen are not sufficiently well off to afford the expense necessarily entailed by having a Guardsman son.'

That same day Stamfordham repeated the King's fears in an official letter to Major-General Sir F. S. Robb, a member of Kitchener's staff at the War Office:

Before war broke out there was a serious deficiency of Officers in the Brigade of Guards, so much so that about a year and a half ago the King sent for the Colonels of the three Regiments, and appealed to them to make special efforts to induce young Officers to join the Brigade.

In the Irish Guards the greatest difficulty was experienced in getting Irish Officers: and the other Regiments complained that young Englishmen were persuaded to join the Irish Guards, who otherwise would have been available for the other three Regiments.

His Majesty was unaware that practical effect had been given to what he imagined was only a pious opinion, and before giving his approval to the appointment of Lieutenant-Colonel W. Murray-Threipland as Lieutenant-Colonel of the Regiment the King would be glad to hear whether Lord Kitchener has fully considered the difficulties which have forcibly suggested themselves to His Majesty.†

* RA GV PS 15246/5.
† RA GV PS 15246/3.

Having seen both letters Kitchener's response was a curt telephone call to Stamfordham repeating his belief that there would be no problems over recruitment and maintaining his confidence in Murray-Threipland's credentials. Could he please have an answer, he added, as he was anxious to proceed without further ado? That same day, 11 February 1915, Stamfordham again wrote to Robb confirming the King's approval of Murray-Threipland as Commanding Officer of the battalion and temporary Regimental Lieutenant-Colonel. At the same time he noted, somewhat wryly, that the King had taken full note of the statement that the new Colonel's 'connection with Wales is that he married a daughter and co-heiress of a Mr W. W. Lewis of New House Glamorgan, and he is willing, if appointed, to adopt the surname of Lewis.'*

And so it was that the Welsh Regiment of Foot Guards came into being by a Royal Warrant of 26 February 1915. What had begun as a fond hope held by several enthusiastic Welsh gentlemen had been nurtured by a private conversation between King George V and his Secretary of State for War and had then come to fruition through Kitchener's indomitable energy. As the King had noted, the idea of the Welsh Guards had only been 'a pious opinion' at the beginning of February, yet, three weeks later, it was an established fact. In the weeks to come King George V was to take a close interest in the progress of his new regiment of foot guards.

On 2 March the King approved the leek as the regiment's cap badge, from a design by the artist Seymour Lucas. Other uniform details were also settled at this time. The peacetime forage cap of officers and men was to have a black band; the tunic was to have buttons in groups of five; the collar badge to be the leek, repeated on the men's shoulders. The bearskin cap would be the same as in the other Guards regiments, but would have a distinctive plume of green and white. The pressing problem, though, was the selection of officers, NCOs and men. The first significant appointment was the selection of W. Stevenson, Scots Guards, to the key post of Regimental Sergeant-Major: he was to serve in that position until his promotion to Quartermaster in 1928 and was known to generations of Welsh Guardsmen as 'Stevo'. 'None of us will ever forget Stevo, as he was affectionately known by all ranks,' remembered Brigadier J. C. Windsor-Lewis, the Regimental Lieutenant-Colonel

* RA GV PS 15246/2.

between 1951 and 1954. 'He was fierce and he looked terrifying, but he was just a man and intensely loyal and nothing was too much for him when the welfare of the regiment was at stake.'

From the very outset it had been agreed by the four other regiments of foot guards that Welshmen within their ranks, or in training, would be allowed to transfer to the new battalion. Around five hundred answered the call almost immediately and on 18 March Murray-Threipland was able to inform the King that the battalion's strength was 763 officers and men and that preparations were in hand to establish a reserve battalion. Officers, though, proved to be a more difficult problem than had been originally anticipated. Although Murray-Threipland had been able to persuade a number of promising Guards and line infantry subalterns (Crawshay from the Welsh Regiment, Fox-Pitt from the Cheshire Regiment) to transfer to the Welsh Guards he admitted in exasperation to his wife that 'seniors are the problem'. When he interviewed candidates he made no secret of the fact that they might have to step down a rank in order to be accepted for he was adamant that a transfer to the Welsh Guards should not be regarded as a stepping stone to promotion. That he found considerable obstacles in winning the confidence of the senior men can be seen in this reply from George Montgomerie, a close friend in the Grenadier Guards:

I do not *want* to leave the Grenadiers now, and as I am not a Welshman I don't think it is in any way my *duty* to do so.

When the thing was first started I was very anxious to move – now I am quite happy where I am and want nothing better.

I should not be *mean* about it and take no interest in Welshmen so I should probably be a failure.

I have stated my intention to take nothing outside and to stick to my company, now I must *do* it.

If it were not for my regret at not helping *you* I should never hesitate for a second.

But I don't believe I should be much help in view of the state of my leanings – so I will definitely decline – and hope you will not hate me for ever after.

Other letters spoke of the disquiet which ambitious officers might feel about joining a new regiment. Far better, they reasoned, to stick with one of the three older established foot guards regiments, all of which had glorious traditions and many battle honours. Of the officers who came to the Welsh Guards from the Brigade of Guards it is interesting to note that the majority were on the reserve list at the start of the war.

Although he worried about the varying military backgrounds and experience of the officers who came to the regiment – they ranged from Scottish regiments like the Seaforth Highlanders and Royal Scots Greys to line regiments like the Royal Fusiliers – Murray-Threipland was fortunate with his key appointments. According to Perrins, Douglas Gordon (Scots Guards) was 'a tower of strength' as adjutant, and Osmond Williams (Royal Scots Greys) proved to be 'a potential future commanding officer' as captain of the Prince of Wales Company. Sadly this 'gallant gentleman', a veteran of the Boer War, was killed in the battalion's first action on Hill 70 during the Battle of Loos in September 1915. Other officers destined to make their names with the regiment included two future commanding officers of the 1st battalion: the Hon. A. G. A. Hore-Ruthven, VC (King's Dragoon Guards) who commanded between May 1919 and December 1920 before holding the appointment of Regimental Lieutenant-Colonel until September 1924, and F. A. V. Copland-Griffiths (Rifle Brigade) who commanded at the outbreak of the Second World War.

Throughout the period Murray-Threipland's wife and family were living at Rottingdean near Brighton, an arrangement which required lengthy periods of separation. As a professional soldier he accepted the situation but there were times when his patience was stretched by the necessary – though 'dreaded' – task of entertaining. 'So sorry I've seen so little of you,' he wrote on 1 March. 'I've a dinner of 20 tonight and I do hate it. These big binges don't suit me a bit.' Present on that occasion were General Lloyd, Murray-Threipland's brother General Scott-Kerr, Lord Kitchener and the Field Marshal's future biographer Sir George Arthur. They were celebrating the first occasion when the Welsh Guards had mounted guard at Buckingham Palace – on St David's Day, just as Lloyd had promised. Murray-Threipland had been Captain of the Guard, the first time in the history of the Brigade of Guards that a commanding officer had gone on duty in that capacity. This was not so much a matter of the colonel stealing the limelight; rather, as Murray-Threipland told his wife, the preferred officer, Rhys Williams, was incapable of the task – 'so that won't do!' Other ceremonial duties included an inspection by the Lord Mayor of Cardiff whose corporation had provided the funds for the regiment to buy instruments for the band. In June the regiment took over the responsibility for routine public duties in London.

On 16 June Lord Harlech, a prominent Welshman, became the regimental lieutenant-colonel in succession to Murray-Threipland and he held the appointment until 14 October 1917. King George V became the regiment's Colonel-in-Chief on 7 August 1915, four days after he had presented the Welsh Guards with their first colours. It was an auspicious occasion, held in the gardens of Buckingham Palace in front of many distinguished guests and it was marred only by a heavy downpour of rain which began when the battalion marched off parade. At the King's special request the regimental choir sang the hymns in Welsh: the following day Stamfordham wrote to Murray-Threipland praising the arrangements which had been made for the ceremony and adding a postscript that 'His Majesty was delighted with the singing'. A fortnight later, the 1st Battalion left London for service on the Western Front.

While the regular battalion remained on active service in France, a second (reserve) battalion came into being; its responsibility was to train the drafts of officers and men who would be required as replacements and reinforcements. Commanded by Lieutenant-Colonel J. B. Stacey Clitheroe (formerly Scots Guards) it was stationed variously at Marlow, Caterham, Tadworth and Ranelagh Camp at Barnes. Regimental Headquarters was established at Wellington Barracks where it remains to this day. A band, too, had been formed as early as October 1915 and under the direction of Andrew Harris LRAM it performed in public throughout the war, both in Britain and France.

Curiously, the battalion had first mustered for training in the unlikely surroundings of White City in west London. Now surrounded by an ugly urban sprawl with the A40 running through it, this 140-acre site had been set aside in 1908 for the purposes of the Franco-British Exhibition of that year. Designed by the Kiralfy Brothers, it was the largest exhibition ever to have been staged in Britain and during the course of the year it attracted over eight million visitors. It was called the White City because it was just that – forty acres of gleaming white-stuccoed buildings, many in the fashionable Indian imperial style, and the centrepiece was a lake with illuminated fountains surrounded by spacious pavilions. That same year it housed the 4th Olympic Games and two years later it staged the Anglo-Japanese Exhibition which had been established to celebrate Britain's recently signed alliance with Japan.

By the time the Welsh Guards moved in, though, the White City was but a shadow of its former glories. The government had taken it over at the beginning of the war and the buildings and trappings had quickly succumbed to the workings of the military machine as the White City was transformed into a training depot for drafts of troops bound for the Western Front. As Dudley Ward remembered it, while the Battle of Neuve Chapelle was being fought in Flanders the Welsh Guards learned about drill and use of the rifle 'on the very ground where the populace used to "wiggle-woggle" and "water-chute" to the strains of brass bands and under the glow of a hundred thousand coloured lights'. For the Welsh Guards it was an unusual initiation to a bold venture.

At the war's end the 1st Welsh Guards advanced to the Rhine with the British forces and formed part of the garrison in Cologne until 6 March 1919 when they left by train for Dunkirk and home. By then the battalion had been reduced to little more than half strength owing to the process of demobilization which accompanied the end of hostilities. When they arrived at Ranelagh Camp six days later the regiment could count the cost of its war. The nominal role of the Welsh Guards showed that 3,853 warrant officers, non-commissioned officers and men, and 195 officers had served with the 1st battalion overseas: of these, 856 had been killed and 1,755 wounded. Of the original battalion which went to France in August 1915 and saw action at Loos a month later only thirteen served from first to last without interruption.

The return to peacetime soldiering was bound to be a difficult transition for the Welsh Guards: having been raised as a wartime formation they had no collective experience of the heavy responsibility of public duties which awaited them in the London area. True, many of the officers and NCOs had served previously with other Guards regiments and had known what it was like to mount King's Guard, but the performance of public duties was going to be a new attainment for the Welsh Guards as a regiment. Fortunately, they still had the 'strong bulwark' of a 'redoubtable

Regimental Sergeant-Major' (Stevenson), an experienced and ener-
getic soldier in the commanding officer Lieutenant-Colonel the
Hon. A. G. A. Hore-Ruthven and the officers and men were full of
confidence after their spell of garrison duties in Germany. As it was
to turn out, though, the regiment would need all the strength of
character and determination at its disposal to meet a rather different
and far more formidable threat. In addition to encountering the
normal problems associated with the end of a conflict – the haemor-
rhage of talent among officers and men caused by routine demobilization, and the need to replace them – the Welsh Guards found that
their very existence had been placed in jeopardy due to cuts in the
nation's defence expenditure.

Traditionally, British political leaders have rarely treated the
army with kindness once the peace treaties have been signed.
Throughout the eighteenth century, for example, the regiments
raised to fight the various European and colonial wars were axed as
rapidly as they had been formed, often with scant regard to history
or reputation. Then if an emergency arose which again demanded
the deployment of British forces in Europe, North America, India
or wherever, the regiments would be raised once more and the
wheel of recruitment and disbandment would be set in motion.
Even the most casual inspection of the histories of some of Britain's
doughtiest regiments reveals the truth that their traditions and
lineage are not always as straightforward as the purists might insist.
Down the years the steady process of formation, disbandment, re-
formation and amalgamation has meant that very few regiments can
claim to have unsullied genealogies. For instance the 20th Hussars,
raised in 1759 as the 20th Inniskilling Light Dragoons, has been
disbanded on three occasions – at the end of the Seven Years War,
the end of the American War of Independence and the end of the
Napoleonic War – and it is only sleight of hand that keeps their
traditions alive today in the 14th/20th King's Hussars.

The same cycle of neglect was visited upon the army after the
First World War which had seen the improvisation of the largest
mass army in the country's history. Many of the men were volunteers who had signed on for the duration, others were conscripts
who had been called up after the passing of the Military Service
Act in 1916; the great majority wanted to be demobilized in 1919
and to get back to their peacetime civilian lives. Having served their
country in a dreadful war they only asked to be granted a quick

return to what they had known before – although for many it was
to mean an unwelcome road which would lead only to unemployment and beggary. A new mood of pacifism began to sweep
through the country and it became fashionable to place the blame
for the heavy casualties of the Somme and Passchendaele on the
army's high command. In such an atmosphere defence expenditure
became an unacceptable concept, one which politicians preferred to
avoid, and the army reverted to what it had always been in
peacetime – short of men and short of money.

In 1919 Lloyd George's government introduced a Ten Year Rule
to govern defence spending: according to this legislation expenditure
on the armed forces was to be planned on the assumption that there
would be no major war for ten years. As a result the army changed
quickly and dramatically, becoming once more a small, tightly knit
professional organization, almost a society apart. The wartime
formations disappeared too, and others underwent curious trans-
formations – five line regiments lost two of their four regular
battalions, five Irish regiments were disbanded and there were a
number of painful shotgun weddings among the cavalry regiments.
Even the Brigade of Guards was not immune from the planners;
their regiments, too, had to face the axe of defence cuts.

The news broke in the *Daily Mail* on 4 June 1920, the day
before the Trooping of the Colour, when Valentine Williams, ex-
Irish Guards, announced that he had seen a sensitive War Office
paper which recommended the disbandment of the Irish Guards
and the Welsh Guards. Specifically, the Irish Guards were to be
brigaded with the Scots Guards as that regiment's 3rd battalion,
the new formation to be known as the Third Regiment of Foot
Guards, and the Welsh Guards were to be reduced to company
strength as part of the Grenadier Guards. Stung into action, the
War Office issued a statement the following day confirming the
report as a paper for discussion and adding the conciliatory thought
that it had not 'directed attention solely or especially to the
Brigade of Guards but has considered that force as part of a general
scheme of review for its object the promotion of every possible
economy consistent with the maintenance of a thoroughly efficient
army of sufficient strength for the requirements of Country and
Empire.'

Economy was the reason given for the exercise – the War Office
suggested that £100,000 a year might be saved if the Welsh Guards

were to surrender their headquarters and depot – but *The Times* thought that there might be other reasons. On 5 June its military correspondent suggested that 'the Grenadiers have never viewed the younger regiments with favour' and pointed to the well-known fact that the officer commanding the Brigade, Major-General Sir George Jeffreys, was a Grenadier who looked on the Welsh Guards as a wartime formation. Furthermore, it was revealed that two separate reports existed on the future shape of the Brigade of Guards – a majority report which supported the planned changes and which had been signed by Jeffreys, the Duke of Connaught (Grenadier Guards), Lieutenant-General Sir Alfred Codrington (Coldstream Guards) and Field Marshal Lord Methuen (Scots Guards). A minority report, opposing the plans, had been signed by Field Marshal Lord French (Irish Guards) and Colonel Murray-Threipland (Welsh Guards). Both reports had been submitted to King George V.

The news brought immediate protests from Wales and from the friends of the Welsh Guards. Sir Francis Lloyd, who had been so instrumental in encouraging the Welsh Guards into being, issued a statement which argued that the war service of the regiment alone meant that its proposed disbandment in peacetime was an insult to the people of Wales:

> There is every reason for maintaining this great regiment in its entirety. A great regiment it is, for we do not base our reasons for its retention on show or parade ceremonial but on the fact that it has proved itself worthy to stand beside the greatest and best fighting troops that carry the King's uniform.

Others who protested strongly included General Owen Thomas who spoke of 'crass stupidity' and a belittling of the sacrifice of the Welsh dead of the war that had just ended, and Captain Philipps of Picton Castle suggested that if the Welsh Guards were to disappear the effect on Welsh recruiting would be disastrous. The Welsh Members of Parliament demanded a meeting with Lloyd George to put forward the national case for retaining the regiment and clamoured for the release of accurate establishment and recruiting figures to prove that the Welsh Guards were up to strength – one of the main points in the majority report had been the so-called low recruiting figures in the Irish and Welsh Guards since the end of the war. When these were released by Churchill it was noted with some satisfaction that the Welsh Guards' strength was 728 with a nominal establishment of 1,101, while the Grenadiers' strength was only 2,317 with a nominal establishment of 3,202. Pressed further by Lieutenant-Colonel Sir John Hope (Conservative, Midlothian), Churchill admitted that during the previous six months 500 recruits had passed into the Brigade of Guards and of these 200 were Welshmen bound for the Welsh Guards.

The uproar caused by the report, and the rumours which surrounded it, took the government by surprise for not only did the opposition come from Wales; the Irish were also incensed, as were many Scots who did not take kindly to the proposal that their country's regiment of Foot Guards should revert to a numbered title it had last held in 1831. As the usually supportive *Daily Telegraph* remarked in an editorial of 7 June, 'A re-organization which affronts the pride of Scotland, Ireland and Wales is hardly to be pronounced a happy invention, and to offend national and local patriotism, at this moment in the history of the Empire is a policy of which it is difficult to speak with moderation.'

The government was on a losing wicket and knew it. On 15 June Winston Churchill rose in the House of Commons to announce the War Office's response: 'This subject has now been considered by the Army Council. There is no intention of disbanding the Irish or Welsh Guards so long as they are able to maintain their recruiting in such a manner as to preserve the national character of the Regiments.'

A few days earlier Churchill had been a guest at the Trooping of the Colour which was held in Hyde Park due to the continuing presence of wartime huts on Horse Guards Parade. *The Times* noted that he stood with his daughter in front of the main stand, behind King George V, and that he watched the proceedings with a gloomy expression, presumably because 'there was more than one challenging glance made by old Irish and Welsh Guards officers at the figure of the Secretary of State for War'. Churchill had been a keen supporter of the majority report and although he had been forced to bow to popular opinion he never lost his suspicions about the Irish and the Welsh Guards. According to his friend Oliver Lyttelton (Lord Chandos), for a long time thereafter Churchill would say of the Brigade of Guards: 'Star, Thistle and Grenade! They should be the only Guardsmen.'

Throughout the 1920s and 1930s there were to be renewed, though less vocal, threats to the existence of the Welsh Guards; partly these were caused by the continuing need to reduce military expenditure and partly too by the lingering belief that they were the junior regiment in the Brigade. Dudley Ward, the regiment's historian of the First World War, firmly believed at the time of the report that its findings had more to do with 'inter-regimental jealousy than a desire for economy' and in later years he saw no reason to change that opinion. The appointment in June 1919 of HRH Prince of Wales, later to become King Edward VIII, as Colonel should have done much to ease matters but in 1920 he was abroad in Australia, undertaking one of the long imperial tours dreamed up for him by Lloyd George. Prince Edward was very fond of his Welsh Guards and as Duke of Windsor he wore the regiment's service dress with the rank of major-general during the Second World War, but as he was also Colonel-in-Chief of other regiments he had to make sure that he did not show them any favouritism. Shortly before leaving for Australia he wrote to Murray-Threipland on 26 January apologizing for his rejection of an invitation to attend the Welsh Guards Old Comrades dinner in Cardiff the following month:

> I am very sorry to fail you and very disappointed, as you know how keen on the regiment I am and all that concerns its welfare. But I am up against it as regards the other important invitations and requests that I have received and had to refuse, and no less than three of these are from Cardiff!! Besides, I am Colonel-in-Chief of several other regiments, and though naturally being a Guardsman the Welsh Guards will always be my special regiment, I have to be careful not to make this too evident and so cause jealousy.

Long after his abdication and his residence abroad, Edward continued to take a close interest in the Welsh Guards: he visited them for the last time at Wuppertal in 1951 when the 1st Battalion was engaged on its first tour of post-war Germany.

Their immediate future assured, the Welsh Guards spent the next nine years on public duties in the London area. In August 1920 they moved to Warley and as the Regimental Sergeant-Major's wife remembered, the regiment settled down to a routine which was as regular as clockwork: 'From then onwards we moved every

year about October, packing up and laying out the utensils and
furniture as per the inventory board for the Quartermaster to
check, and wondering what our next quarters would reveal. Of
course, no one ever left theirs as spic and span as you did, or so we
imagined, but it was all great fun and I thoroughly enjoyed it all,
particularly the Children's Christmas Tree and Party each year.'
During that period the regiment was based at Warley, Windsor,
London and Aldershot.

While they were establishing themselves as a peacetime battalion
the Welsh Guards made many friends through their prowess in
sport. The photograph albums held by Headquarters show that the
officers displayed a good deal of enthusiasm and ability at hunting
and racing, one of their most enthusiastic and dashing riders being
their Colonel, the Prince of Wales. The most active supporter of
field sports, though, was Sir Alexander 'Sammy' Stanier who was
adjutant between 1923 and 1926. He had been associated with the
regiment from the very beginning when Lord Harlech approached
his father in 1915 with the request that the sixteen-year-old Eton
schoolboy should put his name down for the Welsh Guards. After
school and Sandhurst Stanier joined the 1st battalion in December
1917 when, much to his amusement, he found himself travelling to
France as senior officer among a party of forty-year-old second-
lieutenants. On the regiment's return to peacetime soldiering he
was determined that the Welsh Guards should excel at field sports.
In that way, he claimed, the regiment's officers would receive
numerous invitations to ride with the best hunts and in so doing
the Welsh Guards would enjoy enormous prestige as a sporting
regiment. Being a good soldier as well as an excellent horseman,
Stanier was also well aware of the military benefits to be found on
the hunting field:

> You got to know other people and you got to know what the country
> looked like. It's the best way: if you ride a horse you see the whole
> thing in front of you. In a motor car you're going so fast that it's
> impossible to understand what the land looks like. For example, the
> good horseman will know to jump a fence near a tree because it will
> have been weakened by the water dripping from it.

To this day he is convinced that those officers who hunted before
the war made better commanders because they had a good feel for

the lie of the land, especially when they were fighting through the bocage country of Normandy in 1944. 'It's a proud record that the Master and three Whippers-in, all Welsh Guards officers, to the Household Division Draghounds in 1932–33 collected between them one VC and 3 DSOs plus two bars and 2 MCs besides other foreign decorations, all on active service, not on the staff.'

One of those officers was Cyril Heber Percy who won his MC at Boulogne and a DSO while commanding the 1st battalion in north-west Europe. He and his brother Alan were renowned as courageous madcap horsemen who pushed their luck to the limits and, as a result, frequently fell foul of the authorities. On joining the battalion in Aldershot they established a short-lived officers' poaching gang which shot rabbits on army property at night by the light of motor-car headlamps – until the Military Police intervened and gave chase. The gang beat their pursuers back to the mess by the skin of their teeth and were quietly broken up; but it was not the end of the Heber Percys' infatuation with the sporting field.

Hearing that a good horse had been entered in a steeplechase up north and fancying his chances, Alan entered his name and applied to the adjutant for the necessary leave to take part in the race. This was refused but nothing daunted the brothers contacted nearby Farnborough and hired an aeroplane which would take them north after lunch on the day of the race. Quite against military regulations they landed at an RAF aerodrome but managed to escape the wrath of the RAF police when the commanding officer turned out to be a family friend. It was to be their last piece of luck. Alan lost the race by a head and, quite broke, the brothers decided to return to Farnborough at first light. The next morning thick fog enveloped the aerodrome and despite all entreaties and threats the pilot refused to take off until it had cleared. By then the Heber Percys were two hours late for the first parade. There was thick fog, too, at Farnborough but a break in the clouds allowed them to land at a private field in North London where they had breakfast and telephoned the adjutant. 'Report to me as soon as you can,' he told them angrily.

They did just that, although not in the way that the adjutant expected. As they flew over Pirbright they could see the battalion at practice on the ranges. It was too good an opportunity to miss – the pilot was ordered to buzz the ranges and as it flew low over the astonished Welsh Guardsmen Alan leaned out of the cockpit and blew the 'gone away' call on the hunting horn he always carried with him. The result was an unpleasant interview with the commanding officer, a month's stoppage of leave and two weeks additional pickets.

Later, Alan was tragically killed riding in a National Hunt Steeplechase at Cheltenham. Cyril left the army in the 1930s to become Joint Master of the Cotswold Hunt but rejoined the Welsh Guards in 1939 and commanded the joint Irish and Welsh Guards group which was despatched to the Hook of Holland to bring Queen Wilhelmina to Britain. After the war he became Master to the Cottesmore Hunt; he died in 1989 aged 83.

Polo, too, was popular and down the years the Welsh Guards have continued to show a particular excellence at this sport. Being a Welsh regiment, though, the Welsh Guards were expected to excel at rugby football. Welshmen, they say, are born with the ability to pass, tackle and sidestep, and to prove it the Welsh Guards won the Army Cup Final in the 1922–23 season and were runners-up three times during the 1920s. They also had the satisfaction of providing two players for the Welsh national team – T. E. Rees and W. C. 'Guardsman' Powell whom many observers believe was the finest Welsh scrum-half between R. M. Owen and Haydn Tanner. Powell, who won twenty-seven caps for Wales, also played for London Welsh and was a Barbarian in the 1928 and 1929 seasons. Another notable Welsh Guards Barbarian was Lieutenant Gavin Young, the Harlequin player who captained both the regiment's and the army's rugby XVs.

Much help and encouragement was given to regimental rugby by Captain Geoffrey Crawshay. A member of the prominent Welsh family of Crawshay of Cyfarthfa, his name is synonymous with the high romantic appeal of Celtic Wales. Having been badly wounded during the First World War – he was one of the battalion's first officers – he later retired from the army and devoted the rest of his life to his country's cultural and political aspirations. During the 1930s he was a special commissioner in charge of the redevelopment of South Wales during the terrible economic depression and he went on to fill a number of prominent positions in the cultural and social life of Wales. Those who knew him, like John Fothergill, the author of *My Three Inns*, said that he represented the humanity of the Crawshay family, but he was much more than a promoter of social justice. Romantic, idealistic, Welsh-speaking, wearing the green cloak of the Bard Herald at the annual eisteddfod, he appeared to have stepped out of his country's Arthurian past. And like most Welshmen he worshipped rugby, believing that the game transcended social class: for that reason he founded Crawshay's Welsh XV, a touring team which visited the West Country each year from the 1920s onwards. There was more than a touch of corinthian idealism attached to the team. Colliers may have found themselves rubbing shoulders with Welsh Guardsmen or Glamorgan policemen to play rugby football but they were bound together in a fraternity which paid serious attention to the initiation rites and Celtic ritual introduced by Crawshay to the brotherhood.

In 1928 the Welsh Guards trooped the colour for the first time but the following year saw an interruption to their familiar routine when the 1st battalion was posted to Egypt. Their home for the next two years was the famous Kasr-el-Nil barracks in Cairo, which, possessing neither electric lights nor modern sanitary arrangements, had been declared unfit for troops. (They were still the centre of British military power in Egypt during the Second World War but have since been demolished to make way for an international Hilton Hotel.) The Welsh Guards were the first Household regiment to serve in Egypt during the inter-war years; it was also their first peacetime posting abroad and having managed 'to defeat those common enemies, the bug, the shite-hawk and the flies' Windsor Lewis remembered that the men revelled in the conditions. During their stay the regiment again distinguished itself in sport, winning the rugby and boxing cups and reaching the final of the cricket cup.

On their return to Britain the Welsh Guards settled down to the easy routine which was so typical of army life in the 1930s. Field training was kept to a minimum and was hardly ever strenuous; there was much emphasis on bull and drill and the officers were encouraged to adopt an easy-going almost amateurish approach to soldiering. Sammy Stanier remembered being rebuked by the adjutant for working in the company office after lunch, a tradition that continued into the 1950s, it being considered bad form for an officer to appear too serious about his work. Leave was another military matter which attracted weighty consideration. To be seen in London while on leave was a cardinal sin: leave for officers was meant to be spent on the sporting field and commanding officers were known to refuse it to subalterns whom they suspected were poodle-fakers.

Dress, too, both for the officers and for the men was a serious business. Civilian clothes for an officer stationed in London meant a dark suit, stiff collar, umbrella and bowler hat and woe betide the young ensign or subaltern found wanting in this respect. One older officer, now a general, remembers being caught hatless by his commanding officer in Victoria Street and being told sternly, 'You must wear a hat so that you can raise it when you meet me.' Guardsmen walking out of barracks were closely inspected at the guardroom before they were allowed to go any further. They could wear uniform if they so wished – red tunic and peaked cap – otherwise their dress had to be similar to an officer's civilian clothes and the rule about hats was sacrosanct. Being discovered without a hat in London, as a bandsman discovered, was not a matter which was taken lightly by the Welsh Guards. One summer's evening, while walking hatless with his girl-friend in Buckingham Palace Road he met the Regimental Sergeant-Major, then as now an awesome figure. 'Good evening,' the RSM smiled sweetly, doffing his hat to the blushing girl and her suddenly terrified escort. The smile was still on the RSM's face the following morning after the drummer had been sentenced to seven days confined to barracks. 'Nice girl you've got there,' he said. 'Show her some respect next time!'

Although the 1920s and the 1930s are remembered as a time of stagnation in the army there were a number of small but significant changes during the period. A uniform system of numbering soldiers was introduced in 1920, an innovation which meant that RSM Stevenson lost his cherished Welsh Guards regimental number 1. Soldiers had been numbered since 1829 but these were strictly regimental numbers: the confusion of numbers caused by the casualties of the First World War meant that a standard system had to be introduced for the whole of the army. Rates of pay and conditions in some barracks improved – Welsh Guardsmen in Wellington and Chelsea barracks might not have noticed – and some new technology was introduced. The concept of fully mechanized warfare did not win full favour until after the outbreak of war but in 1938 the Welsh Guards formed its first platoon of Bren-gun carriers, the tracked vehicle which was the forerunner of today's armoured personnel carrier. The standard personal weapon throughout the war years remained the tried and tested .303 Lee Enfield rifle.

War, the great creator of change, brought many innovations to the Welsh Guards. Between 1941 and 1945 two additional battalions were formed and the 2nd served throughout the war as an armoured reconnaisance battalion operating Cromwell tanks. The complexion of the regiment underwent further changes in the post-war world. For the first time ever in time of peace there was universal conscription and the manpower of the Welsh Guards was made up mainly of National Servicemen. The majority were Welshmen and as everyone between the ages of eighteen and twenty-six was obliged to serve in the armed forces the standard of recruit was much higher than it had been before the war. National Servicemen tended to have an ambivalent attitude towards conscription and most regarded it as a necessary evil which had to be faced. To their credit the Welsh Guards refused to treat their National Servicemen any differently from their regular volunteers: according to Arthur Rees, RSM in the early days of National Service, the return was a fine soldier:

> They were Guardsman so-and-so and they were treated just the same as a normal regular soldier. I may say that a lot of them were very intelligent and became NCOs: I always had a very high regard for National Servicemen. If they had stayed in longer I'm certain that quite a few of them would have gone all the way through the ranks – but most of them went out after doing their two years. We never treated them as separate entities at all, they were just ordinary Welsh Guardsmen.

One of the benefits of being a National Serviceman was the opportunity to serve abroad – the army then had more overseas stations than they have today – and during the period the Welsh Guards were frequently posted abroad. National Servicemen served with the battalion in Palestine between 1945 and 1948, in Germany 1950–53 and in the Canal Zone 1953–56. Germany meant adapting to the needs of BAOR and the demands of the Cold War but the postings to Palestine and Egypt brought new and often exciting experiences for guardsmen who had never been abroad before. In both places they had to complete internal security duties, in Palestine these were often dangerous and demanding as the British Army attempted to keep the peace between Arab and Jew, but as the adjutant, Peter Leuchars, wrote at the time his guardsmen could also be afforded a glimpse into a different kind of world.

Such was the experience of Support Company in Palestine when they were sent to Aqaba, the first time in the history of the regiment that a complete company had been placed under the operational command of another headquarters in a different country. The highlight was a visit to Amman which allowed them to visit the historic lands of the New Testament:

> The drive down the gorge to the Dead Sea, the ascent to the Mount of Olives, our first view of the Holy City, all we saw of the astonishing life within its walls, the shrines, monuments and churches we visited, gay nights in the hotels and restaurants, the lovely winding road to Bethlehem and the Church of the Nativity – all these sights will remain for ever imprinted in our memories ... Bethlehem will remember Support Company for ringing the church bells at eleven a.m. one Thursday morning, but after all, when a guardsman is shown the bells which are heard all over the world on Christmas Day, it is perhaps too much to expect he will refrain from the temptation of being able to tell his grandchildren that he has not only seen and heard them, but he has actually rung them himself!

Many National Servicemen stayed on as regulars, serving the regiment for three years or more. The Welsh Guards also benefited from an influx of National Service officers who served as ensigns; one of the most notable was Michael Heseltine, the Conservative MP and former Minister for Defence who caused something of a sensation in 1959 when he resigned his commission to stand for parliament. As was the case throughout the army the Welsh Guards benefited greatly from the regular injections of National Servicemen, not least because many of them were fine rugby players.

In 1963 National Service came to an end and the Welsh Guards gradually became the kind of regiment it is today in its 75th anniversary year: small, compact, professional, highly motivated and still capable of turning its hands to the ceremonial duties required of a Household regiment and the operational duties of the infantry. They have served in Aden, Northern Ireland, Kenya, West Germany, Falklands, Belize and Sharjah; they have trained as parachutists and as mechanized infantrymen and they have witnessed many changes, most of them for the better, in the standards of equipment and training in the British Army. When they come together at the meetings of the Association, older members might say that the Welsh Guardsman of today is softer than his predecessors of 1915 or 1940. There might be some truth in this oft-repeated adage, for society itself has changed and the harsh discipline and unnecessary bull of a bygone age are no longer tolerated. But for Arthur Rees, one of the toughest and best respected of Regimental Sergeant-Majors, some things about the regiment and its guardsmen will never change:

> Looking back to the Crimea, people said how wonderful the soldiers had been and then at the time of the Boer War they said, 'Ah, our men aren't as good as they were in the Crimea.' And the boys in the First World War weren't as good as those who fought in South Africa. They even said the same thing during the Second World War that we weren't as good as the last lot. But we were and I think that the Welsh Guardsmen of today are as good as the men of 1939–45 and 1914–18. It's still a matter of discipline, pride and strict training which Welsh Guardsmen will happily adapt themselves to when they join the regiment.

Chapter Three

BATTLE HONOURS

LIKE EVERY OTHER regiment of the British Army the Welsh Guards are fiercely proud of their battle honours. These are borne on both the Queen's Colour and the Regimental Colour and the names of the battles are a solemn reminder of the courage and fortitude which several generations of Welsh Guardsmen have shown under fire in the trying conditions of battle. Unlike line infantry regiments whose Queen's Colour is the Union Flag, foot guards regiments retain their crimson Field Officer's Colour as their first colours; the Regimental Colour is the Union Flag. Because it is a relatively new regiment, formed this century, the Welsh Guards' battle honours reflect the history of the two great world wars – Loos, Somme, Cambrai, Passchendaele, Arras, the Hindenburg Line fought by the 1st battalion between 1915 and 1918; and the campaigns in France, north-west Europe, North Africa and Italy in which three battalions of the regiment saw service between 1939 and 1945.

'A Battle Honour is a public commemoration of a battle, action or engagement of which not only past and present, but also future, generations of the regiment can be proud,' noted the gentlemen of the Battles Nomenclature Committee of the Army Council when they reported their recommendations on 28 January 1956. The committee had been formed to regulate the award of battle honours of the regiments of the British Army which had fought in the Second World War and it followed the rules which had been laid by the Army Council in 1922, namely, that each regiment would be able to select ten honours to be emblazoned on standards, guidons and Queen's Colours. Accordingly, the Welsh Guards carry on their colours the names of ten battle honours from each of the two world wars fought this century: at the same time they were also able to claim ten further honours which are not borne on the colours. Thus, the name of the Battle of the Somme, fought in 1916, is not carried on the colours, but the names of Ginchy, Flers-Courcelette and Morval are. These three related battles were fought in September 1916 on the Somme sector as part of a British attempt to dislodge the Germans from a heavily defended quadrilateral on the high ground between Albert and Bapaume. It was during this phase of the Somme that tanks were used for the first time in battle but the main attack was carried forward by the infantry with predictably high casualties. In all, the Welsh Guards lost seventy-eight officers and men.

All told, 163 battles were selected as honours by the British Army during the First World War and 5,920 separate awards were claimed by 205 regiments. During the Second World War 633 honours were awarded, a reflection perhaps of the global nature of the conflict and of the many fronts on which the army fought. In stark contrast, only three awards had been made by 1800 and it took 190 years for the eight regiments which took part in the combined operations Battle of Belleisle (1761) to claim it as a battle honour.

Given the proliferation of battle honours this century it would be difficult to examine in close detail each of the battle honours won by the Welsh Guards, whether or not they are borne on the colours. In any case, the war histories of the regiment have already been written, respectively by Major C. H. Dudley Ward and Major L. F. Ellis and further investigation falls outwith the intentions of the present book. Instead, there are two battle honours which seem to me to represent the best qualities of the Welsh Guards – determination to carry through a task, however trying the conditions, and the demonstration of courage and *élan* under heavy fire. The first, the Battle of Loos fought in September 1915, is the regiment's first battle honour; and the second, Hechtel, was won by the Welsh Guards Group during the advance to north-west Europe in the autumn of 1944.

LOOS 1915

When the Welsh Guards were formed in the early part of 1915 it had always been the War Office's intention to deploy them on the Western Front at the earliest opportunity. At the time most

Kitchener battalions took six months to be properly trained, but the Welsh Guards were considered to be somewhat different. They were ordered to be ready for active service by the summer of 1915. There were two reasons for this tight schedule. One was that the Welsh Guards was a new regiment and not a service battalion raised for the duration of the war. More was, therefore, expected of them. Secondly, most of the officers and men were trained soldiers, some of whom had already seen action in Flanders. Finally, the Welsh Guards had been allotted to the Guards Division which had been raised in July 1915 as part of Kitchener's plans to reorganize the fighting strength of the British forces on the Western Front.

Kitchener had always held the Foot Guards regiments in high regard and it had long been his personal ambition to draw them together into a single fighting formation. With the approval of King George V the Guards Division was formed from the Foot Guards regiments which were already serving with the British First and Second Armies in France. To them were added the remaining battalions of the older regiments and, finally, the 1st Battalion of the Welsh Guards. The Division's first Commanding Officer was the Earl of Cavan, Grenadier Guards. As was the case in other European armies, the Guards Division was to be known simply by its name and was to have no number. Kitchener was well pleased with the result and countered suggestions that he was creating an elite force, almost a separate army within the army, by reminding Cavan that the Guards' high standards could not fail to have a beneficial effect on the volunteer soldiers of the New Armies.

On 17 August 1915 the battalion moved over to France on board the troopships s.s. *Palm Branch* and s.s. *St Petersburg*, two civilian liners which had been pressed into service to take troops across the Channel. Once in France the battalion joined the Guards Division at St Omer south of Calais. For the generations who grew up after the First World War the Western Front was a shattered landscape dominated by mud, trenches, barbed wire and broken buildings. In those miserable conditions men fought and died, mere cogs in the inhuman machine of warfare. And so it was for the front-line troops. At other times, though, in the rear areas or during training periods, life could be very different and much more pleasant. St Omer, the headquarters of the Guards Division, was also the home of Sir John French's GHQ and it provided an orderly, even idyllic, environment which was very different from the conditions experienced up the line. The landscape around St Omer is flat and pleasantly wooded, with trees breaking up the patterns of fields which stretch beyond the River Aa and canal systems into the far distance. At nearby Arques the Welsh Guards began training in earnest for a forthcoming assault on the German lines.

There was still much to be learned about the two basic skills required by all infantrymen who served on the Western Front in 1915. Firstly, they had to become fit enough to cope with marching in full kit, which weighed around 66 lbs, and secondly, they had to learn how to dig in quickly and efficiently. The capacity to survive depended on the men's ability to create and maintain decent trenches and all front-line troops had to become masters of that art. Marching was a different matter. Although there were some troop trains – made up of cattle trucks for the men – and even London buses as transport, most of the movement had to be done on foot. No one who served with the regiment has ever forgotten the misery of those marches over the uneven roads of France and Flanders. In summer the dry dusty roads made marching an uncomfortable and exhausting chore; in winter the mud made many of the same roads almost impassable. As the Welsh Guards were to discover, the campaign in Flanders was to be dominated by the tiring marches over the long featureless countryside.

There were also brigade and divisional exercises and various schemes designed to bring the men up to combat fitness. Such was the battalion's fighting spirit, though, that there were times when the enthusiasm shown by the Welsh Guardsmen overcame their sense of military decorum. On 6 September, as part of the 3rd Guards Brigade, they had been ordered to make a mock attack on an 'enemy village'. Having failed to carry out a proper reconnaissance, the advancing men found that the ground fell away from two hundred yards in front of their target. In realistic battle conditions, this would have provided the enemy with an ideal opportunity to use his machine guns to enfilade the advancing troops. Undeterred by the obstacle, the Welsh Guards pressed home their attack, whooping and yelling as they approached the target. Their high spirits brought an immediate reprimand from the GO1, Colonel W. P. Hore-Ruthven, Scots Guards:

There is far too much shouting in the Welsh Guards. This is absolutely useless in the din of action and unless men can look to their leaders, whether officers or non-commissioned officers for quiet signs, they cannot be called trained soldiers.

Within a fortnight of receiving that rebuke, the battalion – and its ability to remain quiet in battle – were to be tested to the full in the action that came to be known as the Battle of Loos.

The Loos offensive – which in time came to be known as the 'unwanted battle' – had its origins in the allied talks which had been held at Chantilly in July 1915. By then the war was almost a year old and it is not exaggerating to say that Britain's military resources were stretched to breaking point. Ammunition, especially artillery shells, were in short supply and there was an acute shortage of trained soldiers. The old peacetime Regular Army which had formed the British Expeditionary Force had more or less disappeared by Christmas 1914, having fought the battles of Mons, the Marne, the Aisne and First Ypres; their remnants and some of the best territorial troops had been lost at the battles of Neuve Chapelle and Aubers Ridge in May. Nevertheless, in spite of those shortcomings in men and materiel, the British felt obliged to support their French allies by collaborating in a major autumn offensive on the German lines.

Joffre's plan proposed a French attack on the right in the Champagne country while the British would advance on the left of the line north of Arras. By advancing in a pincer movement to the north and south the allies hoped eventually to converge on the German lines of communication which ran back into Germany. It might have looked good on paper but it turned out in practice to be a rotten plan and from the outset General Douglas Haig, the commander of the British First Army, objected strongly to it. Not only did he entertain grave doubts about the suitability of the terrain – the area around Loos and Lens was dotted with coalfields and mining villages which would make a rapid advance difficult – but he also doubted if the British artillery had sufficient reserves to break the German lines in advance of the infantry attack.

Other tactical considerations crowded in to force mistakes on the British general staff. Gas was to be used for the first time but meteorological conditions did not favour its deployment as autumn days on Flanders tend to be still and windless. No attempt was made to rationalize the British lines of communication. Although the road system around Loos and Lens was adequate, there were no 'up and down' routes, with the result that troops, supplies and transport became hopelessly bogged down when moving between the rear area and the front line during the course of the battle. As the official history was to remark after the war, 'it was like trying to push the Lord Mayor's procession through the streets of London without clearing the route and holding the traffic.' Afterwards, too, it was noted that Sir John French, the British commander-in-Chief, did not possess a telephone, a blunder which was to have a deleterious effect on the course of the battle. Finally, having taken the blunderer's path, French was to continue down it by making the attack with relatively inexperienced troops – raw and untried territorial and Kitchener battalions of the New Army – while the experienced Guards Division was to be kept in reserve as part of IX Corps (General Haking). Nevertheless, political considerations meant that Britain had to co-operate with the French and the matter was settled when Kitchener visited St Omer and told Sir John French: 'we must act with all energy and do our utmost to help France in this offensive, even though by so doing we may suffer very heavy losses.'

As it turned out, when the attacks began on 25 September the first hours of the battle were promising enough. The deployment of gas was a mistake in that it did not unsettle the Germans and in many places remained stationary over the British lines, but the first assaulting divisions quickly reached their objective. For the Guards Division, especially for the Welsh Guards, interest came to be centred on the performance of the 15th (Scottish) Division whose objectives were the Lens Road redoubt and the Loos Road Redoubt, two formidably fortified salients in the German line. Having taken these, the 15th Division was supposed to capture Loos and nearby Hill 70, the one commanding point of any height in the area. Attacking with wild enthusiasm the Scots had taken all their targets and by mid-morning were like a 'bank holiday crowd' on top of Hill 70.

Then things started to go wrong. The 15th Division had become enmeshed with the 47th (London) Division and a gap began to open up between them and the 1st Division to the north. This was exploited by the Germans and by the early evening Hill 70 had been retaken, with the Scots still holding a wobbly line in front of it. It was over that uncertain ground that the 1st Welsh Guards were to win their first battle honour.

By the time that the Welsh Guards and the other battalions of the 3rd Guards Brigade had arrived at Vermelles, two miles short of Loos, on the afternoon of 26 September, the central problem of the British tactics had begun to emerge. The Guards Division, along with the relatively inexperienced 21st and 24th Divisions, had been held in reserve too far behind the battle to be of any effective use. Instead of waiting behind the British lines in open country they had been forced to march to Loos along cluttered roads which were choked with columns of transport and wounded men. Moreover, when they reached the battlefield they found that their role had changed. The expected breakthrough was no longer possible; now the Welsh Guards would be required to support the 4th Grenadiers in their attack to retake Hill 70. If the Grenadiers faltered, then it would be up to the Welsh Guards to consolidate the line.

As soon as the Brigade reached Vermelles the pattern of the battle had become painfully clear – the ruined village was awash with wounded troops and stragglers leaving the line, while in the near distance could be heard the ominous 'short sharp thunderclap of guns'. At 2.30 p.m. Murray-Threipland received orders to move his battalion towards the line in order to commence the attack on Hill 70. To do so his men would have to move up to Loos across a two-mile stretch of open ground in full view of the enemy, and it was then the Welshmen showed their mettle. Private R. Smith, like many another soldier facing combat for the first time, took comfort in the close order drills which had been drummed into him during his basic training:

> It was then that we knew what war was, but every man was ready. A finer sight you would never want to see. On we went, shells and bullets and shrapnel falling all around us but not a man wavered: you would have thought we were on parade at Wellington Barracks.

Having reached Loos the Welsh Guards assembled in the main street to await further instructions and it was at that point that the men had their first experience of a German gas attack. With an ecstasy of fumbling the cumbersome HP helmets were hurriedly put on to meet this new emergency. 'There was the battalion standing about anyhow,' remembered Captain Humphrey Dene, 'and making noises like frogs and penny tin trumpets as they spat and blew down the tubes of their helmets.' In the midst of the chaos Murray-Threipland made his way to the Grenadiers' head-quarters to plan the attack: it was agreed that the Prince of Wales Company would attack on the right with 2 Company in support while 3 Company would support the Grenadiers. The attack was timed for 6.02 p.m., a quarter of an hour before dark.

Many thoughts ran through the minds of the officers and men of the Welsh Guards who pressed home their assault in the face of the German artillery barrage. A curious blend of fear, apprehension and excitement dominated everything but there was, too, an over-whelming desire to do well. Lieutenant J. A. D. Perrins had come to the battalion from the Seaforth Highlanders, a Scots regiment, and it had been made clear to him by other officers in the Guards Division that the Welsh Guards were very much 'a poor relation', an untried formation without battle honours or traditions. His main fear was that the Welsh Guards might let themselves down in the heat of the battle, 'that we should not turn out to be the family skeleton.'

Private David Britton of Swansea felt much the same way. He was in the machine-gun section which was the last to make the assault on Hill 70. While unloading the equipment from the gun limber his section had come under heavy fire. 'I was a bit flurried,' he admitted later, 'but soon got over it. We had to advance along a communication trench and came into a German trench where there were most elaborately fitted out dug-outs. I saw a dead German with his head and leg blown off.' Worse sights were to follow as the battalion reached the upper slopes of the hill. In the early evening darkness the leading sections of the Prince of Wales Company had arrived on the summit where they were subjected to a barrage of artillery and machine-gun fire which Lieutenant F. A. V. Copland-Griffiths thought was more like a tornado or a monsoon downpour than an ordinary bombardment. Forced to dig in as they could the Welsh Guards began to take heavy casualties. Captain O. T. D. Osmond Williams, whom many regarded as a future commanding officer, was mortally wounded and the remainder of his company had been scattered by the suddenness of the German riposte. Lying there in the darkness, under the crest of a hill which gave them some protection but which also denied them sight of the enemy, the Welsh Guards could only take cover and wait. They had been blooded in battle but it was at some cost: when they retired from the line the following morning and regrouped in Loos the battalion's casualties were five officers killed and five wounded and 162 NCOs and men killed, wounded or missing. 'I can't see any of the glory of war that people talk about,' Private G. A. Cooksley wrote to his parents in Cardiff several days later. 'It's all perfectly hellish.' Private A. C. Morgan of Radnor experienced similar feelings once the battle was over. Having told his parents that he was proud of his regiment's conduct he admitted that Hill 70 had been a terrifying experience: 'I don't want to see such a sight again, all the same. The dead, dying and wounded were awful to witness.'

Just as sportsmen who represent their countries in a team game like rugby football always say that their first international match passes in a blur, so too did many Welsh Guardsmen admit that their experience of the Battle of Loos was a mass of noise and confusion. 'It was a most exciting time and one which I will never forget,' recalled the machine-gunner David Britton who eventually reached the top of Hill 70. 'Our casualties were heavy but we had a splendid name which will always remain in a Welsh Guardsman's memory.' The Welsh Guards had pressed home their attack in darkness and under the trying conditions of a heavy artillery bombardment, yet they had reached their objective and in so doing had helped to steady the British front line. For the Commanding Officer that was enough and the following day, 28 September, Murray-Threipland wrote a glowing report to Lord Harlech which spoke only of his men's fortitude and courage under pressure:

> Nothing I can say would represent what I feel at the behaviour of the battalion and the leading of every officer during this trying time. There was no disorder and every platoon appeared to me to be in its place and advancing quietly and in excellent order.

The thought was echoed by Private H. T. Walton of Birmingham: 'I have never witnessed a finer sight. The men swept cross the shrapnel-swept ground as if they were on parade.' Others were less sure that it had been such a famous victory. Although Perrins was pleased that his regiment had proved its worth – 'after Loos there was no more talk of the Welsh Guards being inferior in any way' – like others he was contemptuous of the bungling that had led to so many deaths. 'Loos was yet another instance of the incompetency of the higher command being redeemed by the tenacity and gallantry of the common soldier.'

The Welsh Guards had done well, but in so doing the battalion had suffered heavy casualties. These might not have been as grievous as the British total suggests – 2,013 officers and 48,367 men – but for a young regiment they were bad enough. Loos had been a frightful failure. The line might have been advanced but the winter of 1915–16 brought only stalemate to that sector of the front. And yet, it could have been otherwise. Had French positioned the reserve IX Corps (consisting of five divisions) nearer the front then the early British breakthrough could have been exploited. No doubt, by keeping them twelve miles from the forward areas French thought it might be possible to rush them to the parts of the battlefield which most needed reinforcements but the faulty lines of communication prevented that from happening. He also regarded the Guards Division as an elite formation which should only be used to deliver a knock-out blow: many historians believe that had this experienced division been used in the first attacks on 25 September the result of the battle could have been very different.

When King George V came to present new colours to the regiment on 17 March 1925 (later postponed to 24 June on account of the King's illness) the notes for his speech emphasized the role his Welsh Guards played at Loos – 'the historic march across open country under heavy shellfire from the vicinity of Vermelles to Loos.' While wishing to praise the regiment's achievements throughout the war, the King was also anxious to emphasize three actions which he felt raised the Welsh Guards above the ordinary – Loos, Ginchy ('an instance of severe and successful fighting') and Sambre ('they carried out the difficult task of forming a long flank facing north on the left of the Guards Division attack'):

> From records which are extant it seems certain that the Battalion gained and deserved the confidence of all commanders under whom it served; that they fully maintained the high traditions of the Brigade of Guards; and that they proved themselves worthy of taking their place with the battalions of the older Regiments of the Guards Division.

Ten years earlier, when he presented the Welsh Guards with their first Colours, King George V had reminded the regiment that while 'these Colours bear no names of Battles fought, or of Victories won, your noble deeds in coming days will be inscribed upon them. In

committing these Colours to your care I know that you will look up
to them and prove yourselves true sons of loyal and gallant Wales
and worthy of the glorious traditions of the Brigade of Guards.' It
was a formal gesture, solemnizing the pact that exists between the
monarch and his soldiers, and King George took care to remind the
Welsh Guards that he expected them to be worthy of the trust he
had invested in them. At the war's end the colours showed that the
regiment had indeed kept that faith – in addition to Loos the battle
honours refer to the three battles fought by the regiment during the
Battle of the Somme – Ginchy, Flers-Courcelette and Morval; to
the Pilckem and Poelcappelle actions of Third Ypres (Passchendaele)
and to the Canal du Nord and Sambre battles fought during the
closing stages of the war.

Behind the pride taken in the names of hard-fought battles which
adorned the Welsh Guards' colours lay another emotion, almost
intangible to the outsider, but one deeply felt by the guardsmen
who fought on the Western Front. It was a belief that they had
proved themselves not just in the eyes of the world but in their own
eyes too. Alexander 'Sammy' Stanier joined the battalion in December 1917 as an eighteen-year-old ensign and was posted immediately to the Western Front at Arras. 'There was I only eighteen and
just arrived without any experience at all. Some of the guardsmen
had been there a long time and I couldn't believe it but they
accepted me. The first surprise was that they called me "sir" – up
till then I had been used to saying "sir" to everybody else!' But it
was not just the sense of acceptance which touched him – at his
own admission he had to endure the fierce gaze of a stern adjutant
(Captain G. C. Devas) – what moved him most of all was the fierce
sense of camaraderie in his platoon, the selflessness, pride and
mutual respect which bound them together in a cohesive group:

> The great thing was that they were all Welshmen. Most came from the
> same village. If somebody was left behind wounded everybody would
> volunteer to go and fetch him even under fire, because they couldn't go
> back to the village and say that they'd left Tommy behind.

The next time that the regiment received new colours came on 14
February 1940 when King George VI presented colours to the
recently formed 2nd Battalion at the Tower of London – Sammy
Stanier, now a lieutenant-colonel, commanded and he recalled that

the weather was as unkind as it had been to the 1st battalion in 1915, 'fine but bitterly cold'. Unlike the 1st Battalion whose King's Colour was adorned with the Welsh dragon ensigned by a crown with the motto 'Cymru am byth', the 2nd Battalion's King's Colour had as its badge the Leek within the Garter ensigned by a crown with the motto 'Honi soit qui mal y pense'. It had been decided to raise a 2nd Battalion in the early months of 1939 during the expansion of the army before the outbreak of war and it was formed at the Tower of London that April – 'a great feat on behalf of the regiment to be able to recruit enough good officers and other ranks to supplement the reservists and create this new child.' Many of the men were indeed reservists who had left the Welsh Guards earlier to join the Welsh police forces and although somewhat rusty they were still excellent soldiers who helped to steady the conscripted men and volunteers.

After training in the grounds of the fun fair at Theydon Bois in Epping Forest – shades of the White City experience in 1915 – the 2nd Battalion had to endure a frustrating period of public duties at the Tower of London before joining the 2nd Irish Guards and a territorial battalion of the Loyal Regiment to form the 20th Guards Brigade which was commanded by Brigadier W. A. F. L. Fox-Pitt, a distinguished Welsh Guards officer. One of its first actions was the romantic dash across the channel as part of a composite Irish–Welsh Guards Group to bring the Dutch Royal Family back to Britain after the fall of Holland at the beginning of May 1940. Later that month the battalion was engaged in more serious business during the defence of Boulogne which Fox-Pitt had been ordered to defend 'to the last man and the last round' while the British and French forces were evacuated. As Fox-Pitt later recalled it was a time of confusion – only five 1-inch maps were available for the whole brigade and even these were out of date and he did not receive any orders until after he had crossed the channel. Some idea of the difficulties he experienced in organizing the defence of the town can be seen in the fact that the only vehicle available to him to make a reconnaissance was a French car with one forward gear. Five days after their arrival Fox-Pitt's force withdrew across the Channel but not before the Welsh Guards had delayed the enemy long enough to allow a successful British evacuation. One small Welsh Guards group remained behind under the command of Major J. C. Windsor Lewis and continued fighting the Germans for a further two days before surrendering to avoid unnecessary civilian casualties. 'Boulogne 1940' became the battalion's first battle honour.

While Stanier's men were fighting it out in Boulogne the 1st Battalion was also taking part in a defensive action against the German forces which had pushed into France following the fall of Belgium and Holland. At the outbreak of war the 1st Welsh Guards had been stationed in Gibraltar but on 7 November 1939 they had sailed to Marseilles en route to Arras to reinforce the defence of Lord Gort's GHQ. On 10 May the long-awaited German attack on the Low Countries began and the war started in earnest: as had happened in Poland in the previous September it was characterized by the paralysing speed and daring of its armoured and airborne forces. Within ten days the Germans had reached the Channel coast and had successfully split the French and the British forces leaving Gort with the difficult decision to fight his way back to Dunkirk. During this critical phase the Welsh Guards' transport was attacked by German artillery near Douai on 24 May forcing them to turn. To give the forty vehicles a better chance the Welsh Guards' carrier platoon plus a number of light tanks all under the command of Lieutenant the Honourable Christopher Furness attacked the German positions near a wooded area on the rising high ground above the road. They must have known that the odds were hopelessly stacked against them but Furness and his men pressed home a frontal attack at close quarters, thereby engaging the enemy's attention and allowing the transport to make good their escape. The light tanks had been knocked out early on but attacking in a 'V' formation the carriers circled the German positions until Furness's carrier was put out of action. Undeterred he jumped down and engaged the enemy in hand-to-hand combat. Sergeant G. E. Griffin commanded the second carrier whose driver, Guardsman Griffiths, had been badly wounded in the right arm, and he was never to forget the dash and courage of the men under Furness's command that day:

> Following our leader, we gained the rise, firing and circling the main position which was by now very close.
> By now Driver Griffiths could steer only with his left arm and we were going out of control, firing whenever a target appeared. Those kaleidoscopic images are impressed on my mind: Lieutenant Furness standing up in his carrier, revolver drawn, shooting at a German officer he was holding by the throat. We kept circling – two Germans

appeared from behind the haystacks and made towards the now silent
carrier where the German officer was squirming on the ground in his
death throes. I shot the two just before we crashed into the back of
Lieutenant Furness's carrier which showed no signs of life. There was
now a hail of crossfire from both flanks.

My brave driver had nearly fainted, hence the crash. But he managed
to reverse from the lead carrier. We were the only vehicle moving and
were being struck by armour piercing tracer which set us alight.

Guardsman Griffiths gallantly started our withdrawal down the slope
while I alternately steered and sprayed the fire with an extinguisher.
The fire was too fierce, so I removed the wounded and the dead and
abandoned the carrier.

Of the nine men in the carrier section four were killed, four
wounded and one taken prisoner. For his exploit Furness was
awarded the Victoria Cross posthumously. It was the second such
honour to be won by the regiment.

Like their compatriots in the 2nd Battalion, the 1st Battalion,
commanded by Lieutenant-Colonel F. A. V. Copland-Griffiths,
was able to get back to Britain, having played a valuable role in
stemming the German advance during the retreat to Dunkirk.
Altogether, the battalions had lost seventy-two officers and men
killed, eighty-eight wounded while 453, including many wounded,
had gone into German captivity. Although these losses were made
good by recruits from the Welsh Guards training battalion based at
Sandown Park, there was no denying that both battalions, like the
rest of the British Army at that time, were lacking the equipment
needed to meet any invasion threat, or, indeed, to take the war back
to Germany.

While the 2nd Battalion went to Byfleet, the 1st Battalion was
stationed at Wimbledon as part of the 24th Independent Guards
Brigade. For the first few days 3 Company was billeted in the
grounds of the All England Tennis Club. 'Dare I say it,' remembered one of their number, 'but a game of rugger was played
on the hallowed grass of Centre Court until we were shooed away,
no harm done.' As he was to discover, sleeping in the stand of
Centre Court was not the only luxury afforded to the battalion:

Our transport at that time was a fleet of civilian luxury coaches
commandeered by the military authorities and civilian police motor
cyclists escorted us on our exercises. It was travelling in style but when
equipped in fighting order it was difficult to move. Therefore we

trained for quick embussing and debussing, Major Ashton timing our activities with a stop watch. Later we were issued with workmanlike troop carriers, very draughty but made for the job, they served us well throughout the war. We missed the coaches as not only were they used operationally by the battalion but also for social purposes . . . two were kept and sprayed green to conform with the rest of our transport. They were used throughout the war on diverse duties, often as passion wagons.

As with previous invasion scares during the nation's history there was no shortage of national spirit and the army expanded quickly. A 3rd Battalion of the Welsh Guards was raised a year later, in October 1941, under the command of Lieutenant-Colonel A. M. Bankier: it was destined to spend its war in North Africa and Italy as part of the 1st Guards Brigade and its battle honours are Fondouk and Hammam Lif from the North African campaign and Monte Piccolo, Monte Ornito and Battaglia from Italy. The 3rd Battalion never received colours being a wartime formation which was disbanded in April 1946, but as Major Ellis, the regimental historian for the Second World War, points out, it had a reputation earned in action equal to any other battalion in the Brigade of Guards.

While the 3rd Battalion was taking the war to the enemy a momentous change had taken place in the 1st and 2nd Battalions. In June 1941 a Guards Armoured Division was formed at the instigation of General Sir Alan Brooke who believed that the defence of the country at the time, and the future conduct of the war, should be built around the creation of armoured divisions. At the time the bulk of Britain's armoured troops were in North Africa: initially two infantry divisions would be converted for armoured warfare and Brooke's choice for one fell on the Brigade of Guards because he felt that they possessed the motivation and the high standards of training to change from one type of soldiering to another. Besides, he was aware that most Guards officers, including those of the 1st and 2nd Battalions Welsh Guards, who had already fought in France, had been suitably impressed by the performance of the German panzer groups to believe that armour rather than infantry could be the decisive arm when the allies returned to liberate Europe. King George VI was in favour of the proposal and by the summer's end the new Guards Armoured Division had begun training on the Salisbury Plain area under the command of General Sir Oliver Leese.

It was not an easy process. As Major Ellis remembered in his war history, training as tankmen meant that different skills had to be learned: 'they had to learn first of all how a tank works and how to maintain it in working order, and how to drive it not only on the road but across rough country – in other words to learn Driving and Maintenance, that unfathomable mystery known to tank lovers as D and M. Also they had now to learn to shoot, not with a rifle but a gun (and different sorts of guns at that), and not only when they were stationary and could take careful aim but on the move. And they must learn to use wireless constantly, both to receive orders from outside and to pass orders to each other through the noise inside a tank.'

Not only that but the 2nd Battalion had to reorganize itself to conform with the structure of an armoured regiment – three squadrons each with five troops took the place of four rifle companies each with three platoons. The battalion was equipped with Cromwells, 'a thoroughbred amongst tanks' according to Major Ellis, remarkable for their speed, endurance and impressive firepower and the battalion's duties were to be armoured reconnaissance, a task they shared with the 2nd Battalion Household Cavalry who were equipped with armoured cars. 'It's amusing to look back on our training,' remembered one sergeant. 'For our first few lessons we didn't have tanks so we actually used six-foot long forms which represented tanks and we practised mounting and dismounting on them.'

At the same time the 1st Battalion formed 32nd Guards Brigade with the 5th Battalion Coldstream Guards and the 3rd Battalion Irish Guards; they would be the infantry component of the division. From Salisbury Plain the training continued in Thetford (Norfolk) and Pickering (North Yorkshire) where the final preparations were made for the long-awaited invasion of Europe.

Our exercises continued on the Yorkshire moors, weapon training, battle drill, arms drill, digging and more digging. No doubt about it, the orders given by Lieutenant-Colonel Jefferson in the early days of the war had come to fruition. 3 Company was the best in the battalion: we had a camaraderie par excellence, we were more like brothers and we were itching to go to war. We never doubted our cause, we knew we could beat the Germans and beat them in Europe at that. The Second Front would come soon, it was on all our lips – but when?

Meirion Ellis had joined the 1st Battalion at the outbreak of war: for him and his fellow 'iron men' the waiting came to an end when the Guards Armoured Division crossed to France between 18 and 29 June shortly after the first phase of the fighting in Normandy. At that stage Montgomery's plan was to deploy a show of force in the eastern sector around Caen and to seek a decisive battle with the German panzers which would clear the way into the open country that led to Paris. This was Operation Goodwood, the famous 'Goodwood Meeting' which the Welsh Guards officers faced with the same equanimity as if Ascot were already behind them. It was during this battle that they lost one of their best liked officers, Rex Whistler, who was hit by a fragment of mortar bomb as he moved across open ground near Emieville. A respected artist, he had enlivened regimental life with his many paintings and his last work had been executed in the Prince Regent's Pavilion at Brighton where the 2nd Battalion had been billeted before the invasion – this is the well-known depiction of King George IV as a prince of pleasure. For the Guards Armoured Division he had designed the divisional sign, a reworking of the famous 'eye' which had seen the Guards Division through the First World War.

By August the battle for Normandy had been won but ahead still lay the bitter fighting in Holland and along the German border, the enemy having found the strength to hold the allied advance and to prolong the war until May 1945. Many of the Welsh Guards who served in the campaign in north-west Europe have admitted that they were taken aback by the ferocity and ruthlessness of the German soldiers they met in the field. Whereas most guardsmen felt that they were fighting an unglamorous though necessary battle for democracy against an evil enemy, the Germans seemed to show a single-minded concentration in stemming the allied advance. Often their fanaticism, or devotion to duty, left a deep impression on those who witnessed it. For example, one bizarre incident near Montchamp left an indelible memory for the men of the 1st battalion's 3 Company when they saw their own captured three-ton truck being driven towards them by German soldiers:

We noticed a waggon approaching and as it came nearer it was noticed that it was British – then someone realized it was our own cooker and smelt a rat. We covered it with our PIAT and a Bren gun. Twenty yards or so from our road block it stopped, the canopy was thrown back and a German soldier with a machine-gun sprayed our position – but we beat him to it as a bomb from the PIAT hit the bonnet and at the same time our Bren gun opened fire. The lorry burst into flames, and with it like a torch burned the German soldier. Incredibly, he started to sing and as he sang he fired his gun until he was dead. Those near him looked spellbound by the awesome spectacle. Sounds of screaming, too, came from the rear of the truck which was burning furiously. This prompted 2734503 Guardsman Buckley, a man noted for sensitivity and compassion, to jump out of his slit trench and to clamber on to the rear of the lorry to help the unfortunate man. But a German patrol which had been covering the lorry opened fire and killed this brave unselfish man, an old soldier who had only been married a few weeks.

The Welsh Guards were to meet again that kind of German sacrificial behaviour, so untypical of the British soldier, when they fought the Battle of Hechtel, one of the bloodiest actions experienced by the regiment during the Second World War. By then the 1st and 2nd Battalions had been amalgamated within the Guards Armoured Division to form a Welsh Guards Battle Group and they had been the first allied formation to reach Brussels on 3 September 1944. This heroic dash over ninety-two miles took the better part of a day, the challenge having been thrown down by the divisional commander, Major-General Allan Adair, with the stirring order: 'Intention: Guards Armoured Division will advance and capture Brussels – and a very good intention too.' The gauntlet was picked up by Lieutenant-Colonel J. C. Windsor Lewis who called the officers of the 2nd Battalion and told them, 'Tomorrow night I'll have my dinner in Brussels.' Everyone smiled at the idea but the mission was accomplished without meeting much enemy opposition and by nightfall on 3 September the tanks and tankmen of the 2nd Battalion and the guardsmen of the 1st Battalion were encamped in the streets of Brussels. For Captain R. V. J. Evans, one of the Welsh Guards tank commanders, it was the most joyous moment of the war:

As I started into the outskirts now by myself I saw a fantastic sight, there lining the roads and advancing down the roads thirty or forty deep were thousands and thousands of people all absolutely crazy with joy. From this moment onwards there was chaos. All hope of seeing or moving tactically was finished, at least forty people climbed on my tank, men, women and children embracing me, bottles of wine being broken and poured all over me, boxes of 100 cigars ad lib. The tank was covered nearly 6″ deep with every conceivable type of fruit and flowers, particularly some wonderful gladioli. By this time I was perspiring freely, I could not traverse the turret, nor fire, nor use the wireless as the aerials were having a rough time of it. I went slowly up one road with my human cargo to a crossroads. A column of German transport came across my front, quite slowly. I could do nothing. Eventually I fired a short burst of besa, but it was too late. I was now fired on by some sort of gun and decided to drop back a bit. The chaos became even greater as more and more wildly cheering people rushed into the centre of the town. I was embraced and kissed until nearly suffocated. It was now getting dark and we gave up all ideas of moving far and we harboured in one of the main boulevards, tanks in the trees down the centre and our infantry around us. No one went to bed in the town and we were visited all night by happy people who were laughing for the first time in four years.

The revels continued for a further two days but the people of Brussels were not the only ones to be pleased with the Welsh Guards' achievement; so too was XXX Corps commander Lieutenant-General Brian Horrocks. Describing the capture of the city in a BBC 'War Report' programme the following day, he said that it was all due to the fact that he 'had the pick of the British Army and nothing could stop them.'

To commemorate the event the famous figure of the Mannekin Pis was presented with a Welsh Guards uniform a year later. Also known as the 'Petit Julien', this celebrated chap showers water into a fountain in a most ingenious and entertaining fashion; he represents a popular hero from Brussels' folklore who owned many suits of clothes and each year on 3 September he finds himself wearing the full dress uniform of a regimental sergeant-major of the Welsh Guards in honour of the regiment which had helped to liberate his city all those years ago.

With Brussels taken and Antwerp, too, having fallen the next allied plan was to consolidate a bridgehead on the northern Rhine before the onset of winter.

HECHTEL

Not without reason Hechtel has been called a real Welsh Guards battle, largely because it involved Welsh armour and infantry acting in concert, but also because it brought out in full measure the spirit of resilience and dogged determination which had grown up in the regiment during the three months they had been fighting against the Germans in France and Belgium.

After the fall of Brussels and Antwerp there was a general and understandable tendency to relax and to promote a feeling that the Germans had been defeated and the war won. In his diary Captain Evans describes the mood of euphoria that swept through the Guards Division like wildfire and which made each man a hero – 'we were given grapes, wine, fruit and kisses galore, I found myself signing my name more than a hundred times for all the young women.' It was encouraged by the senior commanders, too; both Eisenhower and Montgomery believed that it would be possible to enter the Ruhr and the Saar by late autumn and that the war could be over by Christmas. This was not idle thinking. The Germans had been decisively beaten and their forces had been broken up and demoralized; the allies held the upper hand and the argument for an all-out thrust into Germany seemed irresistible.

However, there were still logistical problems for the allies to overcome. Because the Germans held the main Channel ports, only Cherbourg, four hundred miles away from the front line, could be used for re-supply, and the lines of communication were over-stretched and liable to break down. Antwerp had been captured, it is true, but it could not come into full use as a port of entry until the Germans had been cleared from the Schelde estuary. This Montgomery declined to do as it would mean turning his men back in their tracks; instead, he determined to keep up the forward momentum. His plan was to leap over the Meuse and the Lower Rhine and to establish a foothold in the north German plain from which he could threaten the Ruhr. This was one of the key moments in the war and it was also the culmination of the dispute between those who favoured a broad front of advance, Eisenhower and Bradley, and those who preferred a lance-like stab along a narrow front, namely Montgomery in the north and Patton in the south. Against all his earlier judgements, Eisenhower, overall commander of the land forces after 10 September, gave the go-ahead to

Montgomery's 'race to the Rhine', the push forward by airborne forces and armoured columns which would lead to the disaster of Arnhem at the month's end.

The allied delay at Antwerp was to have other important tactical considerations for the German Army. They were left free to destroy the bridges over the Albert Canal and, as had happened so often before during the war, they were able to regroup and to reorganize themselves in strong defensive positions. Montgomery's response was to push ahead with plans to deploy an airborne force along a fifty-mile corridor at the bridgeheads at Eindhoven, Nijmegen and Arnhem. The waterways of the Maas, Waal and Neder Rijn having been secured, the armoured and motorized columns would then break out of Belgium to the Zuider Zee and in one stroke Holland would be cut in two, the German defences would be outflanked and the allies would be established in the northern Ruhr.

As part of this plan the Guards Armoured Division, including the Welsh Guards Group, was ordered to cross the Albert Canal and to head towards the Meuse–Escaut Canal which would be the start line for the race to the Rhine. The plans allowed for the taking of the defensively strategic villages of Helchteren and Hechtel which stood in a terrain which lent itself to defence – sandy heath broken by small streams and patches of swamp. Here the Germans had dug themselves in, holding the crossroads and the villages: they were prepared to fight with a fanaticism which surprised the Welsh Guards who soon discovered that they would have to slog it out from street to street and from house to house.

On 6 September the Welsh Guards Group led the Guards Armoured Division's advance towards their first objectives, the bridges over the Albert Canal at Beeringen and Tissenderlo. At Beeringen, the Welsh Guards' crossing point, the group found the bridge partially destroyed and the Germans firmly entrenched on the other side; meanwhile at Tissenderlo the Grenadiers and the Coldstreamers found the bridge there equally badly damaged. Heavy machine-gun fire from the opposite bank at Beeringen prevented any further progress until the Germans made a sudden and unexpected tactical withdrawal which allowed three rifle companies of the 1st Welsh Guards to cross the canal. First on to the bridge were men of Prince of Wales Company with 3 Company close behind and as Meirion Ellis remembered it was a chancy business clambering across the badly broken structure:

Major Miller [commanding Prince of Wales Company] was urging everyone to get across, it was just what we were waiting for. We raced for the bridge in good section order, more like hares or mountain goats, a massive scramble of Welsh Guardsmen, we leapt from board to board doing exactly what Major Miller asked us to do. We were too preoccupied ensuring that we did not fall into the canal to worry about Germans – a slip would have meant certain death as the weight of our kit would have taken us to the bottom of the canal. Yes! Welsh Goats would have been an appropriate word to describe us on that day.

By then a team of Royal Engineers had arrived to repair the bridge and early the following morning the tanks of the 2nd Battalion were able to cross to the other side of the Albert Canal; by then, too, the Germans had returned to mount stiff opposition with mortar fire and artillery fire from a number of self-propelled guns. It was the beginning of five days of fierce fighting against an enemy which was determined to yield ground only after putting up the stoutest resistance.

Having crossed the canal the Welsh Guards columns pushed eastwards towards the village of Helchteren where they again came under heavy fire, much of it from anti-tank guns. It was obvious that the Germans had managed to regroup and were using the flat cultivated countryside with its hedges and woodlands to good advantage. During this advance the Welsh Guards scored an easy if bloody victory over a German cyclists battalion which was resting at the roadside. To the Welsh Guards armoured columns the Commanding Officer's order was clear enough – 'There is a battalion of infantry approaching us down the road. Go and destroy them.' As one of the guardsmen remembered later, what happened next was executed quickly and efficiently, the Germans were surprised and the action lasted barely three minutes:

The orders were simple, no one could have misunderstood them. Within seconds we were on our TCVs, the squadron of tanks leading – we were moving fast, maybe fifty miles an hour. We heard the machine-guns of our tanks and then we were amongst this most unfortunate battalion of the Hermann Goering Regiment. They were cyclists and lay spreadeagled head to toe in the ditches, their cycles alongside them. We threw grenades at them, fired our brens and rifles, grenades thrown by the armour were exploding as we passed, those of us firing could see bodies bouncing up in the air because of the impact of the bullets, those who could not or would not fire quite simply looked with astonishment at this pure act of war and naked aggression. Just as quickly we passed the enemy and our transport stopped. We quickly debussed and lined the side of the road. It was not over as terrified German soldiers ran towards us, hands in the air – they came from all directions, mostly from the roadside scrub; they ran only a few yards yet they were panting and their faces ashen grey. This was pure fear: no one could be surprised at that, they had just witnessed the scene of the crushing of their own battalion, in what must have been the fastest and most efficient destruction of a strong force in any war.

After the guardsmen had rounded up the shaken survivors humanity returned to the battlefield as cigarettes and chocolate were passed to the prisoners who 'seemed pleased that now the war was over for them at least'. In the days to come there would be no other victory so cheaply won.

From Helchteren the heavily defended village of Hechtel lay just four miles to the north and the first attack on it was made by the iron men of 3 Company with the tanks of 1 Squadron in support, but meeting heavy opposition they were forced to withdraw at nightfall. During the evening the Irish Guards relieved the Welsh Guards at Beeringen, allowing the group to concentrate behind the village of Helchteren prior to the following morning's attack on Hechtel. 'We got into the outskirts the first night and couldn't get any further, so we withdrew,' remembered Peter Leuchars who had been with 3 Company since joining up in 1941. 'We then tried a second attack but that got held up and we had to pull out. That was very unpleasant. Meanwhile every night that village was being reinforced.'

Realizing the strategic importance of Hechtel – it lay on the axis of the Beeringen–Eindhoven road which provided a direct corridor into northern Holland – the German commander Field Marshal Model had made strenuous efforts to push experienced reinforcements into this vital defensive position. Facing the Welsh Guards at Hechtel were the 1st Hermann Goering Regiment and the 10th (Grasmel) parachute regiment. There were also elements of the Hitler Youth who fought hard but who then wept tears of mortification upon surrendering – much to the embarrassment of the Welsh Guardsmen who captured them. The German infantrymen in Hechtel had armoured support as well as medium artillery and anti-tank weapons.

At 8.30 a.m. on 8 September the Welsh Guards resumed their attack on Hechtel with Prince of Wales Company and X Company

Scots Guards (attached to the Welsh Guards since August, commanded by Major 'Feathers' Steuart Fotheringham) and the tanks of 2 Squadron. Both groups of infantry encountered determined opposition as they attempted to occupy their sectors, X Company the north-eastern side of the village and Prince of Wales Company the western side; by evening they had dug themselves in and the day ended with a truce which allowed the Welsh Guards to evacuate their wounded. To one eye-witness the scene in Hechtel was one of utter chaos:

> And so night came over Hechtel. In the Kloosterstraat the house of Henri Snoek was on fire and in the Kerkstraat the flames of the house of Hubert Wuyts threw a red colour over the surroundings. In the flickering light of the flames phantoms could be seen of people who tried to save what they could of their possessions and of soldiers who were pulling away wounded. The advance platoons of the Scots limited their movements to a minimum in order not to betray their positions.

During the night both companies had to fight off German attacks on their positions on the outskirts of the village and suffered heavy casualties during the bitter hand-to-hand fighting. To strengthen the Welsh Guards' position the following day (9 September) 3 Company was moved up on the right of Prince of Wales Company. 'I would not say we were looking forward to this second visit,' recalled Meirion Ellis. 'Silent empty villages are never inviting; in any case we could not always be lucky.' Curiously, amid the carnage and destruction the guardsmen found life going on as usual. Those villagers who had not taken to their cellars or air raid shelters remained where they were and while accompanying his company commander Peter Beckwith-Smith, Meirion Ellis was surprised to come across one family still sitting in their kitchen – 'one lady beckoned me over for a coffee. Entering the house I saw five other people, they spoke quietly, the room was highly polished and in the centre was a very ornate shining black stove with a fire burning in it, so the weather was obviously getting colder. We stayed only a few moments and tried to explain to them that they should move out or at least get under the floor boards. They listened intently but I doubt if they understood.' Some idea of the close quarter nature of the fighting which typified Hechtel can be found in the experience of a lance-sergeant who bumped into an equally astonished German soldier while they were searching a house: both let the other go, a short personal truce in the midst of a hard fought battle.

Even the use of the 2nd Battalion's tanks could not break the deadlock. On 9 September six German Panther tanks arrived in the village – huge machines, the outstanding German tank of the campaign in north-west Europe whose fourteen-pound shells could penetrate even the most robust allied tank armour at a distance of 100 yards – and the Welsh Guards' Cromwells were 'ordered up to Hechtel in a hell of a hurry'. One of the Panthers was destroyed by Lieutenant Hugh Griffiths who allowed it to pass by his Cromwell before shooting it up from behind. The next day saw the Welsh Guards' tanks in action again:

> Spent a bloody awful day [diary of Captain Evans], ordered to do a suicidal motor straight through the village from west to east. Poor Sjt Appleby had to lead, he was bazookaed on the main X roads but I think all the crew baled out and are now prisoners. I nearly broke my right arm when the gun recoiled. Nasty situation only just relieved in the evening when the Germans counter-attacked. Our infantry withdrew in haste but were rallied.

The fighting followed the same pattern for the next two days as the three companies supported by armour tried unsuccessfully to move forward into the village. 'Everyone is tired,' noted Evans on 11 September. 'We have all seen enough and heard enough of this bloody village called Hechtel – may it rot in hell and the Germans in it.' That same day 4 Company attacked from the south of the village and linked up with 3 Company but could get no further.

The stalemate was first broken by events elsewhere when the tanks of the Household Cavalry and elements of the Grenadier and Irish Guards broke through the German lines to the west, between Hechtel and Bourg Leopold, a village nearby where the Germans had held up the Coldstream Guards with the same determination they had shown against the Welsh Guards. This initiative allowed the first columns of the Guards Armoured Division to move up to De Groot Barrier, the bridgehead over the Meuse–Escaut Canal. Hechtel had been by-passed and was virtually surrounded but still the Germans refused to surrender; as it was impossible to leave the village in enemy hands the Welsh Guards had to press home a decisive attack. The plan was to mount the assault on 12 September with both battalions supported by machine-guns, mortars and medium artillery, respectively of the Royal Northumberland Fusiliers and 11th Armoured Division (1st Field Regiment RA and 1st Medium Battery RA). During the night of 11/12 September the forward infantry platoons were withdrawn in preparation for the full-scale attack; as Peter Leuchars remembers this was to be the last straw, even for an enemy which had shown many soldierly qualities:

> The Germans were very professional and I'm full of admiration for the people we fought against. It's a very sandy area there and you dig slit trenches in about two minutes, but of course if a shell falls anywhere near them then the whole lot falls in. Once we got medium artillery involved there the young Germans – who weren't really properly trained and it was jolly bad luck putting them in there – were terrified and went and hid in the cellars. So on the last day it became not too difficult a battle.

The artillery barrage began at 8.00 a.m. and by midday Hechtel had fallen into the hands of the Welsh Guards. From the evidence of Dutch eye-witnesses the Germans did not give up the fight without a struggle and as a result the village was badly damaged both by the shell fire and by the fierce house-to-house fighting:

> Five hours after the offensive had started Hechtel had been taken. Dead soldiers and civilians were lying between splintered glass and broken roof tiles, their faces in the dust or towards the sky on a warm September afternoon. Damaged tanks and abandoned guns, rifles and machine guns, helmets and caps were lying around everywhere on and alongside the streets . . .
>   Burning and smoking houses, facades scarred by shell splinter, mutilated treetops and, in between, broken electricity and telephone wires hanging slack over ditches filled with rubble. A sickly smell of blood and soot that testified to the stubbornness of the battle that had just been fought . . . the drone of British vehicles. Raucous commands. Near the church the British and their chaplain were burying their slain comrades. Here and there Germans were still taken out of the cellars of houses. Their mien was so bitter and arrogant that the Welsh Guards forced them to dig their own graves and threatened to kill them. . . . Happy, but also dejected, villagers kept staring at them and sometimes charged at some defenceless and ragged prisoner who in the end would owe his life to a toughly acting British soldier in charge of the prisoners.

The five days of fighting took a heavy toll in terms of lives lost and property destroyed. The British forces lost sixty-two men killed and many more wounded while the Germans suffered around 400 casualties, including 150 dead. A further 500 went into captivity – they were marched off to Edingen near Brussels where they were kept for several days under heavy guard in an open field. As happens when fighting takes place in a built-up area the saddest cuts were reserved for the people of Hechtel: thirty-five civilians were killed, of these eleven had been executed by German firing squad on suspicion of being collaborators and a total of 121 houses were destroyed by artillery and mortar fire.

(In the midst of all the wastefulness there was one moment when tragedy was transformed into common humanity. During the battle one Welsh Guardsman was ordered to watch a row of windows and open fire if he saw any movement. Believing Germans to be inside the house he shot at a window when the curtains moved; then a woman ran from the house shouting that a young boy had been hit in the chest. The shocked guardsman ran into the building to tend the boy who was rushed to hospital in Brussels for emergency treatment. Forty years later when the Welsh Guards Association visited Hechtel to commemorate the battle, the story was told again and fifty-four year old Peter Jensen came face to face with Guardsman Walker – to the surprise of no one present, perhaps, 'they greeted one another as true friends'.)

Arguments still rage about whether or not the Battle of Hechtel should ever have been fought. Had the British not halted in Antwerp and Brussels, it has been claimed, the Germans would not have been presented with the opportunity to destroy the Albert Canal bridges and then to regroup and reinforce their defensive positions in the sector between the Albert Canal and the Maas–Scheldt canals. To General Horrocks, commanding British XXX Corps, this turned out to be one of his great 'if onlys' of the Second World War: 'I believe,' he wrote in 1960 (*A Full Life*), 'that if we had taken the chance and carried straight on with our advance instead of halting at Brussels the whole course of the war in Europe might have been changed.'

Horrocks was writing in the aftermath of war when tempers had cooled and the participants – and students of military history – were able to analyse at leisure the great amphibious, airborne and armoured operations which helped to bring the war to an end. By then it was possible to put in perspective the contrasting claims of the broad front and the narrow front policies, both of which had much in their favour. While it can be claimed that the successful and speedy capture of the Lower Rhine and the Ruhr would have placed an intolerable strain on the German will to carry on the war, the execution of the plan itself posed problems for the allied commanders. That there was a human tendency to halt awhile in Brussels and to soak up the carnival atmosphere generated by the newly liberated Belgians was natural enough, but the delay was also imposed by logistical difficulties. The allied fuel depots were several hundred miles behind the front line and fuel, ammunition, rations and reserves were always going to be in short supply if the British columns over-extended their lines of communication. In that respect it would have made sense, too, to have brought Antwerp into play as a port by clearing the Schelde estuary. This was not done until 29 November.

And then there were the Germans. In Normandy they had been fighting in a foreign country, on the outer edges of their operational area; as they pulled back towards the Rhine they were falling back on their *Heimat*, the German heartland for which they would fight with a tenacity and ferocity that often surprised and dismayed the allied soldiers. The ground-borne 1st Parachute Army, some 30,000 strong, assembled by General Kurt Student to oppose the airborne thrust into northern Holland might have come from many disparate units, many of which were only half-trained, but their determination to resist seems to have been strengthened by the certain knowledge that they were defending the frontier of the Reich.

All these factors combined to make the narrow front strategy difficult to sustain and led ultimately to the tragedy of Arnhem, the one large error of judgement Montgomery was to make during the war. Instead of relying on his previous tactics which had served the British so well – the build up of logistical support and reserves and the application of superior firepower – he was tempted by the possibilities of a short sharp thrust into well defended territory. Although his ground troops linked with the American parachutists at Eindhoven and Nijmegen, the Guards Armoured Division failed to reach the British 1st Airborne Division at Arnhem. This was not their fault: having to operate along a single road which ran through inundated fields, they simply could not keep to the agreed timetable and the surrounded airborne troops were forced to retreat as best they could. Only 2,000 men of the 9,000-strong division managed to fight their way back to the allied lines. An imaginative plan it might have been but it came at the wrong time and the wrong place in the war.

For all that the strategy can still be questioned, no one can deny the fortitude and determination shown by the Welsh Guards at Hechtel. They were facing a tough enemy which had been given ample opportunity to take up superior defensive positions but by refusing to be daunted the Welsh Guards resolutely wore down the opposition eventually with the deployment of superior firepower. The fall of Hechtel secured a vital part of the corridor towards Eindhoven, a large German force had been defeated and a substantial quantity of German equipment had been destroyed. On thanking the Welsh Guards, Lieutenant-General Sir Richard O'Connor, commanding VIII Corps, said, 'It is one thing to gain ground but it is quite another to destroy a complete enemy battalion.' This the Welsh Guards had done at Hechtel.

The Welsh Guards Group remained together until 12 March 1945 when the 1st Battalion returned to Britain to be replaced by 2nd Scots Guards; the rest of their war was to be spent at Stobo Camp near Hawick in the Scottish Borders. Plans were afoot to send them to America as part of a British expeditionary force to take the war to the Japanese in the Pacific, but before that happened the bombs on Hiroshima and Nagasaki brought the war against Japan to an end. For the 2nd Battalion the war ended on the banks of the Elbe twenty miles from Hamburg, and the 3rd Battalion's last action came on the banks of the Adige in northern Italy on 27 April 1945. During the course of the war the Welsh Guards lost 633 killed and 1,306 wounded; 170 personal awards were made for gallantry and 133 officers and men were mentioned in despatches.

The experiences of all three battalions were very different. The 1st and 2nd Battalions, united by their actions during the fall of France and by their later service with the Guards Armoured Division, seemed to have the most in common, but one battalion served as infantrymen and the other as tankmen. Not surprisingly, given their service in Italy and North Africa with the 6th Armoured Division, the 3rd Battalion was the odd man out, but whatever their experiences the Welsh Guardsmen who fought in the Second World War are united by the common factor of having served in a regiment whose fighting spirit depended ultimately on its own character, one born of tradition and national pride. For Peter Leuchars, later to rise to the rank of major-general and to become GOC Wales, this was the true strength of being a Welsh Guardsman:

> I've always said that if you're in a really sticky position I would sooner be there with Welshmen than with anybody else. They have extraordinary determination. If they are really miserable they start to sing and they sing so beautifully. That happened frequently in the war when we were in a miserable position – suddenly they would start singing and everything would be fine.

From Sammy Stanier listening to his men vowing never to leave a boy from the village wounded in no man's land, to Peter Leuchars hearing his men singing after Hechtel, in a mere thirty years the fighting spirit of the Welsh Guards had been proved beyond any possible doubt.

Chapter Four

MORE OF A
FAMILY REALLY

THE STRUCTURE OF the regular British Army of today is firmly regimental. A man might join the army and swear his soldier's oath of allegiance to the Queen but he will then belong to a regiment which he will find is more of a home than a military formation. He will learn to think of himself as a Green Jacket, a Welch Fusilier or a Gordon and he will take a special interest and pride in the niceties of uniform, the battle honours and the traditions that make him different from a Royal Anglian, an Irish Ranger or an Argyll. As a creator of morale, the alliance between the man and his regiment has no equal: it is claimed that it will stiffen a man's courage in time of war and offer a sense of belonging in time of peace. But there is more than group loyalty at work here, an artificial bond imposed by the army to keep its men under control. A civilian might smile at the notion of a young Welsh Guardsman being imbued with the courage of the men who broke the German defences at Hammam Lif but as George Younger, a former Argyll officer and one time Minister of Defence, has pointed out, there are good practical reasons for allowing the idea to persist. If men behave well under fire their bravery will be praised by later generations; but if they let down their comrades on the battlefield, then that will also be remembered.

Although the regimental system has been tried and tested over the years and is held in high regard by senior infantrymen, this does not mean that it is sacrosanct. Zealous army reformers have frequently promoted the concept of a Corps of Infantry, similar to the Corps of Engineers or Corps of Transport in which the regiments or battalions are numbered and there is a central reservoir of reinforcements with a free transfer of officers and men from unit to unit as the need arises. They also add that the strong regimental spirit fostered by the infantry, inspiring though it might be, can lead to a lack of co-operation with the rest of the army. Needless to say, the attempts to form a corps establishment have been stoutly resisted by the hierarchies of the line infantry regiments who have fought long and hard to retain the hallmarks which make them different from their neighbours. The principal argument for retaining their territorial designations is that these have been evolved over the years and they help to produce a sense of group identity and loyalty. To take one example: the Duke of Wellington's Regiment, a Yorkshire based regiment, is still the only line infantry regiment in the British Army to bear the name of a commoner in its title, a distinction of which it is rightly proud, and few people outside the army know, or even care, that it is numbered 33rd and 76th.

Nevertheless, ever since the Second World War when the regimental system broke down temporarily owing to the need to provide regular drafts of men to the infantry, there have been several far-reaching changes to the line regiments. In a typically British compromise the line regiments remained, but they became mutually supporting units of five large infantry divisions and during the process many regiments became unrecognizable. A handful of eleven remained more or less intact: one of these is the Royal Scots, the 1st of Foot and the oldest line infantry regiment in the British Army, older than the Guards, having been formed by a Scots aristocrat in 1633 for service in the pay of the King of France. Others helped to form 'large' regiments like the Royal Anglian Regiment which is a hybrid made up of nine old English county regiments, including the Royal Norfolk and the Royal Leicestershire both of which date from the 1680s. It was formed in 1964 when the army planners believed that the creation of larger formations would improve recruitment, training and the prospects for promotion. During the same period eleven more regiments were formed by amalgamation and two, the Cameronians and the York and Lancaster Regiment, disappeared altogether.

By a process of concession, compromise and amalgamation, therefore, the line regiments managed to avoid the awful fate of the formation of a Corps of Infantry such as the Americans possess. Purists might protest that the Royal Regiment of Wales, formed in 1969, has neither identity nor traditions, whereas its component parts the South Wales Borderers and the Welch Regiment possessed these in abundance, but there is little doubt that the continuing links with Wales enjoyed by the regiment are central to its recruiting policies. A young man, newly volunteered, will be trained centrally at the depot of the Prince of Wales's Division but from day one, if he is a Welshman and that is his choice, he will be badged into the Royal Regiment of Wales. Although he might be cross-posted within the Division later in his career he will continue to think of himself as a soldier of his original regiment and his name will still appear on its roll.

For the British infantryman this is the apogee of the regimental system and from the very outset of his career the recruit will be well versed in the history and traditions of the regiment of his choice. He will learn about the battle honours and about the pride, if he is of their number, of being one of the six Minden regiments. He will be told about the peculiarities and the significance of the uniform he wears, whether it be a badge worn at the back of the collar or the black buttons on his spats. He will be shown the regimental silver and the trophies and later he might be quizzed about the origins of the silver Gateway to India which sits in the officers' mess. All these customs and traditions help to reinforce his sense of belonging. Senior officers and NCOs have the greatest interest in promoting this *esprit de corps* but when they describe their regiment as more of a family than a military formation, they mean what they say. The regiment, said Field Marshal Sir William Slim, was undoubtedly 'the moral strength of the British Army'.

Unlike the experiences of the line regiments, the regiments of the Guards Division – and the battalions of the Parachute Regiment – survived intact the process of amalgamation and disbandment. The Welsh Guards might have lost their wartime 2nd and 3rd battalions but they remain in essence very much the regiment that was formed in 1915. The regimental spirit survives too. When Brigadier M. C. Thursby-Pelham, a distinguished former Regimental Lieutenant-Colonel, presented the traditional leeks to the 1st battalion in 1988 he said, 'The feeling of being a family regiment was stronger than ever, and that is just what it should be.' Speak to most Welsh Guards today about the ties which bind them to the regiment and they will reply, 'we're more of a family really', or as one former guardsman who became an officer put it, 'we're brothers in arms – the first thing I noticed was the sense of comradeship amongst the men in the regiment'. He joined the Welsh Guards in

1. King George V investing Sergeant Robert Bye with the Victoria Cross on 27 September 1917.

2. 'You have to raise a regiment of Welsh Guards.' Lord Kitchener in 1915.

4

6

3. Colonel William Murray-Threipland, DSO.

4. Colonel Lord Harlech.

5. Lieutenant The Hon. Christopher Furness, VC.

6. The Victoria Cross.

7. Prince Edward was very fond of his Welsh Guards. Colonel M. B. Beckwith-Smith, HRH The Prince of Wales, Colonel R. E. K. Leatham and Sergeant-Major Stevenson.

8. The Welsh Guards won the Army Rugby Cup Final in the 1922–23 season and were runners-up three times during the 1920s. Lieutenant Gavin Young, in the stripes, captained both the regiment's and the army's rugby XVs.

9. The Guards Armoured Division crossed to France between 18 and 29 June, shortly after the first phase of the fighting in Normandy. These are Cromwell tanks of the 2nd Battalion Welsh Guards.

10. En route to Hechtel across the Escaut canal. Hechtel was one of the bloodiest actions experienced by the regiment during the Second World War.

11. 'Intention: Guards Armoured Division will advance and capture Brussels – and a very good intention too.' Nurses cheer the Welsh Guards on their way to Brussels in September 1944.

12. The Mannekin Pis of Brussels being dressed in the uniform of a Regimental Sergeant-Major, Welsh Guards.

13. Men of the 16th Independent Parachute Company taking over from the Welsh Guards at Buckingham Palace on 24 August 1948. Their uniforms show the austerity of the war years.

14. King George VI presents new Colours to the regiment.

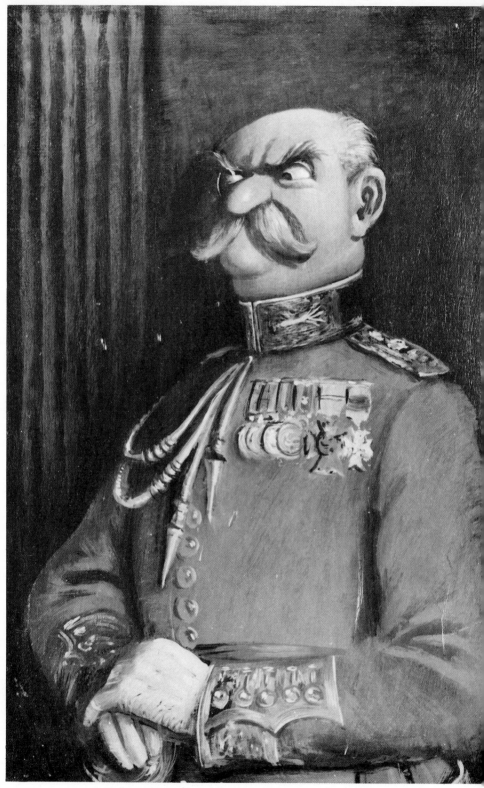

15. Colonel Blimp painted by Rex Whistler. The artist left much of his work to the regiment.

1944 as a conscript and immediately felt accepted; despite differences of age and background among the men in the platoon, he
sensed that he had 'come home'. One night in Germany that belief
was put to the test:

> I can remember an occasion going out before orders had been put up
> and getting back before midnight to find that I was on guard the next
> morning. When I went to my room there was all my kit pressed, ironed
> and cleaned and ready to go on guard. They had noticed it and had this
> feeling that they had to look after their own.

One strand of this family loyalty comes from the Welsh people
themselves. Some eight hundred years ago the historian Giraldus
Cambrensis noted that his fellow countrymen 'consider liberality
and hospitality among the first virtues'. He also wrote that in war
the Welsh are 'bold in the first onset, but cannot bear a repulse';
however, it is not the Welshman's ability in combat that concerns us
here; it is his sense of family and his love of community.

As with the other Celtic peoples of Britain, the Irish and the
Scots, the family is an important symbol in Wales; the Welsh word
for nation is *cenedl*, meaning 'generation', the mother is often the
most important member of the family and Welsh people are generally very interested in their pedigrees. This has less to do with the
fact that most Welshmen recognize themselves through their names
– all those Rhyses, Joneses, Williamses, Robertses and Evanses – but
more to do with the fact that whether living in the industrial
settlements of the south or in the open moorlands of the back
country they place great store by a sense of community. 'The most
obvious expression of this lies in the Welsh gift for hospitality,'
claimed the novelist Wyn Griffith. 'No one can visit the country
without being impressed by this trait, whether he be an exile in
time of war, an evacuated child from the slums of big cities whose
foster-parents denied themselves to clothe him, a casual visitor
detained by chance in a remote hamlet, or a professed student of
social conditions staying in a mining valley.' The by-product of this
open-handedness, he continued, is a genuine interest in other people,
not just in those who live within the community but also in those
who visit it. *Dewch i mewn* – 'Come in!' – is a familiar, yet genuine,
greeting of welcome throughout Wales and writers as different as
George Borrow and Gerard Manley Hopkins have written glowing
tributes to Welsh hospitality and kindness.

Further evidence of that intimacy is a deep love of the country, another trait which the Welsh share with their Celtic near-neighbours. Far from home they will wax sentimental about the valleys of their childhood years, about the long pull up Cadair Idris or about the small village in the hills with the wind whistling around it. They will sing sentimentally about such places in their songs: often, to an Englishman, these sound like dirges, tuneful and melodic in their own right and beautifully sung, but mournful to the ear. Wyn Griffith served with the Royal Welch Fusiliers in the First World War and during the Battle of the Somme he was asked by an English brigadier why the men sang so sadly. 'They are being themselves, not men in uniform,' he replied. 'They are back home, with their families, in the valleys.' Singing has always been one way for the Welsh to express their love of country, that extended family which is their home. After the Welsh Guards' attack on the Gouzeau-court Ridge in December 1917, a bloody action which cost them 278 casualties, an officer listened to the survivors singing softly in unison 'In the sweet bye and bye we shall meet on that beautiful shore.' 'To those listening silently,' he remembered, 'the song was a triumphal tribute to the indomitable spirit of the Welshmen. Many were missing from the voices of the previous week's gathering, voices which were in some cases stilled for ever; but the gaps had already been closed. And so in song, these men were showing yet again in their traditional manner that Welshmen are a people whom no terrible power can still for long.'

The army, so it is claimed, is only the nation in uniform. When the raw recruit joins the Welsh Guards he takes that sense of family, and the extended family that is Wales, with him into the army. There it is merged with another kind of family, the regiment, which he learns to regard as home. He might have to watch his step in the early days and learn not to speak out of turn, there are sure to be rebuffs before he is fully accepted but one day, as many have discovered, he will realize that he is among friends, men who accept him for what he is.

From the day that he took command Murray-Threipland was determined that the Welsh Guards should foster that sense of belonging. Many of the Grenadier and Scots Guards who joined the regiment at the beginning were Welshmen who were more than happy to generate a family feeling and to promote the idea of

Welshness. A glance at the records, though, shows that many other recruits came from Liverpool or London, two came from Airdrie in Scotland, one from Cambridge: they too had to be instilled with the kind of regimental pride insisted upon by their colonel. Small but important reminders that they were a Welsh regiment helped them along the way – the gold leek is the most easily recognized of the foot guards' cap badges, the Welsh Guards' quick march is 'The Rising of the Lark', the slow march the patriotic 'Men of Harlech' and the St David's Day parade and reunion quickly established itself among the regiment's calendar of events.

Although he was not a Welshman himself Murray-Threipland's wife was and she took a deep interest in the welfare of the regiment. She knew many of the men in the battalion by their name and number and was never slow to act on their behalf. During the First World War, with her husband in France, she was responsible for organizing the parcels of comforts which were sent to the fifteen Welsh Guards' prisoners of war who had been captured during operations against the enemy in 1915 and 1916. Throughout the war it was possible for families in Britain to communicate with fathers, husbands or sons who had been taken prisoner and were being held either in enemy prisoner of war camps or in captivity in neutral countries. It was also possible to send, post-free, parcels weighing up to 11 lbs provided that the contents met with the regulations laid down by the Central Prisoners of War Committee. There were also a number of charitable associations which had been established to provide parcels of comforts and foodstuffs on a regular basis; one such, the Royal Savoy Association for the Relief of British Prisoners of War was chosen by Lord Harlech as the most suitable for those Welsh Guardsmen who were in German captivity but were not receiving parcels from their own families. On 4 February 1916 he asked Mrs Murray-Threipland if she would get the scheme off to a good start by adopting one of the prisoners of war who were in need:

I propose asking wives of officers to be responsible for 1 prisoner of war. There are at present 15 of our men prisoners, only 5 of whom are at present being provided with food. If you would care to join in this I would send you name and full particulars. The parcels we send cost about 6s. 6d. each and we send them once a fortnight . . . if you have any choice of any particular individual please let me know.

The soldier whom she chose was one Private Fowler of Cadoxton near Neath who had previously been one of her husband's orderlies: he was being held in a German prisoner of war camp in Munster, Westphalen. All that was required of her was to send a monthly cheque to the Savoy Association so that parcels could be sent to Fowler but Mrs Murray-Threipland did not let the matter stop there. A year later, on 15 May 1917 she received a card from Fowler saying, 'I haven't received any parcels for two months now, nor no bread from Berne Switz since the last week in March. Hoping you will intercede and to hear from you shortly.'

She did just that and wrote immediately to Wilfred Brook, the Secretary of the Savoy, demanding to know why her husband's orderly was being omitted from the association's fortnightly supply of food parcels. (The bread was sent separately from an agency in Switzerland.) This brought an anodyne reply noting Fowler's complaints and promising some action should it be needed. Privately, Brook took up the matter with Lord Harlech, suggesting that Fowler was either not receiving his parcels regularly or that he was making up the story in order to get additional rations. Harlech was inclined to agree because he thought it strange that Fowler was the only Welsh Guardsman to be treated in this way, but the suggestion was too much for the colonel's wife. On 29 June she returned to the attack:

> The last paragraph in your letter, I am sorry to say, it makes me despair. You quote the dates of Fowler's postcards as showing that he was wrong in his statements but you do not *read* those postcards . . . possibly you are quoting his remarks to others and making your monthly returns misleading to those who have not had the opportunity, as you have, of seeing what he really says.

A second check by Brook proved the colonel's wife right; Fowler's parcels had not been sent for a number of weeks and he was justified in making his complaints. Suitably chastened Brook wrote to Mrs Murray-Threipland apologizing for putting her to so much trouble and promising that Fowler would not go short of parcels again. Once the supply had been restored Fowler's mother learned of the regiment's intervention and wrote to thank her son's benefactor: only a family set-up, she said, would have shown such kindness to her son. Similar duties were undertaken by officers' wives during the Second World War, most notably by Lady Stanier, the wife of the commanding officer of the 2nd Battalion, and throughout the war they worked hard to send comforts to those Welsh Guardsmen who had been taken prisoner and to those who were preparing to fight in North Africa, Italy or France:

> Our welfare was always in the minds of the regiment . . . to the benefit of the majority [at Radstock] a comfortable room was set aside in the large house for our leisure. Here we could not only sit in the comfortable chairs provided, but we could also use the free writing paper, headed with the regimental motif, which had been provided for us. Of course, full use was made of this facility.

The same sergeant (1st Battalion) admitted that comforts apart, what held the men together during the Second World War was a sense of belonging which was almost tangible. Even if the guardsmen were not Welsh – many were recruited from the north of England – they were soon made to feel that they were part of a goodly Welsh fellowship. 'They are Welsh Guardsmen and once they joined us they were treated equally, the same as if they had been born and bred in Wales. They also learned that the family spirit is more binding in the Welsh Guards than in any other regiment. How? Well, I think it's just the way we are in Wales. I mean if you go to visit anyone in Wales the first thing they say to you is, "Come in and have a cup of tea."' And, as he says, the intensity of feeling injected by the war meant that a firm sense of regimental pride was quickly built up – it was almost as if the Welsh Guards had become an extended family for the Welsh and for the many orphans who joined it from the other parts of Britain.

War is of course an important watershed in the lives of ordinary men. For those who have served as combat soldiers it is an experience which they can never forget and their memories tend to be the sharpest. While they will agree that war is a nasty, cruel and brutish business, they will also admit that it changed not only their lives but the way they looked at life. One Welsh Guardsman of the First World War said that he was only able to cope with the economic horrors of the Great Depression of the 1930s because he had survived the savage fighting on the Pilcken Ridge in 1917. After that nothing could be worse for at least there was comradeship and *esprit de corps* on the Western Front, so much stronger and more acutely felt because all the Welsh Guardsmen were experiencing a common danger. Yes, it was ghastly and yes it was a hateful terrifying experience but many of the Welsh Guardsmen who served in the First World War have admitted that the fellowship within the regiment would stiffen their resolve, making it easier for them to face the mud, the danger and the ever-present fear of death. Curiously, few felt badly about the hardships and the dangers at the time and there was a tendency to put to the back of the mind the death and disfigurement of friends and comrades. The time for mourning would come later – one Welsh Guards sergeant who was at Hechtel during the Second World War remembered a friend weeping silently during a reunion while the names of the German casualties were being read out. 'It was because I was thinking of the young German lad I shot in the face with my Sten gun,' he explained. 'I can see him now and I wondered if he was amongst those whose names were read.'

Repression of war experience is also common among soldiers who have been in combat – some Welsh Guardsmen have admitted that it took many years before they were able to discuss their experiences because it was impossible for family and friends to comprehend what they had encountered. The people at home in Wales could not understand the mud of the Somme and Third Ypres, the harsh conditions of the Italian mountains or the fierce fighting in the bocage country of Normandy. For that reason many soldiers only recall their memories with reluctance, feeling, not without reason that civilians, not having been there, cannot understand them.

Simon Weston, for example, who had been badly burned after the bombing of *Sir Galahad* during the Falklands campaign of 1982, admitted that he could not even tell his mother about what had happened to him and his mates on the landing craft. When he did, it was a moment of catharsis:

One night after I'd had too much to drink again I went into Mam's bedroom and stood over her, sobbing. 'Don't you realize how my hands got burned?' I cried, putting my hands out in front of her.

'Well, you got burned with the bomb.'

'No, Mam. There were boys there and I was trying to push them out, and why do you think my hands are all burned? Because when you go down you clench your hands, but I tried to push them out and they wouldn't come, Mam, they just wouldn't come and they were on fire and I had to stop it and all the skin was dropping off my hands – and those boys died and I ran, and I should be dead with them.'

At the time Weston had more or less recovered from the many operations to save him but by his own admission he was becoming lazy and lethargic and he was drinking heavily. During his time in hospital he had been greatly sustained by regular visits from Welsh Guardsmen, including some who had fought – and had been injured themselves – in the Second World War. Having been discharged from the army he had to come to terms with the fact that not only had he been transformed, mentally as well as physically, but that he was also a civilian. No longer was the regiment there to look after him, no longer did he have his mates beside him to sustain him when his new life created problems and no longer did he live in the controlled and tightly-knit ambience of the 1st battalion Welsh Guards; it was a difficult transition and he handled it badly. 'I still had to come to terms with getting up every day and looking in the mirror and saying, "That's you, you're still ugly, you still look the same way, you haven't changed."'

Shortly afterwards, Weston's mother contacted her son's 'other family' to ask for help and the regiment acted quickly and tactfully. Weston was invited to spend some time with the battalion in Germany and they provided the necessary catharsis:

> Just the thought of going cheered me up. I travelled on my own and collected my usual round of stares. But this time I didn't care. Depression is a circle and you're a pea in the centre, rattling around. You're stuck. But there is a chink in that circle, and everyone has a key to open it. My regiment was the key. And when I got there and discovered that they hadn't forgotten me and they were still my mates and treated me quite normally, I was cured.

A long road lay ahead for Simon Weston before he felt that he had conquered the burns which had disfigured him and had come to terms with the skin grafts that had changed his appearance for ever. There would still be troughs of depression and times when life would seem unjust but the despair had gone and that sense of renewal had begun with the regiment. No one pandered to his needs, he had to look after himself and he was treated as an equal. One sergeant who had played rugby with him ordered him to shake hands properly after Weston offered him a clenched fist, a habit he had started after the grafts to his hands – 'I was mortified, as I had allowed myself to be disabled in a handshake. It was another moment of truth, another lesson learned.'

No one is claiming that the Welsh Guards cured Simon Weston – he had to do that himself – but they did provide the impetus. Other Welsh Guardsmen injured in the Second World War have made similar comments about the importance of being made to feel that they still belonged, long after their demobilization. A former sergeant in the 2nd Battalion who was badly wounded in Normandy in 1944 said that it was enough for him to wear the Brigade tie, the deep red and blue stripes which are instantly recognizable. 'You're never alone when you wear this. You can be anywhere in the world and soon as they see it someone will talk to you. If you get stopped by the police or a traffic warden and they've been in the Brigade, they'll let you off with a warning!' Beneath the casual self-deprecation, though, lie emotional ties stronger than many civilians experience in the daily round. You see, he said, those men who served with me in the war are closer to me than many friends I've met before or since. They never let me down because we were all Welshmen together, we were a family.

It was that need to keep intact the togetherness and the fellowship of the wartime years that led to the creation of the Welsh Guards Comrades Association – now called the Welsh Guards Association, in deference to the Great War connotations of the word 'comrade'. The first of these clubs were founded in Cardiff, East Glamorgan and Monmouthshire in 1920 and others came into being over the years: today there are sixteen branches, including one in North America. As the regimental hierarchy admits, these local associations owe their strength to the men who served during the Second World War and to those who saw long-term service during the peacetime years. It is not easy to suggest to young men still in their twenties that they should join what is in essence an ex-servicemen's club when their own interests are bound to lie in other directions. The same holds true for the National Servicemen who served in the Welsh Guards during the 1940s and 1950s for their military service often seemed to be an intrusion and there was little reason to be reminded of it when they returned to civilian life after two years with the colours.

Yet for all that the Association might be regarded as an anachronism in the lives of young men it, too, plays a part in fostering the sense of family. This comes not only from the comradeship which exists among the dwindling band who served with the 1st

Battalion on the Western Front in Flanders or the larger group of men who served with all three battalions during the Second World War, but also from the strong links which have been forged with the regiment and its regular battalion. 'Once a Welsh Guard, always a Welsh Guard,' they will say and to prove the point the Association takes a close interest in the exploits of the younger generation of Welsh Guardsmen. They visit the battalion on St David's Day and are regular visitors at other formal and informal occasions throughout the year and most will admit that it is good to be back and to see the young men carrying forward the old traditions. It is a comforting feeling born largely of sentimentality but there is also another powerful ingredient – a need to recapture or to recreate the comradeship and the security of being with their own kind.

This is not an emotion generally associated with peacetime soldiering – although many Welsh Guardsmen who served as National Servicemen with the battalion in Palestine and the Canal Zone own up to understanding its pull. It has more to do with being at the sharp end of war among the exclusive fraternity of the front-line soldier. The men who served with the 3rd Battalion during the Second World War still feel that they are very different from the other Welsh Guardsmen who fought in Europe with the 1st and 2nd Battalions; their war was fought with the 8th Army in North Africa and Italy which by the middle of 1944 was a theatre of war much neglected by the people at home. 'Which D-Day can they mean?' they joked after the Normandy landings. 'Sicily? Salerno or Anzio?' And like the rest of the 5th and the 8th Armies they were delighted when Lady Docker remarked that the men in Italy were nothing but 'D-Day Dodgers', a description the men adopted with self-conscious pride. Within days of her making this unfortunate comment it had become the basis for one of the best known soldiers' songs of the Second World War, sung to the tune of 'Lili Marlene':

> We're the D-Day Dodgers out in Italy,
> Always drinking vino, always on the spree.
> Eighth Army skivers and the Yanks,
> We live in Rome, we laugh at tanks,
> For we're the D-Day Dodgers, in Sunny Italy.

The men in the 1st and 2nd Battalions felt no less strongly the bonds that bound them together during the fighting in France and north-west Europe between June 1944 and May 1945. For Peter Leuchars these had been forged during the years of training: when the time came to go into action his platoon was like a finely tuned machine:

> I enjoyed a very close relationship with my men because we had done a great deal of training together and had therefore got to know each other extremely well. I suppose I knew many of them better than my own family. You lived so close to them and did so many odd things and adventurous things together – and you underwent a certain amount of hardship as well.

When the time came to leave his men later in the war he admitted that it was a terrible moment, almost like the private grief of a death in the family. Men in front-line positions, he felt, were drawn more closely together because they took a fierce pride in themselves and in their regiment and the worst fear was that they might let down either of them:

> We preferred to think of ourselves as a family, not as an organization. People do things because they're part of that family. I think that some of the actions which people took during the war, actions of incredible bravery, were for that reason – because they were part of this family and must not let it down.

The feeling was shared by Meirion Ellis, a sergeant in 3 Company, Leuchars' own company, who believed that the almost fanatical desire to succeed in Normandy was prompted by an inner motivation, itself created by love and concern for the men who were sharing a common danger:

> We developed an obsession to help each other, sharing ourselves without expecting reward. A magnificent obsession with a determination to conquer, to succeed: there were no obstacles that were insurmountable. We were in essence a proud band of men who found satisfaction in our jobs and no goal was too high. The higher it was, the better the sense of satisfaction.

It was the same feeling which Sammy Stanier had experienced

during the First World War when he overheard his men telling each other that they could not show their faces again in their villages if it was ever known that they had left a wounded boy lying in no-man's-land.

Welsh Guardsmen who fought with the battalion during the Falklands War have admitted to similar feelings. When the *Galahad* was hit by enemy bombs it was a savage blow not just because lives had been lost but because the men felt so helpless in the aftermath. Their kit had been destroyed and they were left without the means to take the war back to the Argentines and to gain thereby some measure of revenge. During the first long night after the action some of the survivors slept in a large sheep shed where, as one platoon commander admitted, the mood was one of 'sadness and melancholy'. He felt at the time that the regiment might never recover from the blow but as the night wore on the mood turned to one of defiance. 'I was really angry, absolutely livid, and I just thought, "Well, I'm going to get somebody for this. It's ridiculous, I'll get the Argentines for what they've done to us."' The worst moments had come when the platoons first formed up on the shore:

> The new Company Sergeant-Major – the old one had been badly injured, burned – said, 'Right, One platoon there, Two platoon there, Three platoon there,' in good army fashion. So I said to my radio operator, 'OK, fall in there and I'll go and round up the rest.' It was only then, within a matter of ten minutes that I realized that no one else was going to join him – the final tally was three of my platoon killed and twenty-two wounded out of a full platoon of twenty-seven, leaving one guy and myself who were all right.

It was then that regimental spirit began to rally the men. The Commanding Officer, alerted at battalion headquarters by the scream of jets and the pall of smoke from Port Pleasant, had rushed to the scene and was busy pulling the men together. 'I remember the Commanding Officer landing and going up to the company commander. "Hello boy, how are you?" And then he came up to me and said, "Hello boy, how are you?" And then to my great delight he pulled a small bottle of whisky out of his smock and gave me a wee dram. It was lovely – he called everyone "boy", and still does.'

Discipline began to take over as the officers and NCOs pulled their men together, coaxing them out of the depths of shock with familiar words of command. Even those who were wounded, many of them badly burned, kept themselves going by joking among themselves and making sure that no one wavered or cracked. Simon Weston remembered crying out in agony while waiting to be treated at Fitzroy and being told by one of his mates, 'Come on Squeaky, you're a Welsh Guardsman. Stick with it.' One of the more poignant scenes from the casualty clearing station at Ajax Bay was the sight of 'stoical and cheery' Welsh Guardsmen waiting outside in the bitter cold, 'blowing on their tattered and painful hands to keep them cool.' Surgeon Commander Rick Jolly had to break the news to them that they would have to endure a half-hour journey by landing craft to the better facilities on board the assault ships *Fearless* and *Intrepid* before they could be treated. 'But by God, they're brave,' he wrote in his diary. 'The bad news of another half hour in an LCU before they can be treated is simply and willingly accepted. Each man seems to know someone else in the building more seriously injured than himself, and all would rather see him treated first.' Without that ability to pull themselves together by putting others first, claims one of their company commanders, the pain of the accident would have been too great to bear:

> If it hadn't been a family regiment I think we would have been in all manner of problems after the *Galahad*. Without that bond and without the discipline they had, we would have been in a lot of trouble. They performed exceptionally well in that respect, because it was a great deal to take.

The simple and unaffected comradeship of men who have endured the terrors of death or injury in action is a well-known and well-attested military phenomenon. It accounts for the courage and stoicism with which men will willingly face extreme discomfort and danger, and throughout the Welsh Guards' short life there have been numerous occasions when mutual self-respect and pride in the regiment have persuaded men to press on, whatever the odds. In that respect the notion of the regiment as extended family is of paramount importance and many Welsh Guardsmen have responded to it by admitting that they were sustained mightily by relationships formed during the months of training and forged in the heat of battle. For one young lance-sergeant who served in the Falklands as a guardsman the experience meant that his life had changed utterly. 'In spite of the cold and the discomfort and the horrors of the *Galahad*, I have to say that the Falklands brought the best out of the battalion. We put the pride back into Wales and the Welsh Guards – I consider myself a real Welshman and it gave my family a lot of real pride to know that I had been down there. We can hold our heads up high, all of us; it's something that can never be taken away.' As happened to many of his friends in the same platoon he found it difficult to break away from the tight little group when the battalion arrived back at RAF Brize Norton. 'The truth was that we really wanted to be by ourselves, to hold the pain to us. It was difficult to let others intrude, even though we were delighted to see our family and loved ones again.' One of his officers said that he could well understand the feeling and admitted that he spent a few long minutes 'counting the rivets on the wing of the VC10' before making his way to the terminal building.

Not everyone who served in the Falklands feels so sanguine about the idea of the Welsh Guards as a family regiment. Although Simon Weston, for one, has been fulsome in his praise about the regiment's part in rebuilding his shattered confidence after the incident on the *Galahad*, there was a tendency for the survivors who were unscathed to forget the survivors who had been badly injured. After the battalion had returned to Britain the Regimental Lieutenant-Colonel had to write a stern letter to the officers reminding them of their responsibility to visit the wounded Welsh Guardsmen who were languishing in the Queen Elizabeth Military Hospital at Woolwich. All too often, he warned, the men had been forgotten; some would return to the battalion to pick up again the threads of their army careers and it was bad for *esprit de corps* if the regiment ignored them in their hour of need. One guardsman at the time, now a platoon sergeant with twelve years' experience, still feels that his mates were let down by the Welsh Guards when they were in hospital after the Falklands and that the much-vaunted family concept has a hollow ring. 'I mean, if I was to get out tomorrow, nobody's going to get in touch with me. The people at the top may say it's a family regiment but I disagree. I may be going against the grain when I say this, but I'm talking from the shop floor.'

The theme was given a more public airing in 1987 when Yorkshire Television screened *The Falklands War: The Untold Story*, a documentary about the campaign based largely on the evidence of a number of people who had served with the British task force or whose lives had been changed by the war. One widow, the wife of a Welsh Guardsman who had been killed on the *Galahad*, was particularly vehement in her claims that she had not been well treated by the Welsh Guards. 'You always got the feeling that it was a family unit and they always looked after their own. But my feeling is that when things go wrong then they are not a family unit. I certainly found the family unit lacking when I needed help.' Although she admitted that her husband's officers had been supportive at the beginning, this help had soon tailed off; her principal objection was the casual malignity with which she was treated by the military authorities. Her husband's pay was stopped on the day that he was killed and she ran into difficulties over the payment of rent for her army quarters. While this was a matter somewhat outside the purlieu of Welsh Guards' authority, its disclosure did help to prompt a rash of similar complaints in the Welsh press from guardsmen's families who believed that they had been let down by the regiment. Many of these were unjustified or caused by a breakdown in communications but they were vociferous enough to tarnish, however briefly, the Welsh Guards' high reputation in the Welsh community. Like ordinary families, it seems that regimental families can have their share of skeletons and difficult or ramshackle human relationships.

Fortunately for the Welsh Guards Britain has only been at war officially for nine of their seventy-five years of existence. There have been the so-called 'savage wars of peace' which accompanied the British withdrawal from empire and the violence created in Northern Ireland has caused lingering problems for the whole of the British Army but for the better part of its life the Welsh Guards has been a peacetime regiment. How then does the family relationship operate outside the camaraderie and togetherness of the front line? For one of the battalion's recent commanding officers it manifests itself as a mixture of social work and pastoral care:

> The regiment behaves rather like a family inasmuch as it doesn't make a great fuss of those who are in it and are happy and are getting along all right. It only makes a fuss of those who are doing particularly well and, more importantly, those who are doing particularly badly or, indeed, have come across misfortunes which need larger help than they

can provide. It is under those circumstances that the Welsh Guards come out in the most favourable light. I know of many occasions when people who have come across hard times have received – without asking – very timely and generous help. This is neither exaggerated nor over the top and it's not continued when it's not needed but the regiment behaves exactly as a family would do, diverting its resources to those who need the most. It doesn't make a great song and dance about it, and it's normally done privately, but it's there and it's a great comfort to know that one belongs to an organization that is based on true Christian caring.

What this means in essence is that the commanding officer, his company commanders and his senior NCOs keep their eyes and ears open when they are in barracks. In that way, for example, a guardsman in financial difficulties or another with marriage problems can be helped quickly and discreetly without the need for formal inquiries. By the same token a guardsman who had distinguished himself in sport would be congratulated immediately and made something of a pet. For the Commanding Officer this is a matter of good management and like other officers in the Welsh Guards he resists the comparison with the well-run school, he playing the role of headmaster and his company commanders the housemasters. 'That's only part of the story. If any organization is to be well run you have to care deeply about the lives of the men who come under your control. Listen to what they have to say. They might talk about the Welsh Guards, or the regiment, or the battalion, but you hear the word "family" used very often. I like to encourage that.' It's difficult to imagine the managing director of a business or manufacturing concern making the same connection between his position and the workforce in his employment.

For some Welsh Guardsmen the family relationship is closely entwined with a military mystique that outsiders can never fully comprehend. Often it is a deeply personal revelation, all the stronger when it is least expected. One ensign, having heard he might be in for a rough reception from the younger officers, arrived at Pirbright to find most of the battalion away at the Cardiff Tattoo. But he had not been forgotten:

I had a wonderful evening arriving there, just two nights after I had passed out of Sandhurst. It was a summer's evening, middle of August, and I pulled up outside the mess at about half-past nine with a car full of uniform and junk for my room. Then, stamp-stamp, just outside the car door, hardly as I shut it, there was my Orderly. My platoon sergeant had told him to turn up as soon as the new officer arrived and he had obviously been waiting for me. And there he was. 'May I help you with your stuff up to your room, sir?' he asked. Which I thought was really nice and, my God, I knew that I was a Welsh Guards officer then . . . it was a lovely feeling.

It cuts across rank too. A similar experience happened to a young guardsman from a remote North Walian village. He arrived at Pirbright to find the whole battalion away on exercise and as he sat alone in the barrackroom a dreadful tide of homesickness threatened to overwhelm him. A passing NCO from the depot happened to see him head in hands; he greeted him in Welsh and took him out for an evening in Guildford. Such a thing would have been unheard of not so long ago when it was a punishable offence for an NCO to fraternize with his men. Indeed a Welsh Guards sergeant who served with the 1st battalion in the 1930s said that he was hauled up in front of the commanding officer and reprimanded all because he had met some guardsmen by chance in a London pub. That they came from his village cut no ice with the colonel who informed him that he had committed a 'terrible crime'. A more recent commanding officer shuddered when he heard the sergeant's story but then cheered up when he was told the North Walian guardsman's account of his reception in the battalion. 'I am very cheered by the love of people for people within the Welsh Guards family especially when the chips are down. It's all very underplayed, all very understated, much of it one never hears of. It is very sincere and rarely given but given when it's needed. And if that's Christianity, well it's good enough for me in command of the Welsh Guards.'

Much of the effort which goes into keeping alive the family spirit is engendered at Headquarters where the staff are well placed to take a more detached view of what is happening. They were able to co-ordinate the help that was given to Welsh Guards' families in the aftermath of the Falklands; to assist with applications to the South Atlantic Fund and to give immediate help where it was most needed. The Welsh Guards obviously made some mistakes in handling the situation – which organization would not? – and there were needless misunderstandings, but the overall impression is that the regiment worked hard to alleviate the personal suffering that accompanies many people's experience of war.

After the hostilities had come to an end the Prime Minister, Mrs Margaret Thatcher, announced that funds would be made available to allow those families who had lost loved ones to make a pilgrimage to the battlefields of the South Atlantic. This offer required the regiment to put in a good deal of organizational effort as a total of 651 people would be travelling south for the two-week trip in April 1983. Three Welsh Guards officers accompanied the party as escorts to assist the regiment's families as well as those from the REME and ACC who had lost sons and husbands aboard the *Galahad*: the entire party travelled by British Airways' charter flights to Montevideo where they joined the MV *Cunard Countess* for the onward voyage to the Falklands. It could have been a trying experience as the grief was still raw but everyone was agreed that the sadness they felt was partly assuaged by being members of a large group. Just as their sons and husbands had gone to war as members of a tightly knit community, so too did they feel drawn together by the same bonds.

The most moving moment came on 11 April when the ship passed near *Galahad*'s last resting place in San Carlos deep and wreathes were thrown into the dark water – after her destruction the LCL was towed eighty miles out to sea from the East Falklands and scuttled as a war grave. The next day the families visited Fitzroy where the Welsh Guards had a temporary memorial, a simple cairn, a wooden cross and the regimental badge picked out with white stones, 'a patch of red and white in the dull green of the boggy soil'. Afterwards many families were to remark that the landscapes of the Falklands were comforting and familiar, reminding them of the hills and moorlands of home, 'the panorama we are accustomed to around Sennybridge and the Brecon Beacons and the area of Anglesey and the Snowdonia range in North Wales'. At the end of the trip the senior officer of the escort agreed that it had been a cathartic experience for everyone: during the campaign he had been the Welsh Guards Liaison Officer in Wales and it had fallen to him to break the news of Welsh Guards losses to families there:

Those who made the pilgrimage were glad that they had made it. They had crossed the world, travelled to those southernmost populated islands and they had done their duty to their relatives. They will never forget the journey and they shared their grief with hundreds of others. Time will bring them peace in their hearts.

A similar amount of care and attention was put into helping the families of the Welsh Guardsmen who were injured in the IRA bomb attack on the Caterham Arms in Guildford. This shocking incident happened in the late evening of 27 August 1975 when the popular public house was full of customers. Many of them were guardsmen and of these twenty were badly hurt: among their number were three Welsh Guardsmen who suffered terrible injuries. (Guardsman Thomas lost both legs and an arm, Lance-Sergeant Ollerhead lost a leg, as did Guardsman Watkins.) So shocked was the public by the indiscriminate barbarity of the attack that a considerable sum of money was raised for the regiment to ease the difficulties their men would face in the future. The Association also threw in its support and Welsh Guardsmen who had been similarly injured during the Second World War were quick to offer practical help and advice. Perhaps the most spectacular event of all took place on 30 June 1976 when the wounded guardsmen and others made an emotional pilgrimage to the top of Snowdon in North Wales. In their company was the regiment's Colonel, the Prince of Wales, and although the route to the top was aided by the famous mountain railway and a helicopter of the Royal Flight the final triumphant stretch was covered by foot – or in some cases on false limbs. For all who took part – and for those who witnessed it – the pilgrimage was a solemn reminder of the brotherhood that exists within the regiment.

There is another sense in which the Welsh Guards rightly consider themselves to be a family regiment. Throughout their existence sons have followed fathers into the Welsh Guards and it is not unusual to hear a guardsman claiming that his father and grandfather were in the regiment and that his brother will be joining next year. Family ties are greatly encouraged by the regimental hierarchy for the very good reason that they help to maintain a steady supply of recruits from the Welsh heartlands. If one member of a family enjoys his service in the regiment, runs the argument, then he may persuade others to join; or his nostalgic tales of military service in later life might well encourage a son to join the regiment. The same holds true of the officers. Sammy Stanier is not the only distinguished Welsh Guards officer to have experienced the satisfaction of seeing his son and grandson enter the regiment and at any given time there is at least one set of brothers in the mess. One officer who joined in the late 1970s really wanted to join a Scottish regiment but when his brother went into the Welsh Guards steps were taken to encourage him to follow suit. 'The commanding officer at the time was a fairly forceful personality and he said that brothers go into the same regiments. I don't regret it for a minute actually. Although the Black Watch is a very good regiment I'm very pleased that I joined the Welsh Guards.'

Although the family connections within the battalion are as strong as they ever were they were more noticeable perhaps in the past when men signed on for longer periods. Because they could stay with the battalion for up to twenty years they were steeped in its ways and as 'trained soldiers' they were used to helping the young recruits ease themselves into army life. Many had turned down the chance of promotion or had refused to sit the necessary tests which would take them up the ladder; this did not make them any less cunning, as recruits who joined the 1st Battalion in 1940 discovered to their cost:

I noticed that the old soldiers pooled their cleaning kit, calling themselves 'The Inner Circle'. I was anxious to join them and to be made a member of this august body of men. But they were good psychologists, they made me understand that I was a raw recruit, that the ink on my AB64 was not even dry and that it would take a long time before I would be admitted. But within a couple of weeks one of them took me to one side and told me that as they liked me so much I could join them. The membership fee was ten shillings. I would also have to buy a new set of dusters, blanco, Kiwi (black and brown), metal polish and a burnisher. Pleased to be accepted I willingly obliged. But I noticed that as the weeks went by I was the only one renewing stock which by then was used by the whole platoon. Young soldiers are a little frightened of these characters so I kept it up until another innocent arrived.

The passing of the years have no doubt lent some enchantment to that view of army life. Indeed, there is a tendency for old soldiers to view their service through rose-tinted glasses, to claim that they were enjoying the best years of their lives and that nothing can beat the comradeship and group loyalties they encountered in the army. As a consequence some found it difficult to re-adapt to civilian life and even today it is not unusual in the Welsh Guards to come across officers and men who have rejoined the regiment because they missed the friendships and the camaraderie and found the outside world to be a poor substitute. 'I was jealous of all the yuppies and what have you,' admitted one officer. 'So I left and got a job in a merchant bank selling warrants and bonds and so on. And then after about a year I suddenly realized that I couldn't bear working there any longer. The major reason, even though I was paid quite a lot better than I am now, was that I missed the battalion. I didn't miss the army hugely, but in the short term I missed the battalion and the people I had known.'

Would he have felt the same way about any other unit? The young officer thought not because his adult life had been the Welsh Guards ever since he had visited them as a schoolboy. An older officer, no longer with the battalion, was inclined to be iconoclastic. 'Yes,' he admitted, 'the family is everything but the name doesn't matter. Let's be frank about it, it's your mates, your muckers and your buddies who count, not what they are or what they were.' An admirer of the Parachute Regiment, he points out that they recruit from all over the country, yet they quickly build up and establish a sense of *esprit de corps* and take a fierce pride in wearing the 'cherry beret'. During the Falklands War, for example, officers and men of 2nd Parachute Regiment could be heard exhorting each other to remember Arnhem. This could have sounded like ancient history to men who had not even been born at the time but to the paratroops it was a solemn reminder of their battalion's gallant behaviour in the face of impossible odds. 'And remember too,' he warned, 'during the Second World War the Welsh Guards had three very different battalions and many of their officers and men had no connections with Wales whatsoever. Yet they retain great pride in the regiment and a loyalty which transcends national boundaries. You have to provide a sense of belonging, however artificial, so that when they come back to the regiment they feel they are coming home.'

The men who served in the Falklands knew what the brigadier was talking about. When they went off to war, they were not going to fight for an abstract idea like Queen and Country or for Margaret Thatcher's ideological dogma. They were going off to fight, and if necessary to die, for each other, for the brotherhood of the Welsh Guards. A sergeant from South Wales encapsulated the feeling of togetherness which drew the men in his company into a tightly knit group. 'We like to think of ourselves as a family, not as an official organization. People will always do things for a family and I think that some of the acts of bravery on the *Galahad* were done for that very reason. Because the men were members of a family, they didn't want to let it down.'

To the outsider, though, the idea of the organization as family, and the importance placed upon the concept by the army, can be mystifying or just faintly ridiculous. It can smack too much of other establishment rituals designed to bond men together, of the kind evolved in public schools and Oxbridge colleges and which may seem out of place in our more egalitarian times. Families, too, might not provide the best analogy: they can have fairly tenuous kinships, with brothers and sisters falling out with one another, galleries of ghastly cousins and a whole range of ramshackle relationships. Some of the family customs and traditions can be based on fairly dubious history, too. The Welsh Guards never stand to drink the loyal toast but that custom was borrowed from the Grenadiers, and the ceremony of the 'brick' practised each year in the Sergeants' Mess seems to have evolved from the Scots and Coldstream Guards who shut the gates at Hougoumont during the Battle of Waterloo in 1815, a hundred years before the Welsh Guards were born.

For all that the family relationship might be ambiguous the feeling that the officers and men of the Welsh Guards have for their regiment is almost tangible. It might be the delight experienced by a retired officer when he returns to the mess and finds the same silver in the same place and the same *solidas* among the younger men. Or it might be the relief of a guardsman returning late to Pirbright to find that his mates have cleaned his kit ready for the next morning's parade. Or it might be the lump in the throat when the band breaks into 'Men of Harlech' or it might be the shout of encouragement from a former guardsman as the Queen's Guard marches out of Wellington Barracks.

However small these expressions of loyalty might seem, they have assumed a significance which is respected by all ranks and which has helped to make the Welsh Guards the regiment it is today. And as a senior NCO reminded me, deride the system if you will, but so far no one within the army or outside it has come up with a better one.

Chapter Five

GUARDS OF WALES

WHEN HE JOINS the Welsh Guards the recruit is not just entering a regiment which will provide him with a home and a sense of belonging throughout his army career, in some small measure he is also becoming heir to a long and proud Welsh military tradition. Although there is a lingering prejudice against the practice of 'going away for a soldier' in Wales, largely due to eighteenth and nineteenth century religious teachings and to the more recent twentieth century prejudice against the use of the military to quell political disturbances in the South Wales valleys, the history of soldiering in Wales goes back much further in time.

Like the Scots, the Welsh fought against each other for well over a hundred years, family against family, tribe against tribe, until the rival princedoms were united under English rule. Then, like the Scots too, they served abroad as mercenaries: at the Battle of Poitiers in 1356 there were Welsh captains serving in both the armies of the Black Prince of England and King John II of France. The tradition continued into the sixteenth and seventeenth centuries and Welshmen who followed the career of the mercenary found a ready market for their services. Because the expense of maintaining a national standing army was beyond most states in this period rulers relied on mercenary companies to fill out their ranks in time of war. The Swiss and the Germans were the first to capitalize on this trend and the Welsh captains followed closely behind. Henry Lloyd of Gwynedd, for example, fought in the armies of Austria, Prussia and Russia and his fellow countryman Thomas Morgan of Gwent served in Turenne's army where he gained a fearsome reputation for his belligerent behaviour.

Poverty, adventure, love of fighting were all important considerations in the making of the Welsh mercenaries but money was always the deciding factor. A well regarded soldier could offer his services to the highest bidder and, like the football star of today, he could offer himself for transfer if the price were right. Small wonder that the soldiers of fortune were so savagely attacked by Nicolo Machiavelli in his study *The Art of War*: 'They are disunited, ambitious, without discipline, faithless, bold among friends, cowardly among enemies, they have no fear of God and keep no faith with men.'

The idea that all soldiers were mercenaries was one of the tenets of the Nonconformist objections to soldiering – when Robert Graves joined the Royal Welch Fusiliers in 1914 prayers were said in the chapels of Merioneth, not for his physical safety, but for the moral welfare of his soul. In more recent times, though, money, or more precisely, the lack of it, has been the most immediate reason why young Welshmen have turned to the army for a career. During the periods of economic depression during the 1930s and 1970s unemployment and redundancy proved to be first-rate recruiting sergeants and the army prospered from a regular supply of Welsh recruits. The Great Depression of the 1930s was the worst; 400,000 people left the valleys of South Wales to seek work in England or overseas and most never returned. The tide of unemployment swept over other parts of Wales, too, leaving poverty and hardship in its wake; even in a relatively prosperous place like the village of Ffynnongroew situated between the Point of Ayr coalmines and the Mostyn iron works, life could be hard:

> Few in the village were well off, no one was rich, one could see that by looking around and observing what people wore. While I would say that there was no poverty, it would be true to say that life was hard for the parents whose job it was to bring up the children in a decent manner.

Like many others of his generation, Meirion Ellis gravitated towards the army, joining first the Royal Welch Fusiliers and then the Welsh Guards in August 1939.

War was another reason why so many Welshmen joined the army. Around 280,000 Welshmen served in the armed forces during the First World War – a higher proportion of the population than in England – and of these 35,000 died. Lloyd George eventually had his wish granted that a separate Welsh Division should be formed – the 38th Division which was commanded by one of the

Philipps of Picton Castle who had pushed so hard for the formation of the Welsh Guards. It fought its first battle at Mametz Wood in July 1916 during the Battle of the Somme and lost 4,000 casualties. To many of the Welshmen who served during the First World War their struggle was part of a greater struggle for the rights of small nations, 'the little five foot five nations' as Lloyd George called them. Naturally enough, in the aftermath of the killing, a reaction set in, and in the Welsh Guards in the 1920s recruiting became a problem. Just as King George V had forecast, it was not always easy for the regiment to maintain its full complement of guardsmen. (After the war the King had instructed that all private soldiers in the Brigade of Guards should be known as guardsmen.) Had it not been for the strenuous efforts made by Regimental Headquarters and the battalion's senior officers to play up the Welshness of the regiment then there is little doubt that the political threat to close down the Welsh Guards would have succeeded during the course of the decade.

At the same time life in the army went back to what it had been in Victorian and Edwardian times; for the Welsh Guards that meant smartness on parade and a reliance on the customs and etiquette of the Brigade of Guards. As the wartime enlisted men returned to their civilian lives the regiment became an older place too. There were more 'old soldiers' in the battalion and a bottleneck in promotion prospects meant that officers could only reach higher rank after their seniors had retired. Pacifism, or at least public disgust with the high casualties of the First World War, also meant that the nation lost interest in defence matters and throughout the 1920s and 1930s the army stagnated.

As remembered by Brigadier Windsor Lewis this was a time when 'very little field training was done apart from a concentrated month at Pirbright, followed by two or three weeks Battalion, Brigade and Higher Formation training in September. Even the Machine-Gun Company ceased to exist after 1935.' Instead the battalion excelled at sport, particularly at rugby football, a game naturally conducive to the Welsh national spirit, and for the officers there was 'much enthusiasm for hunting and racing'. When the battalion was stationed in Egypt, one officer, Peter Ackroyd, was allowed to spend his winters in Britain and his summers in Egypt all because he was Master of the Belvoir hounds. As Windsor Lewis wryly recorded, Ackroyd was indeed a fine sportsman but it was 'doubtful whether such consideration could be given these days [1960s] to an officer's sporting activities'.

To a large extent the Great Depression of the 1930s helped army recruiting, especially in Scotland, the north of England and South Wales which had to bear the brunt of the recession in the traditional heavy industries. Whereas the proportion of unemployment among insured workers in London and South-East England was 13.7 per cent in 1932 and 6.4 per cent in 1937, in Wales it was 36.5 per cent in 1932 and 22.3 per cent in 1937. Small wonder that men turned to the army for a career, even though the basic daily rate of pay for a private soldier had only been raised from 2*s*. (10p) to 2*s*. 9*d*. (13p) in 1937. (With allowances for educational ability or skill at arms, though, the trained soldier could earn 4*s*. a day after three years service.) Most men going to the army recruiting offices in Cardiff or Chester would try for one of the corps, the engineers or the RASC, which would give them a trade but many of these would succumb to the blandishments of the Welsh Guards recruiting sergeants and the posters of smart red-tunicked guardsmen. Even lack of inches, a common Welsh failing, was not always a problem – in 1939 the minimum height was reduced to 5′ 9″ – as recruiters, tongue in cheek, would tell a growing lad, not to worry they have a stretching machine for the Guards at Wrexham!

> I was a Welshman. I went to the recruiting office in St John Street in Chester and there were five photographs of His Majesty's Brigade of Guards with the Welsh Guards in the middle and the recruiting sergeant said to me, 'Are you Welsh?' Yes, I replied. 'Then you must join the Taffs.' And that's what I did.

Elwyn Roberts joined the Welsh Guards in March 1943 and served with the regiment throughout the war until he was demobilized in 1946. He was one of the 2.68 million men who had been called up into the army that year – the figure was to rise to a maximum of 3,007,300 in April 1945 – because from the very beginning the British government had realized that its manpower needs for the services could only be met by conscription, or national service as it was better known. Unlike the First World War when the forces had relied on the voluntary principle until May 1916, the Second World War was to be a 'people's war' in that very few citizens escaped an obligation to serve their country. (In 1941 the maximum age for service was increased from forty-one to fifty-one and, in all, 16,416,000 men and women registered for non-military service.)

For the first time, too, families found themselves in the front line. Cardiff and Swansea were both bombed heavily with the loss of over seven hundred casualties and the stricken petrol tanks at Pembroke Dock went on burning for three weeks before the blaze could be extinguished. The ordnance factory at Bridgend employed 35,000 workers and was reckoned to be the largest in Britain; the long Welsh coastline had to be guarded and defended against invasion, and, paradoxically, the war brought new hope to the faltering coal and steel industries of South Wales. During the Second World War, as was the case in other parts of Britain, hardly any Welsh families were left unaffected by the hostilities.

For the Welsh Guardsmen who joined the regiment during the war the basic training was completed at the Guards Depot at Caterham: this was their first experience of military service and it could be an unnerving rite of passage:

> The Guards Depot at Caterham was a terrible place – you wouldn't believe it. Next door there was a mental asylum and the first thing the sergeant said to me was, 'You'd be better off on that side. They're madder here, I promise you.' When I heard the sergeants shouting and bawling at us from all angles, I thought he was right.

In fact the first day spent at the Reception Centre was a relatively good-humoured business with the NCOs doing their best to chivvy the young men into a semblance of order. The real training began the next day when everything had to be done at the double. Major J. C. Buckland remembered it as a time when life was dominated by a litany of confused orders and strange-sounding names: 'The instructors, the drill, the discipline, and above all the spirit and determination of the individual not to be defeated by any power, spiritual or temporal. The training, extended order, Coulsdon Common, kit inspection, pay parade, saluting for something you hoped you would get, saluting for a meagre 1s. 1d. a day, the fear of losing one's name, the Short Arm Inspection in the shivering hut, the baths, "Tin Town", the wet canteen, the fatigues.' What this meant in reality can be seen in Meirion Ellis's recollections of an average day during basic training, a regime which he admitted could reduce grown men to tears, particularly the more sensitive who hated the way NCOs would push their faces in front of them before letting loose a stream of insults and obscenities:

Breakfasts, dinners and tea were good but there was little time to enjoy the menus. After tea we held our cleaning parade, each recruit sat astride his own bed under the eagle eye of the Trained Soldiers, spitting, polishing and burning our boots with a hot spoon, scrubbing and blancoing our webbing, polishing and burnishing our rifle and bayonet, brass work had to glitter, everything had to be perfect for the preliminary inspection by our trained soldiers, then Sergeant Bates, lastly an officer. If Hector Smith [the trained soldier] was not satisfied he simply threw the equipment into the coal bunker, bad in this case was known as 'shit order'. This was not the end as we finally washed and scrubbed ourselves, fingernails, toenails for a body inspection by 8 p.m. If we were lucky we could go to the NAAFI for a well deserved pie and chips.

What kept many of them going was a growing realization that they were all in it together, that they were Welshmen serving a common purpose and that for one of them to let down the side was the most heinous of crimes. The humour also helped, for if Caterham was a place of burnished boots, spotless uniforms and screamed inhuman commands, the ridiculous was never far away:

You go down to the Guards Depot today and you still get a tingle down your spine. I'd been in two days and had just been squadded which meant that I could go down to the NAAFI for the first time. I crossed the square, the parade ground, and there was this Irish Guards RSM who screamed at me from about half a mile away. 'Oo are you?' he roared. 'Ow long 'ave you been in?' Two days, I replied. 'O f-ing old soldier are you? Well, get off my bastard parade ground!'

Other old Welsh Guardsmen, including the National Servicemen who served with the regiment and were trained at Caterham in the post-war years, carry similar memories with them into the meetings of the Regimental Association. With the passing of the years it becomes easier to forget the horrors, the rough woollen shirts, the shapeless battle dress with its gaiters and webbing and the hard unyielding boots. Yes, they will say, it was tough, it was meant to be, the training turned us into Guardsmen; it gave us the discipline and the tenacity to fight a determined enemy and then to face up to the problems of remaking post-war Britain. Like old soldiers everywhere they worry about the training that is given to the young Welsh Guardsmen of today. Curiously, the sentiment that it is not as tough as it should be is shared by some of the NCOs of the present 1st Battalion:

When you tell a guy, 'Right, get over there, I want you to cover me,' he'll reply, 'Why? What do you mean?' 'Why, because I'm telling you, that's why. When I shout shit you jump on the shovel.' These guys are so intelligent – and that's not a bad thing – but they don't always do as they're told by the NCOs. Slowly but surely discipline is breaking down now. The powers of a sergeant are being eroded. For example, on the drill square, drilling a squad, and you see an idle guardsman, you can't say, 'Get your shoulder higher, or I'll lock you up.' The guy says, 'Where?' That was never heard in my day: you just did it. You can't keep bucking the system, and that's what these guys do, buck the system.

As the sergeant is quick to acknowledge, every old soldier feels that way about basic training: it was always tougher in his day and the youngsters of today have it far too easy. In one respect he might be right. There was a time, not so long ago, when the training at the Guards Depot was tough and uncompromising and the instructors indulged in a kind of casual brutality which would not be tolerated today. Meirion Ellis had completed his basic training with the Royal Welch Fusiliers before joining the Welsh Guards and found the Guards Depot easier to cope with than some of the others in his squad. But even he was slightly shocked by the odd blow on the head for having a dirty rifle or being kicked in the body while lying in the prone position during musketry drill. Even worse was the tendency to pick on the odd-man-out, the one soldier in the squad who could not, or would not, conform mentally or physically to the Welsh Guards' code of discipline:

Every squad would inevitably have one recruit normally known as a 'blemster' – in our case a lad from Anglesey who was scruffy, inadequate and unable to cope with the rigours of the Guards. It was obvious from the word go that he would never make it. Consequently he got us into trouble. This did not in itself bother us very much, although it is possible that some would have wished he had joined the Grenadiers. He was a born loser, a target for the NCOs, hated by the Trained Soldiers and tailor-made for the venom of Sergeant Bates.

'Roberts!' he would shout, 'get on that table. What are you?' Poor Roberts would get on the table and say, 'I am a sow from sowland.'

'Now flap your arms and mark time and say, "I am a sow from sowland,"' demanded Sergeant Bates and Roberts very sensibly did as he was told.

We approved by our smiles and carried on polishing our boots. It was bullying all right, even terrorizing.

Bullying is an emotive subject in the British Army. In recent years scandals about initiation ceremonies and casual brutality have rocked several training depots and military formations, most notably one distinguished Scottish infantry regiment. The Guards Depot, based at Pirbright since 1959, has also been singled out for media attention, and disaffected recruits have willingly sold stories about 'beasting' to the tabloid press. These can range from a simple dislike of the strict regime of discipline and bull to the other extreme – allegations of harsh or uncompromising treatment involving physical or mental cruelty. Naturally enough, the Guards regiments are keen to play down the minor complaints but, sensibly, they also make sure that offenders found guilty of bullying are punished. For example, an offender discovered kicking a recruit – as happened in Meirion Ellis's day – would possibly be reduced to the ranks and perhaps even sentenced to a spell at the army's rehabilitation centre at Colchester.

One reason for the prevalence of bullying during these early weeks is that basic training is designed to be tough because it marks the transition from civilian life to the disciplined world of a Guards regiment. It is designed to give the embryo soldier an introduction to weapons training and minor tactics and to instil the sense of tradition, *esprit de corps*, morale and group identity which makes up the military ethos. For much of the time there is a concentration on drill and because the Welsh Guards are a ceremonial regiment, the close order drill has to be well-night perfect by the time the recruit passes out at the end of his twenty-one weeks of basic training. Given the concentrated effort that has to be put into the training it is hardly surprising, perhaps, that evidence of bullying comes to the surface. Often this is little more than over-zealous instruction but in recent times stories about brutality have turned out to have a solid basis in ugly facts. One young officer – not a Welsh Guardsman – was dismissed from the Depot after he was discovered putting hot potatoes down the backs of recalcitrant recruits and then punching them into a hot burning mass.

On this score the Welsh Guards have an exellent record of prevention – according to one CQMS this is because it is a tightly- knit regiment in which officers and NCOs are constantly alert to the problem. When he first joined up in the early 1970s he was greeted with the threat of a thumping from a trained soldier for no other reason than he was a new boy.

I never got thumped by him and I think to a large extent the same sort of thing will happen nowadays. The older guardsmen will say, 'New draft, go and fetch me a pie up at the NAAFI, go and get me a cup of tea or a pint of milk.' That sort of stuff. But I think very little actual bullying takes place because there's been so much publicity in the newspapers and on the television. There's been a big crackdown in the army too and the commanding officers nowadays, and particularly this commanding officer, are very sharp on the matter. Anyone put in front of him for bullying is guaranteed at least fourteen days detention, possibly twenty-eight. So I don't think actual bullying takes place. The threats probably do, but not the thumpings.

Another senior NCO who joined in the early 1970s regarded the casual brutality as simply part and parcel of army life at the time. If that was the army way, then it had to be accepted and in any case Welsh society in his native South Wales tended to be equally well-ordered and strict. When he joined the Welsh Guards he was not at all surprised to discover that the regime was just as rigorous as the one he had left behind. It was much like joining a rugby club and learning the hard way how to be accepted – not by being boastful but by proving one's worth.

When I first appeared in the battalion I didn't get a name; I was the 'new draft' and looking back at it now none of the duties were shared fairly. It was, 'We've got a dirty job to do, put the new draft on it.' And that was the way it worked. In fact, looking back, I agree with some of the system now because it got you into the swing of things. You learned to keep your mouth shut, you didn't speak to half the guys because you got beaten up. When I say 'beaten up' it meant a smack around the head. You knew when you'd been hit around the head a couple of times but it wasn't done with malice; it was more or less part of your training.

Nowadays, of course, any physical contact of that kind would be met with equally severe punishment, and NCOs tend to be wary in their dealings with lazy recruits. Most will agree that bullying has gone for ever and has no part to play in modern military training, yet, pushed further, some will also admit that, yes, on a training run for example a boot up the backside has never done anyone any harm if they look like giving up and letting down the side. On the debit side, though, there is a tendency in the Sergeants' Mess to wax sentimental about the old days and to regret the passing of the hard physical training that marked out the Guards Depot as being rather different from the other training depots of the British Army.

Another CSM, with ambitions to 'go all the way' to a commission disagrees vehemently with this view – that because it did me no harm it is a good thing. He believes that the Welsh as a people are hard but fair – look at the national rugby team, he says, and the phrase 'fair play' falls easily from Welsh lips – and there are other methods such as sarcasm and irony, both of which are well respected by Welshmen:

> We'd obviously been doing something wrong on the square this one particular day and the platoon sergeant – he later became our RSM – decided that there was only one way to cure that. He marched us into the drill shed, stood us with our noses to the walls and just made us mark time while he went outside to chat with the others. It was nothing difficult, we could have marked time on the square but he decided it would be better if we just marked time looking at a wall. Our performance improved no end after that.

In the year 1987–88 813 guardsmen passed out of the Guards Depot. Of these, 132 were bound for the Welsh Guards, a healthy enough figure and indeed the regiment remains the best recruited of the regiments in the Guards Division. That this should be so can be partially explained by the fact that the Welsh Guards have only a single battalion whereas the Grenadiers, Coldstreamers and Scots have two and in the latter regiment recruiting is fast becoming something of a problem. With only one battalion and an establishment of 550 officers, NCOs and men when engaged on public duties, there are fewer vacancies to be filled and in recent years manpower levels have remained reasonably high. This is also due to the economic recession which has enveloped Wales throughout the 1980s but as the situation improves in the country so too does the concern begin to grow within the regimental hierarchy that sooner or later, the Guards Division, like the other infantry divisions of the British Army might have to accept the principle of cross-posting. If that were to happen then it might be difficult for the regiment to keep its national identity. A company sergeant-major's post, for example, might have to be filled by a Coldstreamer, or the clerks in Headquarters Company might be a composite mix from other Guards' regiments and by the same token, in order to gain promotion a Welsh Guardsman might well have to consider an appointment elsewhere outside the regiment he calls home. This happens in other infantry divisions, why should the Welsh Guards be so different, even exclusive, in their approach?

> I can't really speak for the other regiments but we are very much a family and we should preserve that. There are three main reasons for this. Firstly we're a one-battalion regiment; secondly we're very Welsh, whether it be North Wales or South Wales, we are a Welsh regiment and thirdly all our officers, NCOs and guardsmen see their service in the Welsh Guards. I mean, sixteen or twenty years from now, the people in the battalion might have seen service elsewhere but they'll always come back to the regiment. All that helps to create the spirit of the family and I don't think I've ever known it not to be a fairly closely knit battalion.

That sense of clannishness described by the second in command of the battalion is central to Welsh Guards' thinking. The fact that a Welsh Guardsman will always retain his cap badge is regarded as one of the great selling points when it comes to recruiting. The Royal Regiment of Wales might have a greater public presence in Wales but it cannot promise its recruits that they will not be transferred to the Gloucestershire Regiment or the Royal Hampshires or to any of the other regiments in the Prince of Wales's Division. On the other hand, the Welsh Guards can and this point is taken very seriously by Regimental Headquarters.

Whether or not this approach, however admirable it might be, means much to the potential recruit when he goes to the Army Recruiting Offices in Cardiff is a moot point. Unless he has a family connection with the Welsh Guards then his choice of regiment can be much of a lottery. For every Welsh Guardsman who says that he joined because he had a father, brother or cousin in the regiment and would have been devastated had he been turned down there will be many more who put down as their first choice an elite macho fighting force like the Parachute Regiment or a corps which would offer a trade:

> I basically wanted to join the Military Police and when I didn't make the grade, they said, 'How about joining a Welsh regiment?' Being sort of wet behind the ears I didn't realize it was a Welsh Guards recruiting sergeant at the desk and he said, 'OK, Welsh Guards, that's the regiment for you.' (Lance-Sergeant, Headquarters Company.)

I originally wanted to go into a tank regiment and was accepted but then I was told I would have to wait six months to start training. I said I didn't want to wait that long and was offered either the Royal Regiment of Wales or the Welsh Guards. Knowing that the RRW isn't strictly a Welsh regiment I decided to go into the Welsh Guards. (Company Sergeant-Major.)

I went into the Recruiting Office to join the Parachute Regiment – the reasons for which totally elude me now – but a Welsh Guards recruiter talked me into joining his regiment. It's as simple as that. (Company Sergeant-Major.)

I didn't know anything about the Guards, only what I'd seen on the telly but I thought they were smart. I'm tall too, that's why they put me here. (Guardsman, Prince of Wales's Company.)

Very few guardsmen, other than those with family connections, can explain the precise reasons that took them into the Welsh Guards. For some it might have been a spur of the moment decision on seeing a recruiting poster outside the swimming baths, for others it was simply the culmination of a long-held wish. These are easy meat for the Welsh Guards recruiting sergeants: for the others they have to try a little harder:

Everybody else had to be steered in the right direction. I know it was wrong but in the office where I worked we had three recruiters, myself, an officer from the Royal Regiment of Wales and a sergeant from the Royal Welch Fusiliers. We had a saying that if a boy was over five-foot-eight he went to the Welsh Guards, if he was under five-foot-eight and a boxer he went to the Royal Welch Fusiliers and if he played rugby I had to fight it out with the Royal Regiment of Wales. You had to decide for them where they wanted to go. Only later on would they realize why.

About six weeks after being selected the potential recruit is passed on to the Army Recruit Selection centre at St George's Barracks at Sutton Coldfield near Birmingham in the heart of the West Midlands. Established in 1971, this is where the army really meets the civilian and where the young lad has his first taste of military life. There will be intelligence tests to gauge his SSG (Summed Selection Group) and he will be rated on a scale of one to five, the rationale being the lower the mark the better the job offered to him. The Welsh Guards, like most infantry regiments, prefer to have a good mixture with a leavening of threes and fours. Grade ones usually become clerks and stand a fair chance of becoming, in time, senior warrant officers. But brains are not everything: one officer admitted that a lad might well be brimming over with intellectual capacity yet still be a liability on a street patrol in West Belfast. There are also interviews and aptitude tests and it is at Sutton Coldfield that they are given their first uniforms. By the time they reach Pirbright they know that they are bound for a Household Division regiment, some may still decide to change at the last minute from the Scots to the Coldstream Guards or find that an officer persuades them to join a regiment which is short of recruits but it is almost unheard of for a Welshman *not* to join the Welsh Guards if that is his choice. And why not? After all, the recruiters have insisted that it is *the* Welsh regiment.

Curiously, very few recruits had given two thoughts at this stage to the possibility of doing public duties and the idea of wearing a bearskin and tunic is rarely a factor. Because the Welsh Guards have no base in Wales and only visit the principality infrequently the uniform matters little because it seems to be associated with distant London. Whereas a young Scot might be lured by the kilt to join a Highland regiment, the call of the Guards' red tunic appears to be surprisingly muted in Wales. The main reasons which drive young Welshmen into the army are as old as time: a sense of adventure, a desire to get away from the small towns or remote country areas which make up so much of the country and the spectre of unemployment. 'You know,' they will say, 'the pits are closing down, the jobs are going, so you might as well try for the army.'

The gloom that permeated Wales in the 1980s was almost tangible. Reductions in steel production and the closure of previously profitable coalmines meant that the old industries had to be drastically reorganized and new industries had to be introduced and developed. Before the decline really set in around 1979 a Welsh Guards officer at the Guards Depot noted that recruiting had fallen off to such an extent that the Division was almost a battalion – some 500 men – short of its establishment. Then, with 'Cardiff moribund and North Wales dying on its feet there was suddenly not a bed space to be found in Pirbright'. Throughout the decade recruiting remained high, especially in North Wales which provided the Welsh Guards with fifty per cent of its recruits. (Normally only twenty per cent come from that area.) Whether that situation will continue depends largely on the economy and in Wales in 1989 it was definitely on the up-turn. Ford, the motor car manufacturers had developed a £750 million plant in Bridgend, Japanese investment in Clwyd had pulled in some seventy companies with 5,000 new jobs and unemployment between 1987 and 1989 had fallen to 9.5 per cent. Endowed with good communications as well as cheaper land than many other parts of Britain, South Wales suddenly became an attractive base for industries that wanted to stay within hailing distance of London.

The transformation of Wales to a modern high-technology economy will have an obvious effect on recruiting into the Welsh Guards. So, too, will the demographic though which will influence recruitment into other sectors of British commercial and professional life. For the first time since the 1930s the falling birth-rate of the past quarter of a century will make its mark on the employment market with fewer young people competing for more jobs. To counteract these trends the Welsh Guards plan to go back to their roots and to reinforce their position in Welsh society for as the Regimental Lieutenant-Colonel admits, 'our links with Wales are terribly important and we would be lost without them'. One way of keeping them secure is through the infrequent KAPE tours which keep the army – in this case the Welsh Guards – in the public eye and in 1988 Number 2 Company visited North Wales for a week with a programme of marches and demonstrations designed to introduce the regiment to the Welsh public. In the old days it was called 'showing the flag' and it was often the only way for a regiment to get fresh recruits. According to one of the officers involved in the modern tour, keeping the army in the public eye can achieve the same function: 'The week was a most enjoyable one and some useful recruiting work was done. As one measure of the success of the visits, the Wrexham recruiting sergeant reported that after the first day fifteen children went to his office next day and sat their tests the following week.'

Although the Welsh Guards are aware that they have to work hard and to compete with other organizations if they are to keep recruiting figures up to acceptable levels, the Commanding Officer is alert to the fact that it is not enough to appeal only to national sentiments or to rely on the vagaries of the British economy. Recruits have to be given the tangible return of a worthwhile career:

Be we in Northern Ireland or be we a mechanized infantry battalion in Germany, or indeed in front of St James's Palace, we do equally well because the intakes are trained to a particularly high standard. The man we actually get into the battalion on successful completion of his training I think is truly above the average of the rest of the army and can cope with any dual responsibilities or dual trades. The difficulty we have at the moment, in common with every part of the army, is that we have trouble recruiting him. But that's not our fault. It's nobody's fault. There just happen to be fewer young people available in this country for any sort of work. We're not helped by having a rather uncompetitive salary, but once somebody's in and if the management is right, then, my goodness, we can offer a most splendid career.

The career begins at Pirbright on a Monday morning when four times a year two dozen or so boys from Wales arrive at the Guards Depot. For many this will be their first time away from home and there is a gradual breaking-in time for documentation, haircuts and necessary administration before training proper begins on the Thursday. Ahead lies twenty-one weeks of basic training which will turn the lads into competent infantrymen. They will still have much to learn and as they will be told when they join the battalion the learning process will continue throughout their army lives but for the staff at the Guards Depot, if they have done their job properly, the transformation is much more than a simple sea change:

The transition is extraordinary, it's so dramatic it's wonderful to see. We produce a marvellous product: he's got self-respect and confidence, he looks smart, holds himself well, talks confidently and answers up. All the old qualities which the country has lost – it makes the job very worthwhile.

Before they reach that happy stage some twenty-five per cent of the original intake will have dropped out, either because of an untreatable medical complaint, epilepsy or asthma, is discovered, or a previous criminal record is made known, or simply because the recruit does not take to army life. The armed forces are perhaps the one public establishment which cannot soft-sell itself, and were the army to give a rosy picture of basic training promising an easy life, it would be guilty of deception. Basic training is hard, it is meant to be and no amount of flannel can disguise that fact. For that reason the army allows the older recruits to leave at any time beween week nine and week twelve and those under eighteen can leave after the twenty-eighth day. A proportion take that option although the Guards Depot does all that it can to prevent the recruits from reaching that stage of despair and rigorous steps are taken to improve remedial care. Fortunately, the Welsh Guards do rather better than the other regiments on that score. If a Welsh recruit feels homesick or threatens to throw in the towel the Welsh Guards personnel at the depot will contact his family to try to find a solution to the problem. Usually, the parents will back the army and persuade the boy to give it a go – the most persuasive is often the mother and many Welsh Guardsmen will put down their mother's name as next-of-kin, 'mam' being the dominating figure in most Welsh families. Often, too, a sympathetic word or two of Welsh can work wonders as can appeals not to let down the side. It's noticeable that the Welsh Guards recruits tend to stick together during basic training:

They come from a wide and varied background. You could have a lad of seventeen from an unstable background who was looking to the army as a last resort; then there is the exact opposite, a young lad of twenty-two with six or seven 'O' levels unhappy with civilian life who wants something completely different. Being Welsh I have to say that the Welsh Guards recruits are different and the majority come from good supportive backgrounds. They are fairly quiet; they like to be praised a great deal when they've done something really well. If they have a good night out together the majority end up singing or crying, not in a fighting mood. They don't have a rough edge. They're much more mellow and for that reason the discipline in the Welsh Guards is less severe than in many other regiments. It's a much nicer and more workable system.

Although the Welsh Guards personnel selection officer at Pirbright admitted that there is a noticeable clannishness among the Welsh recruits it is not as strong as it used to be in days gone by when each Guards regiment had its own training company. Nowadays all Guards recruits are mixed up among the eight platoons which make up Caterham Company and, for example, there could be a Household Cavalry platoon commander, a Scots Guards platoon sergeant and instructors from the different regiments. The only common factor is that all training personnel come from the regiments of the Household Division. However, the old system of

regimental affiliations – Welsh Guards always made up 8 Company
– still remain in theory and for the Welsh Guards training officer at
the depot in 1988 'its most important role is to ensure that Welsh
Guards trainees passing through the Depot really do get taught the
traditions and customs of the Regiment before passing out and
joining the Battalion. This is achieved by organizing centralized
regimental history evenings run by 8 Company staff and by arranging outings and talks. Here presentations by ex-members of the
Regiment, visits to the battalion and trips to Old Deer Park to
watch London Welsh playing teams from the principality have all
been a success.'

What that reduces itself to in human terms is a desire to look
after your own. A senior NCO admitted that he was terribly
homesick after joining up in 1971, mainly because he arrived at the
Depot before his intake's programme had started. Sitting miserably
in his barrack room he was shaken out of his lethargy by a young
Welsh Guards lieutenant who was passing by. 'Did you see the
Audie Murphy film on television last night?' he asked. 'Yes, sir.'
'Good,' came the reply, 'go down to the stores and get a rifle, you
can pretend to be him for the day.' Although it was a cold
November day the officer gave up his spare time to teach the young
Welsh recruit basic weapons drill and more importantly perhaps he
gave him the confidence and determination to stay in the army.
The lesson was not lost on the recruit when, eventually, he was
promoted Company Sergeant-Major:

> I always try to look after the men who are in my care. If someone were
> to try to give us more duties than I thought fair, say we had three more
> duties than another company, then I would complain about it because it
> would, ultimately, mean that the men underneath me would be doing
> more duties than they should be. That would then go to the Company
> Commander who would take it to the Adjutant or to the Second-in-
> Command and he would then say, 'yes, that's true', and it would be
> reallocated. So everyone gets a fair deal across the board.

In some respects, it is little more than 'fair play', the words the
warrant officer had used to describe Welsh attitudes towards discipline. The days of the doffed cap in South Wales disappeared
many years ago, he claimed. Today, Welsh Guardsmen are encouraged to speak up, not to be disloyal or cheeky, but to possess
the confidence to speak to Royalty if necessary, which being

Household troops, they may well have to during the course of their army careers. His fellow countrymen, confides the same man, are rather better in that respect and in turn their attitude affects the tone of the Welsh Guards. Whereas English soldiers can appear slow and taciturn, Scots truculent or aggressive, the Irish too reckless by half, the Welsh have an easy-going attitude which commends itself to their superiors. The point is taken up by one of that number, an officer, Oxford graduate, with no Welsh connections whatsoever. He was thrown in at the deep end when the battalion was in Belfast:

> Just because we were in Belfast they don't stop taking the Mickey. When we were going out on patrol and I was giving orders the banter would be good. They'd spent most of the tour trying to find out what my third Christian name was and one of them, a bit of a Cardiff wide boy, had managed to bribe someone in the Orderly Room. I was just getting to the end and said, 'Any questions?' and he said, 'Just one, Ambrose.' You know, everyone dissolved with laughter, but that's fine.

And that was one of the reasons why this officer had decided to join the Welsh Guards in the first place. After looking at the Green Jackets he had visited the Welsh Guards as a potential officer and had been greatly amused by the genial relationship that existed between the officers and men. For him it was exactly the right balance between aloofness and familiarity and later it taught him how different was his own life style. While out on patrol in Belfast his platoon sergeant said to him, 'You realize, sir, that most of the men would be very happy to live in a street like this?'

The Welsh Guards found themselves on a short operational tour of Northern Ireland in the spring of 1986 while the battalion was still stationed in Germany. It was their first time in the province since 1979 when they had been stationed in South Armagh and for many of the guardsmen it was their introduction to internal security duties. Being Welshmen most of them found it particularly difficult to understand that a fellow Celtic race who can be so friendly and uproarious at rugby matches in Cardiff could also provide such a hard-bitten and sullen enemy in Republican West Belfast:

> We are blamed for everything in the Nationalist (IRA sympathizing) population of West Belfast. If you have a hangover, if you live in a self-

made slum, if one of your children is sick or even if you are browned off with the world, you can blame the Brits and especially the British Soldier. A funny custom really. Most of us, in even the smallest adversity, would blame ourselves or perhaps the gods, but not the Republican parts of Northern Ireland. The fault is entirely with the British – even those most charming and engaging of fellow Celts, the Welsh.

The same officer also found the behaviour of the children unsettling: up to the age of twelve they were fascinated by the soldiers but once into their teens they turned into urban gangsters and accurate throwers of stones. Even the Belfast women caused strained nerves, perhaps for different reasons, with their 'preference for extremely tight jeans and strong scent'.

And then there were the patrols, each of which would be accompanied by one or two policemen who would generally decide the route and duration. The patrols employ the standard 'brick' formation which has been tried and tested over the years. (A brick is a four-man team, consisting of an irregular rectangle, two men walking ahead and two walking backwards. They are staggered to prevent one man walking in line with another or walking directly behind another.) Each patrol is composed of seven bricks, four of which cover the primary brick on foot while two more provide greater mobility in armoured Land Rovers. 'Although a number of attempts were made to attack our patrols and bases,' noted the Commanding Officer at the end of the tour, 'and although tension was high "post-Hillsborough", no member of the battalion was injured.' Because it seems such a strange environment, part of Britain yet perversely hostile with a hidden enemy ready to strike without warning, a tour of Northern Ireland might put a strain on the battalion but it also helps to pull it together. While they were in South Armagh a newly joined second-lieutenant, fresh from Sandhurst, spent his first few days as an ordinary guardsman in a platoon: this was the only way he could learn the ropes in a bandit country where one mistake or lapse in concentration could be fatal.

Very few of the older guardsmen or NCOs will admit that they actually hate Northern Ireland. One sergeant said that as far as he was concerned the place could be towed out to sea and sunk by naval gunfire, but he was an exception. The men might not like the crowded living conditions in the Springfield Road or in Musgrove Park Hospital but when pressed further they say that Belfast gives them a buzz that cannot be gained pounding the streets outside St James's Palace. 'I think we were at our fittest, the fittest I've ever experienced,' a CSM explained. 'Everybody was fit and there were no slugs around the battalion because there was so much work to be done.' There were even times when the barriers came down and there would be an unexpected point of connection between the Welsh Guardsmen and the local people:

> I remember being out on patrol in a Catholic area on Christmas Eve and as we were patrolling along this guy called me over and said, 'Would you like to come in for a drink.' I hesitated, 'I don't know' and then to be sociable said, 'Aye, all right.' And he said to go and get the guys and to come in, so I called the other three over and went up to the door. He then shouted, 'F--- off you British bastards,' but at the same time he was standing in his doorway waving us in. When we'd got in and he'd shut the door he said, 'I'm sorry about that but I've got to do it to keep up appearances for the rest of the street. When you leave I'll tell you to f--- off again and don't keep pestering me.' Then he gave us a drink and wished us a Merry Christmas and Happy New Year. . . . People like that are worth going over for, even if it's just one of them. If it means stopping one person being mucked about, I think it's well worthwhile.

Apart from the threat of retaliation and the pretended abuse, it was an incident which could just as easily have happened in civilian life on the streets of Llanelli for while most Welsh Guards are bemused by the hostility shown to them in republican areas they also like to feel that they are wanted. Whereas the English and Scottish regiments, for example, tend to be cold and standoffish, even in loyalist areas, Welshmen have an openness and curiosity which their officers often have to curb – for safety's sake. Certainly the CSM was chancing his and his men's luck by accepting the albeit well-intentioned Christmas Eve invitation.

So far the Welsh Guards have had five emergency tours of Northern Ireland and as these are unaccompanied the older married men find it irksome to be separated from their families. The younger men tend to like the experience because after the intensive basic training at the Guards Depot life with the battalion can seem rather staid especially when the Welsh Guards are stationed in the London area on public duties. For that reason Chelsea Barracks is every Welsh Guardsman's least favourite place. 'If you come off

Queen's Guard,' one older guardsman said, 'you just laze around
on your bed. Looking at it now we were at the most untrained I've
ever known the battalion to be. There was no way to do anything
and you couldn't really do much fitness training.'

The difficulty lay in the fact that it was almost impossible to go
running in the busy streets nearby and even to go shooting at the
ranges in Pirfleet meant a two-hour drive through heavy traffic.
Yes, the social life was good because you were in London 'but for
guys who wanted to stay fit and be soldiers it was a bloody awful
posting'. When the Welsh Guards are in the London area most
guardsmen – officers less so – prefer Pirbright, the home of the
Guards Depot, which also has a barracks for one Guards battalion.
Built in the early 1960s, Elizabeth Barracks is at first glance an
imposing modern military base but like many other buildings of that
vintage it suffers from poor design and faulty building techniques.
The married quarters are small and cramped; they are prone to
heavy condensation and have many other defects associated with
poor design and lackadaisical workmanship. In the barracks themselves the men sleep eight to a room in airy two-storey blocks with
their own bath and shower areas and laundry rooms. But what
makes Pirbright such a favourite with the Welsh Guards is its
proximity to the M4 motorway: South Wales is only a couple of
hours away by car and each weekend there is a steady migration
back home to the family. 'Most will say that they're going to see
their girl-friends,' confided one sergeant, 'but it's really to see their
mams.'

In the past Welsh Guardsmen going home on leave would have
worn their uniforms but the modern threat of attack by terrorists
has ended that ritual; in any case all young men prefer wearing
civilian clothes nowadays. Nevertheless, most will admit that there
is a certain kudos attached to being a Welsh Guardsman and take
pride in hearing older men in the local pubs saying things like,
'Flipping heck, look at him, he's in the Welsh Guards. Never knew
he had it in him!' The same guardsman admitted that in some pubs
in the Guildford area being a Welsh Guardsman could provoke the
opposite effect. 'Some people when they hear you're in the Guards
want to fight you straightaway. You walk into a pub and that's it,
especially if it's full of Paras or Green Jackets.' Although the
Commanding Officer is anxious to play down any inter-regimental
rivalry which spills over into violence, Welsh Guardsmen drinking

in local civilian pubs regularly get into fights. (A standing order on each company noticeboard reminds them that offenders will be severely punished and tells them that they are letting down the army, the regiment and Wales.) Because nearby Aldershot is the home of the Parachute Regiment and because there is still a lingering belief held by the Paras that the Welsh Guards did not perform well in the Falklands War, the arrival of Welsh Guardsmen in the wrong pub can lead to taunts followed by a punch-up. Those officers who feel that as the conflict passes into memory time will erase this particular problem can take little comfort from the lessons of history. The cry of 'Broken square!' will still start a fight when it is shouted at the men of the Black Watch – the regiment faltered and allowed the square, then the basic defensive formation for infantry, to break at the Battle of Tamai in 1884. 'If there's ever a war against the Russians,' one Welsh Guardsman told me, 'once you get all the regiments on the battlefield the Russians won't have to do anything, we'll all be fighting each other'.

There is a tendency, too, for some civilian pubs in the Guildford area to refuse to serve soldiers and Welsh Guardsmen are particularly conspicuous because of their bearing and their accents. The problem affects some of the North Walians who cannot get home at weekends; some go to Cardiff rather than stay in Pirbright at weekends but for the rest it's a case of make or mend. There are, of course, local clubs and discos which offer the kind of lifestyle they would enjoy as civilians but there is a tendency which worries the NCOs for the younger North Walians to retreat into themselves and to stay in barracks. North Walians are often native Welsh speakers, too, who use the language in their own company and some experience difficulties with English, not unnaturally since it is their second language. When they leave the army they might go back to a Welsh-speaking community and they remember the famous story – told tongue-in-cheek but still true – of the Welsh Guardsman who went back to his civilian employment at the Point of Ayr colliery and discovered that all the pit ponies refused to obey his orders. They only understood Welsh, you see, and during his time with the Guards he had lost his command of the native tongue.

Quite apart from the language it is noticeable that the North Walians are different from their southern counterparts in many other respects. The North Walians tend to be more solid, country lads who can appear at first meeting to be taciturn or shy; while the South Walians are sharper, more streetwise perhaps and certainly more open and superficially friendly. Far from taking away a sense of cohesion from the battalion the differences only serve to give the Welsh Guards an indefinable zest or 'a fizz' as many of the guardsmen would say. In the company of strangers or outsiders like myself they appear uninhibited, anxious to please and overwhelmingly hospitable yet they rarely commit themselves to any definite point of view and are initially reticent about their own feelings. They will have opinions a-plenty but what they think themselves, they keep to themselves. One senses that it would take a definite breaking-in period before a new officer was accepted, acceptance depending not on any personal quality or military virtue but on a common understanding:

> It's rather like a Scottish clan. It's the valley community – a common dislike of the English which binds the Welsh together, a love of rugby and everybody knowing everybody's brother. Well, the Welsh do, regardless of whether they're soldiers. They are a very close people – one of the first things a Welshman will say, or I will say to him, is 'Where do you come from?' I'm much less likely to ask an Englishman that.

The same company commander admitted that his men took great strength from being Welsh and carried their nationality like a talisman throughout their military careers. When he first visited the valley communities in the early 1980s he was shocked by the obvious signs of economic depression – the industrial wastelands, groups of unemployed men standing at glum street corners, the absence of activity and the general air of neglect. Coming from a well-to-do middle-class English family, he was astounded that such scenes could exist in Britain; then he began to realize that those same conditions had helped to mould his men's characters. 'They have an inbuilt resistance which I think they must have gathered over generations of quite hard life and that's given them a resilience to help them cope with real disasters like the *Sir Galahad*.'

While it is easy to romanticize the idea of the hard-bitten working man or the stolid son of the soil who are immune from hardship because they are used to it, there is a kind of truth in the major's observation. Despite the redundancy and the unemployment which have hit the valleys, despite the decline of the heavy industries and the loss of human dignity which accompanied them, despite all the hardships, there is a sense of community in South Walian towns like Aberdare, Treorchy or Pontypridd which is stronger than in many other parts of Britain. It surfaces in the way the guardsmen regard Wales as home and never really feel at ease in the fleshpots of the south-east. Once the excitement – and the expense – of a few nights on the town has worn off most want nothing better than to go home for the weekend. One reason why, for some, Germany was such an unpopular posting was that it was just too far away. 'It was a pain. You'd always have to spend one day's leave travelling home and another travelling back. What a waste.' Quite simply, many of the younger Welsh Guardsmen found that they were homesick. The Scots, those archetypal empire builders who first peopled and then administered Britain's colonies, emigrated in droves and then settled happily enough in foreign lands; the Welsh, though, have rarely preferred the world outside to what they have at home. Simon Weston spoke for many Welsh Guardsmen when he described his emotions on returning to his native Nelson after being so badly wounded during the Falklands War:

Wales is my country. It's a marvellous place to come from. As Mam drove me through the valleys that day, I realized just how much I value the place and its people. There will always be a lot for me, and a lot of me, in Nelson. It's our stamping ground, the place we jacked up our silly little plans to go somewhere and do something. I'll never really leave Wales. I'll keep travelling now, because I know there's a lot more for me to see and do, but my heart and soul will be for ever in the place I grew up.

The aftermath of the war was a testing time for the regiment. The *Galahad* incident had left mental and physical scars which would take time to heal and there was a lingering sense of anger and betrayal that the worst setback to the British war effort in the South Atlantic had been visited upon the Welsh Guards. Older Welsh Guardsmen, many of whom had fought in the Second World War and knew what front-line combat was like, were equally concerned. Proud they might have been that the regiment was taking part in the campaign, but the news of heavy casualties was a hard cross to bear. 'I cannot say that during the war I had any feeling whatsoever of distress at my own friends who were casualties,' said one veteran of the 1st Battalion about his part in the fighting in north-west Europe, 'I do not think I was the only one either. But if ever there was a time when I was hurt it was hearing the news of *Galahad*. Yes, I was really and truly hurt, and it was painful.' It was also a time when the officers and NCOs feared that their men's spirits might sink beyond recall but as one young officer noted, 'they might have been very shocked by what happened on *Galahad* but they also had an inner determination to succeed. And that helped a lot!'

What also helps to keep the Welsh Guardsmen going when the going gets tough is *hwyl*, an almost indefinable sense of well being. At its most basic the word means 'mood' or 'spirit' but even that bland translation cannot do justice to an exuberance which, while it lasts, suggests that all is for the best in the best of all possible worlds. Its polar opposite is *hiraeth*, a mood so obscure that it has no exact equivalent in English and means many things to many Welshmen. The atmosphere it conjures up is nostalgia and yearning for things and times past accompanied by a sense of desolation which paints the world black. It is the difference between *sol* and *sombra*, light and shade, for the Spanish, or the contrast which their fellow Celts, the Scots and the Irish, will make between the heart and the mind, the emotions and the intellect. Welshmen tend to fluctuate between *hwyl* and *hiraeth* – it is almost a national pre-occupation – and Welsh Guardsmen are no different:

> Oh, bloody Welshmen! Yes, without a doubt, one's got to be very careful about them. It can be seen very easily on something like the rugby field. When things are going badly they get in a real gloom and just do worse. When things are going well, it's hunky-dory, it's marvellous.

The officers admit that it is something they have to look out for in their men. If heads start to drop or if the men start grumbling then morale suffers and there is a decided tendency to give up. Not surprisingly perhaps, most officers and NCOs draw an analogy with the national rugby team for in recent years Wales have not done well in the international championships. It is not that the players are poor – far from it – but they lacked belief in themselves and in their ability to win. The same holds true of the Welsh Guardsmen. If they are feeling self-confident and are sure of their capacity to perform any task that is thrown at them then they are first-rate soldiers, but if there are any setbacks doubt sets in and according to one experienced company commander 'they panic, get over-excited about the thing and try too hard; then things can start to go a bit wrong.' For that reason, he says, 'you've got to keep the team running at a peak for most of the time.' In that way *hwyl* is maintained, *hiraeth* is kept at bay and the Welsh Guardsman is seen at his best:

> One of the most outstanding qualities of the Welsh Guardsmen is what they – if correctly led – are prepared to endure. I think that the pain and misery they'll go through to achieve an aim is wonderful because quite often they have really rough conditions. They might murmur amongst themselves but soldiers always do that whether it be good times or bad times. They'll always get on with the task in hand and that is one of their outstanding attributes.

One former RSM with a reputation for being a hard man, hard but fair – 'all blokes hated and loved him on alternate days it seemed' – found that the best way to treat the Welsh Guardsmen was to offer incentives to make them do better. Shouting at them rarely did any good – and this comment comes from a man who was much feared in his day both for his strictness on the parade ground and his prowess on the rugby field – rather, he preferred to leaven strict discipline with the occasional helping of encouragement:

> When the Commanding Officer was on parade, having given the men a good drilling and then calmed them down my favourite saying was, 'Right, we'll do a present arms. If it's good enough, I'll ask the Commanding Officer to dismiss you.' Now this may seem to be a little thing, but it's not, because I said it ten minutes before the end of the parade. If they did a good present, they got off drill ten minutes earlier. I found that little things like that would bring them on – and they used to love it.

And he feels that pattern has not been altered with the passing of the years. The men in the battalion today might be better educated and better off than ever before and their intelligence and maturity might lead them to question some aspects of military life but some strands of their behaviour have not lost their colour. They still need encouragement and look for it from their superior officers, they are still as cocky as they ever were and they still think that they are the best battalion in the British Army – 'if they can't say that, then somebody's not doing his job!'

Chapter Six

OFFICERS AND
GENTLEMEN

WHEN ASKED IF they are different from officers in the other regiments and corps of the British Army most Welsh Guards officers will either sidestep the question or politely disclaim the suggestion. Pressed further some will admit that, yes, perhaps they do have their peculiarities but so too do the other chaps and, in any case, who wants to be dull standard issue? By way of further explanation a recently retired Welsh Guards officer related an anecdote which has a wide currency within the regiments not only of the Guards Division but also of the whole British Army.

A young Welsh Guards officer had been sent on an anti-tank weapons course which meant living in a mess among fellow officers from the army and the Royal Marines. Although he felt that he fitted in perfectly well he noticed that one or two of his colleagues took exception to him and seemed to resent his presence on the course. They would make sure that he overheard jokes about thick guardees and whispered loud asides about chocolate-box soldiers, all right for ceremonial duties but useless when the going got tough. One in particular, a Royal Marine, went out of his way to be unpleasant, boasting about his own corps and belittling the infantry, especially the Guards for whom he entertained a special dislike. The crunch came one morning at breakfast when the two men found themselves alone in the dining room.

At that hour of the day the Welsh Guards officer was sitting at one end of the table wearing his cap, the peak pulled firmly over his eyes. He ignored the Marine officer's morning greeting and continued reading his newspaper. He ignored him again when the Marine, having sat himself at the opposite end of the long table loudly called for the sugar. A second request brought no response, nor did a third. Instead he turned wearily to the Marine and said, 'Look here, when a Welsh Guards officer wears his cap at breakfast it's a sign that he does not wish to speak – or be spoken to. It's a tradition of the Regiment.'

This sepulchral utterance left the Marine dumbfounded – but not for long. Recovering his wits, he jumped on to the table, stamped down to the Guards officer and slowly ground his boot on to his plate. 'When a Royal Marine officer puts his boot in your cornflakes,' he bellowed, 'it means pass the bloody sugar. It's a tradition of the Corps!'

Not strictly true of course – the same story is told of a Cameronian officer at breakfast with a Para officer – but by telling the story against his regiment the Welsh Guards officer was making a point. Had his colleague been so inclined, he suggested, he could have criticized the Marine's accent or pulled his leg because he held his knife like a pencil but that would have been discourteous. Even when he was provoked beyond endurance at breakfast he still refused to retaliate because to have taken any action would have reduced him to the same level and that was unthinkable. Welsh Guards officers, I was reminded, were far too independent: picking up his newspaper, he simply walked out of the dining room leaving the Marine to wipe the cornflakes from his ammunition boots. The moral high ground, it seemed, had been left intact.

Even if the story is apocryphal, it deserves to be true for whether they like it or not, the Welsh Guards are regarded as a different species. All officers in the British Army are held to be equal and discrepancies in social background, upbringing, education or accent are supposed to count for little. A glossy recruiting brochure says as much: 'Class distinction is a meaningless term in the modern army. Candidates are judged on their merits, regardless of background, accent or any other purely incidental factor.' That disclaimer, however democratic it might appear, has a hollow ring when the complement of an average officers mess is examined. There will be more officers from independent schools in the smarter Highland and English line infantry regiments, fewer in corps like the Royal Corps of Transport or the Royal Electrical and Mechanical Engineers. In the cavalry regiments and the regiments of the Household Division, the officers mess is purely the preserve of the public schoolboy. A glimpse at the destinations of the officer cadets passing out from Sandhurst proves the point. Alongside the names of Eton,

Ampleforth, Radley or Fettes will appear an acronymic code which speaks volumes about the pecking order for the army's better connected young officers: LG (Life Guards), QOH (Queen's Own Hussars), BW (Black Watch), GR (Gurkha Rifles), RGJ (Royal Green Jackets) and, of course, WG (Welsh Guards).

There was a time, not so long ago, when such a process would have been unremarkable; indeed no one would have suggested that Guards officers should come from anything other than a wealthy, preferably landed background. When the Welsh Guards came back to England at the end of the First World War they quickly settled down to the easy routine of public duties in the London area – interrupted only by a spell in Egypt between 1929 and 1931 – and the complexion of the regular battalion began to change. During the war, when the regiment had given three years unbroken service in France, there had been little opportunity, or need, to pay attention to social niceties. With the return to peacetime soldiering, though, Welsh Guards officers soon fell back into the relaxed assumption of duty and responsibility which was the hallmark of an officer in the Brigade of Guards.

On exercises it was a case of making sure that the men had put down their groundsheets and then passing the port. In London they were expected to afford a style of living considered appropriate to officers of His Majesty's Foot Guards. Dress, including civilian clothes, had to be correct to the minutest detail; an officer was expected to travel first class by rail and never to be seen carrying a parcel or a suitcase. Above all he was expected by his behaviour and demeanour to exemplify the English aristocratic habit of never appearing to take things seriously. Living in London provided access to a full social life; officers were only on parade when required and rarely wore uniform. It was often sufficient to inspect the men in the morning wearing a civilian suit and bowler hat and the rest of the day would be free. Leave, too, was generous especially if an officer were a keen athlete with an interest in field sports. Those were the days when it was considered essential for a Guards officer to be able to ride to hounds. It was said – not without reason – that hunting gave a man a feeling for the lie of the land, an essential attribute in military operations.

Although the Welsh Guards never considered themselves to be a particularly wealthy regiment in that the officers were not expected to have large private incomes, they did place great importance on background and being able 'to fit in'. That being said, there have been occasions when officers found that financial limitations could cause problems. In 1919 Murray-Threipland reported to the Prince of Wales that 'a promising young officer, who was to have transferred to the line, finds he will now be able to carry on with the Regiment, and although he is not well off, he is an excellent young officer and I am very glad he has been able to remain.' The officer concerned went on to command the 1st Battalion. Almost thirty years later, in 1947, the Commanding Officer of the 1st Battalion reported to the Regimental Lieutenant-Colonel from Palestine that he was mildly surprised by the parsimonious mess bills run up by his young officers; in his day, he recalled, ensigns were much better off and behaved accordingly.

Selection to such a narrow elite was an elaborate procedure which involved a thorough check being made on the candidate's credentials. There would be a formal interview with the Regimental Lieutenant-Colonel but before that stage had been reached many soundings would have been made to ensure that the boy was the right stuff for the Welsh Guards. As a matter of course his headmaster or housemaster at school would have been consulted but, more importantly if he were not already known to the regiment, discreet enquiries would have been made of friends of the regiment who might know the boy and his family. Did he have good manners? Was he sufficiently reserved yet possessed of enough self-confidence? Did he take an interest in sport? Were his cultural interests confined to *The Times* or *Country Life*? In short, was he a decent chap? If the answer was yes, he was likely to be accepted. A boy who was cocky, too charming by half, brash or talkative would fail to make the grade and it would be suggested that he try his luck elsewhere, perhaps with the Rifle Brigade. (Welsh Guards officers affect to pour scorn on this regiment: even today they will greet pomposity or cleverness as 'typical Green Jacket behaviour'.)

Candidates could also apply directly to the regiment, as they can today, but that was a chancy business: Evelyn Waugh's experience in 1939 is a fair illustration of the difficulties the outsider was likely to face. According to those who knew him, Waugh had professed to take little interest in the deteriorating international situation and had refused to take part in alarmist conversations; privately, though, he had foreseen that war would break out and had attempted to find employment in the Ministry of Information. When war was declared he quickly bent his energies to gaining a commission and began to fret that he would be unable to make a useful contribution in a military capacity. In his diary for September and October 1939 there are recurring references to the twinges of resentment he felt at seeing friends like Frank Pakenham 'in uniform' and being the man he was, he decided that life would be miserable unless he joined them. There followed a series of expeditions to London from his Gloucestershire home to browbeat his contacts in high places.

An attempt to join Naval Intelligence on 17 October was deflected by Ian Fleming with the comforting reassurance that Waugh was 'on his list' and later that day he was equally unsuccessful in finding employment at the War Office. Somewhat depressed Waugh retreated to the St James's Club 'where I had half a dozen oysters, half a grouse, a whole partridge, and a peach, half bottle of white wine and half Pontet Canet 1924. From then my day began to improve.'

It was not just the food and the drink which renewed his sense of well-being. An interview with the Welsh Guards had been confirmed and during the course of the evening friends told Waugh that the Brigade was short of officers of the type normally required by them in peacetime, that is, well connected, reasonably intelligent and affable former public schoolboys. Waugh felt confident enough on that score and, accordingly, he presented himself at Wellington Barracks the following day 'where two distinguished officers of enormous age interviewed and accepted me.'

Much comforted Waugh returned home to Gloucestershire, 'sustained by inward satisfaction having arranged things with Welsh Guards.' It was not to be: three days later the Regimental Lieutenant-Colonel, Colonel R. E. K. Leatham, wrote to Waugh advising him that the regiment's list was full and that there was no place for him. 'My first feeling was that there must be someone at the War Office occupied in blocking my chances; my second that Colonel Leatham had become notorious for his generosity in giving commissions and had been rebuked. Whatever the reason, I was thrown into despair. I now had no irons in the fire.'

Waugh's rejection is still a matter for some conjecture. There is a story in the Welsh Guards that he tried each regiment of Foot Guards in turn and no sooner had he left the Grenadiers than their Regimental Lieutenant-Colonel telephoned his opposite number in the Coldstream Guards to warn him of the novelist's approach.

The same message, it is said, was then passed on to the Scots, the Irish and the Welsh Guards. This seems unlikely, as according to Waugh's diaries, his only appointment was with Colonel Leatham; and it is clear that he was stunned by the subsequent letter of rejection: Given the difficulties that Waugh encountered in gaining a commission – it was only with Brendan Bracken's help that he eventually fetched up in the Royal Marines – there are good reasons for believing that his name was being blocked by someone at the War Office. His most recent publications had shown him to be out of sympathy with the western liberal tradition and in *Waugh in Abyssinia* he had expressed some admiration for certain aspects of fascism. At the beginning of the Second World War, as tends to happen at the outbreak of any war, there was a spy mania and it may be that Evelyn Waugh's name was caught up in it. His brother Alec, on the other hand, was given an immediate commission with the British Army in France.

Of course, it was not impossible to apply for, and gain, a direct commission into the Welsh Guards during the Second World War. The artist Rex Whistler did just that. According to his brother Laurence, he possessed neither family background nor money and the Welsh Guards had to rely on 'his unimpeachable friends, reinforced by keenness and a gentleman's accent'. A near contemporary of Waugh's, Whistler had made his name as an artist and designer and moved easily in London's social circles where his boyish good looks and easy charm were much admired. Like Waugh he had enjoyed a good deal of public success and like Waugh too, he had a wide range of friends and acquaintances in high places who were prepared to be helpful. Both men applied for a commission in the Welsh Guards during the same month, October 1939, yet Whistler was accepted while Waugh was rejected.

Quite apart from the fact that Waugh's name might have been blocked by the War Office – and there is no hard evidence to prove this – the reasons for the Welsh Guards' choice boiled down to the attitude taken by the two men to the army and to the war. Evelyn Waugh regarded the outbreak of hostilities as the opportunity for the intellectual to slough off his theories and plunge into action. He also looked on the army, or more accurately the officers' mess, as a natural extension of the clubland life he lived when in London. To him there was something glorious about being an officer and when he joined the Royal Marines at Chatham he revelled in the good living, quiet courtesies and gentlemanly ambience of the mess. Later, he was to come to the conclusion that the writer was not a man of action and could only write about it, and to his cost he learned the lesson that it was just as easy to be excluded from the mess as it was to be blackballed from a West End club. In his novel *Put Out More Flags*, which was published in 1942, Waugh wrote a hilarious account of the seedy Basil Seal's interview with a crusty old Guards colonel 'whose scarcely human croak and eloquent gesture of hand' indicated that the meeting was over and that there was no place for such a candidate in his regiment. It remains one of Waugh's great comic novels and a classic recreation of the high hopes and enthusiasm with which Britain went to war.

Whistler, on the other hand, was perplexed by the war. He hated it yet felt that it was wrong for young people to bear the brunt of the fighting – he was thirty-four at the time and believed that in some small way his generation was responsible for the policy of appeasement which preceded Britain's declaration of war in September 1939. When he failed to find a place on the register of Official War Artists he tried for a staff job with the help of Duff Cooper, and when that failed he applied, also unsuccessfully, for a commission in the Grenadier Guards. It was as a last resort that he wrote to the Welsh Guards cleverly illustrating his letter with a military landscape and suggesting that his skill at drawing might give him 'some slight qualification'. To his surprise, as he told a friend, he was interviewed by Colonel Leatham and accepted:

I was taken by Leatham on the grounds of being a decent fellow and rather a good cartoonist! (I have never done a cartoon in my life.) I have kept very dark about my drawing and painting, of which he has only the faintest idea that I have some hobby of that kind! Hobby my foot. There was a blood–curdling moment when I heard he would take me on at once, in which case I was *absolument dans la consommé*.

As it turned out Whistler was not commissioned until May 1940 and he was posted to the 2nd Battalion. Although older than the other subalterns he refused a safe job when the time came to go into action and he was one of the first Welsh Guards casualties during the battle for Normandy in July 1944.

According to those who knew him Whistler was, on the surface, an unlikely officer. In the early days he was inclined to be scruffy and on one occasion committed the unthinkable by turning up on parade without a tie. Much of his spare time was spent painting and when the battalion was training at Pickering from July 1943 to May 1944 he spent his leisure hours designing the sets for a production of Wilde's *An Ideal Husband* and the ballet *La Spectre de la Rose*. A substantial amount of this private work was bequeathed to the regiment for wherever he was stationed Whistler decorated the rooms occupied by his fellow officers and men, including a Welsh Guards crest painted on the wallpaper of 'an unlovely chamber' at 39 Preston Park Avenue in Brighton, prior to the Guards Armoured Division crossing over to France in June 1944. What seems to have saved him on many an occasion when lack of military know-how might have told against him was his self-effacing charm and easy temperament. In other words, he had no problem fitting in.

The same quality holds good today. The army might have changed its process of officer selection quite dramatically during the past quarter of a century but for the Welsh Guards at least, 'fitting in' remains one of the main criteria for choosing their officers. Family background and education play an important role but as one career officer with a degree in law puts it, those count for nothing if the man does not conform:

> I mean one makes no bones about our officer selection – we're quite choosy about the people we have. One would never say so publicly but, socially, one's careful. But it is for a very realistic reason. If you were, say, in Germany for five years – and this is a very good example – and someone who comes from a very different background were to live with us and work with us and we're stuck in Belsen miles from anywhere and he's completely different, he isn't going to be relaxed, and we're not going to relax with him. What eventually happens is we're bigger than that person and we will continue to enjoy life but he won't . . . If someone's not going to fit in then you should jolly well say so.

The analogy he would draw is with the family who wants to employ an au pair – the only way that relationship can work is when both hired hand and family feel happy in each other's company. The secret, he says, lies in determining whether or not the outsider will fit into the family group.

Fitting in can mean many things to different officers. At its most basic it can simply be a matter of knowing the same kind of people and understanding the unwritten social rules or mores which govern their lives. In a young man it can be a matter of being suitably reserved, of not exuding too much charm, of being confident yet not over-talkative, of never being pompous or bumptious, of never being indiscreet or over friendly at first acquaintance. The selection, therefore, can be something of a minefield for the unwary, a curious blend of unspoken interest in behaviour with a mix of personnel management techniques and psychology thrown in for good measure: a process without rules which can still make or break a candidate. How then does the potential officer convince the Welsh Guards that he has the qualifications to join their number?

In common with the rest of the British Army the Welsh Guards have a formalized approach to the selection of officers. They interview suitable candidates and invite them to visit the battalion before they decide whether or not to sponsor them through the rest of their training. In the case of the Welsh Guards the initial interviews are undertaken at Regimental Headquarters by the Regimental Adjutant and the Regimental Lieutenant-Colonel who make the first early decisions about whether or not a candidate will fit in. 'One tends to try to get people who have a common interest and a common background because they will get on well together and like each other as a result.' At this stage the Regimental Lieutenant-Colonel hopes that the boys will have other irons in the fire, as Evelyn Waugh did not, and that they will be looking at other regiments, too, perhaps another Guards regiment or a suitably distinguished line infantry regiment like the Royal Green Jackets or the Black Watch. Once over this hurdle – and for the unprepared a visit to Regimental Headquarters at Wellington Barracks could be a daunting experience – the candidate is invited to visit the battalion, usually in the company of a group of other potential officers. The same process happens with other regiments and corps for it is a fundamental tenet of officer selection in the modern army that the candidate must be sponsored by the unit of his choice – or the one that has chosen him.

What makes the Welsh Guards slightly different from the rest of the army outside the Household Division is that they work quite hard at getting hold of the right people at an early stage. Instead of getting their au pair from an agency they rely on having the connections and knowing the kind of people who can help with pre-judgement before an approach is made. For many of the Welsh

Guards officers this process will begin while they are still at school. The Regimental Lieutenant-Colonel makes regular visits to the country's top public schools to keep in touch with boys who might be suitable and younger officers are encouraged to go back to their old schools to extol the virtues of the Welsh Guards. It is also the custom to keep in touch with officers who have served in the regiment previously and to invite them to put down their sons' names as suitable candidates. The line of succession is a task which the Regimental Lieutenant-Colonel takes very seriously:

> We are always talent spotting. I have just written to 450 of the Welsh Guards Officers Club saying, please if you see suitable boys who you think would fit in do point them towards us. You have to look after yourselves in this way. We encourage the officers themselves to find their successors. I would like to say that you can't leave until you've found someone to replace you. We also do our best to retain our links with our officer-producing schools: any way we can we encourage people to send suitable candidates towards us.

To the outsider the system could appear to be little more than a self-perpetuating oligarchy but, perversely, by taking such an active interest in seeking out officer material the Regimental Lieutenant-Colonel feels that the Welsh Guards have succeeded where the other regiments of the Guards Division, with their narrow focus on Eton and Harrow, have failed:

> In many ways we've always been more prepared to go wider than the other Guards regiments and I think as a result we've managed to keep up the standards of our officers. In some cases they are most interesting young officers. For instance our officers now come from a broader selection of schools but whether the general background has changed I don't know. They're not perhaps as well off as they used to be but that's the same generally throughout the army – but we've never been a particularly rich regiment anyway.

The Regimental Lieutenant-Colonel's views are generally shared by the officers serving in the battalion today. One company commander who cheerfully explained that he had no connections whatsoever with the regiment also admitted that his family was quite alarmed when he announced his intention of trying for a commission in the Welsh Guards. An uncle offered some well-meaning advice: 'Just have a look and see what kind of cars all the officers have parked outside the mess and that'll give some idea whether you're going to be able to cope.' Expecting to find the car-park crowded with Porsches and drophead BMWs he was not disappointed to see several cars of that type, but he also noticed that there were quite a few 'beaten up Ford Escorts'.

The days are long past when an army officer in a smart regiment needed a private income in order to sustain the rigours of a busy social life. One reason for their disappearance is that the army has become a busier and more professional place: after dinner officers are more likely to spend their time studying or planning the next day's activities than to hit the port. Social activities are more limited, too, because they are expensive in money and time, and the drink-drive laws have meant that the road from London to Pirbright is 'full of all sorts of traps for the unwary in the early morning'. Although some of the retired Welsh Guards officers sigh for the more relaxed days of past years when fun was paramount, they can also see that as times have changed so have the attitudes of the younger men:

> The days of the extravagant large balls and dances would appear to be over and they [the younger officers] basically lead humbler but, I would guess, much happier, normal social lives than they once did. I see it in the way they arrange their parties in the mess which are more informal, much happier and totally unstuffy. I find that their girl-friends and their guests are refreshingly brighter, and of course some of them come themselves from a different academic background than their predecessors. Our officer intake now has a high proportion of graduates, they're obviously much older by the time they get to us and they tend to have girl-friends who are graduates too. This changes the whole social scene and we find our parties are infinitely more gregarious, more fun, more witty and more enjoyable. And what I personally notice in comparison to my own early days is that drink is very much more moderately consumed and basically the whole thing is one deal more civilized.

Now this is not to say that young Welsh Guards officers have embraced lives of unrelieved celibacy or that they regard themselves as some sort of praetorian guard which can never relax. When they are stationed in the London area their lives off-duty are their own and so are their friends. 'My social life when I arrive in London is entirely my own and revolves around people who were at university with me,' said an Oxford graduate who decided against making the Welsh Guards his career. 'I like to keep my private life very much separate.' The trouble lies, he continues, in other people's perceptions of him. 'They tend to say, "My God, not another thick army officer," or, "Oh, that's smart, but why aren't you in barracks?"' Quite often they will expect a younger Welsh Guards officer to be something of a fop or an eccentric and are disappointed when they discover just another ordinary young man going about his business or determined to enjoy himself. Quite often, too, the young men will play up to the image for all that they are worth and give a passable imitation of the laid-back, ever so vague guardee but then, I was assured, it was always done with 'a huge twinkle in the eye'.

At other times the opinions of some outsiders can be downright hostile. One company commander who worked at a Ministry of Defence desk for a spell shared his room with an officer from an English line infantry regiment and was at first disconcerted and then angered when he discovered the strength of the man's dislike of the Household troops. It was quite in order for him to be offhand to me and rude about my regiment, he confided, but had I responded in kind not only would it have been bad manners on my part but I would then have been thought a typically arrogant Guards officer. Even having two cars could be a disadvantage:

> Last year when I was at Staff College I used to give someone a lift down to Shrivenham in my car which is an Audi estate and which we had bought terribly cheaply in Germany. Then one day I took my wife's car which she had been given when we got married – it's a tiny little Volkswagen Polo – and when I picked him up he called his wife out and said, 'Hey, look at this, here's a Guards officer with two cars.'

What he finds is that quite a few people want to believe the popular idea of a Guards officer that has been fostered by the media, in fiction and, it has to be admitted, by the Guards themselves. Like any other elite group – and Welsh Guards officers certainly believe that they are just that – they have a good conceit of themselves but to allow any sign of that superiority to show would be considered bad form. 'I think that the appearance of an arrogant young man is almost self-inflicted,' confided a recently commissioned subaltern, 'because if you are told you are the best you start to believe it. Unfortunately when you're nineteen you can be pretty immature and can't keep that confidently and quietly to yourself.' Equally unfortunately, he continues, outsiders tend to remember the silly show-offs 'whereas I think that most of us, hopefully, are quiet, mild-mannered and normal people'.

The route into that charmed circle begins, as we have seen, with the Regimental Lieutenant-Colonel's interview at Wellington Barracks. Some candidates will have met him before during one of his periodic visits to their schools and will have already made up their minds about the Welsh Guards. For others, the uncommitted, the visit to the battalion is of prime importance for, as most officers readily admit, at that stage of their lives boys are easily impressed and if they are given a good time by a particular organization they will tend to favour joining it. 'I had a good friend at school who was going to the Welsh Guards; I enjoy the game of rugby; I was attracted to the Welsh as a people and when I visited the Welsh Guards as a schoolboy I was suitably impressed.'

Not unexpectedly, the Welsh Guards like to put on a show and to give their potential officers a good time when they visit the battalion. Quite a number of officers admitted that this was the stage when they decided that only the Welsh Guards would do and then prayed fervently that not only would they be accepted but that they would then get through all the hoops that would lead to a commission. In recent years cuts in defence expenditure have meant that some of the glitter has been shaken off the visit of potential officers to the regiments of their choice – older officers still speak with no little reverence of visits to the battalion when they were in postings outside Britain. Even so, a visit to the battalion in the late 1980s is not without a touch of glamour, as I myself discovered. True, the boys are put through a busy programme which normally lasts three days – they have to see all aspects of the battalion at work and at play – but they are also well entertained. There is one modest semi-formal dinner which the boys and the officers attend wearing lounge suits – 'Now that's a real Eton suit and no mistake,' whispered one of the subalterns to me when the boys came into the mess. Contrary to popular belief neither their table manners nor their ability to hold drink are under scrutiny, both are taken for granted, but it is another part of the process of discovering whether or not they will fit in. As the

Commanding Officer explained, each moment of their visit has been under scrutiny and it is up to them to make the most of their opportunity:

> At the end of this three day period every officer who has met them will have a pro forma and he will frequently leave bits blank because he simply will not know the answer. But if he has an opinion over one or more of these young men he will write it down and in confidence it will come to me. I will collate these views and it will become very clear, after twenty officers have commented on their sheets of paper, which of these young men would be happy with us. They themselves will go away knowing in their heart of hearts whether they would be happy as Welsh Guards officers. Of quite delightfully little interest to the officers in the mess is where they came from, or what school they were at, or who their parents were. It couldn't matter less. What really matters is whether the fellow looks like somebody you would like to be next to in a tight spot, and somebody who really cares for other people apart from himself.

That may be true but it was also clear that during the visit by potential officers there was no need to raise any of those issues – one candidate admitted that he was relieved to find a former prefect among the subalterns; another made polite enquiries about someone else's cousin. It made them feel more at home, they said.

Being judged by one's peers is as democratic a process as any and it was clear to me that all five candidates had much to offer the Welsh Guards. One professed an engaging interest in being near to the West End for much of his army career, a second put forward the claims of rugby football, another hoped that his interest in the fine arts would not tell against him, only one had any family connections with Wales: all were very different, all seemed to be perfectly agreeable and polite young men yet three would fall by the wayside. For one of the older officers present that was just as it should be:

> Funnily enough, I think that although we have people from roughly the same kind of background we certainly don't have people with the same interests or attitude to life and we have a very broad mixture of types in the mess which I think is a thoroughly good thing, and I think it's our preparedness to accept people who are not necessarily what one might expect the orthodox Guards officer to be which has stood us in good stead.

At present, and for some years past, the Welsh Guards have flourished as far as officer selection is concerned. On the one hand they have been prepared to look a little further than other Guards regiments, and on the other they have balanced this liberal tendency with a strengthening of the home base. If the regiment is a good one, runs the argument, then people will get to hear about it and will vie to join it. Presumably, too, if the regiment has a bad name then candidates will steer well clear of it.

According to the army's book of rules the next stage after sponsorship is an appointment with the Regular Commissions Board (RCB) which determines whether or not the candidate has the potential to train to be an army officer. Being a Welsh Guards candidate cuts no ice here: the three-and-a-half day course is designed to test intelligence, confidence, fitness and initiative, all the component parts of demonstrating leadership potential and everyone has the same chance. Designed by psychologists in the 1940s to bring some cohesion to officer selection the process has changed over the years but basically its aims remain the same – to weed out those young men who have the best chance of benefitting from officer training. Each candidate is assessed on his own merits and is not in direct competition with the others on the course, but the assessment is continual and one big blunder, compounded by an indifferent showing in other tasks, could lead him to being judged a 'fox' (fail) instead of a 'dog' (pass) at the final board. It is a tough course, and most regiments and corps offer their candidates a pre-RCB course to familiarize them with the tasks they will meet. The Welsh Guards, like the other Guards regiments, go one step further: their potential officers have to go through Brigade Squad:

> Brigade Squad. Some might say eight weeks of sheer hell. I wouldn't say that. I'd say that it was a challenging experience because one was going to something you knew nothing about apart from hearing the most dreadful things about it from people who wanted you to sweat a bit. You were joining an organization as the lowest form of life. At the Guards Depot you were slightly apart from the soldiers. You occasionally came into contact with them but because you were men with a mission, that is motivated into trying to get into the army, you could to a large extent be given a harder time.

Like all seasons in hell the hardships of the Brigade Squad period of training get rosier as the years go by. One Welsh Guards potential officer arriving at the Guards Depot was confronted by an angry-looking Scots Guards NCO with the welcome, 'I know you. Your father was in the navy, wasn't he ... so I thought. Well, I was too and he once gave me ninety days. We're going to get on well, petal, aren't we?' As all Welsh Guards will admit, Brigade Squad is a wonderful opportunity for the training sergeants at the Depot to have complete power and authority over a group of young men who may one day be in charge of them. Being a fairly tightly knit regiment, the odds are high that a young officer will meet again one of the sergeants who helped to put him through eight weeks of hard graft. 'I remember being locked up by a man who has just finished being our quartermaster. He took great delight in locking up the Welsh Guards, him being a Welshman, and he seemed to think, "Well, they're coming to us. He might be an officer in a year's time, let's do him now." So in the clink I went for doing something totally correctly on the drill square – but once they have their eyes on you there's nothing you can do.'

As well as giving the boys a short sharp introduction to army life – the Brigade Squad training is a much condensed version of the basic training given to the guardsmen – it provides ample opportunity for the potential officer to see what his own men have been through. For that reason, because it is unlike any other experience they will encounter in the army, Brigade Squad is also an important part of the bonding process: once you've been through, they say, you know a little bit more about yourself and the men with whom you will serve.

From Brigade Squad to RCB the path continues to the Royal Military Academy Sandhurst which trains all officers for service in the British Army. It occupies nearly 900 acres of land on the Surrey-Berkshire border and is best known perhaps for the stately Doric columns of Old College which was built by King George III and then bought by William Pitt the Younger who sold it to the War Office at a handsome profit. Sandhurst is a curious mixture of university college and military academy whose course combines spartan vigour with high professional standards. Training takes forty-two weeks, except for graduates who do a shorter Standard Graduate Course.

While at Sandhurst cadets of all military persuasions share the same training but there is an understandable tendency for those bound for Household Divison regiments to stick together. It is also a time when close friendships are made and these can influence minds which are still not one hundred per cent certain about their futures. One officer admitted that he almost gave up the chance to join the Welsh Guards because he found that the cavalry cadets at Sandhurst seemed more fun; by the same token it has happened that Grenadier officer cadets have switched to the Welsh Guards for precisely the same reason. As one of them admitted, they were still young, immature and impressionable and if one regiment seemed to offer a better home then wasn't it a good thing that the army was flexible enough to allow them to change horses in mid-stream? On both counts the Welsh Guards have done rather better than other Guards regiments over the years.

If Sandhurst is the training ground which takes the young man out of civilian life and gives him his first taste of living in a military environment, then joining the regiment completes the transition. It can be a daunting experience for however exalted he might have been at Sandhurst and however brightly might have burned the memory of the Sovereign's Parade and the Commissioning Ball, life as a newly arrived second-lieutenant definitely begins on the bottom rung – professionally and socially. Many Welsh Guards ensigns (second-lieutenants) have admitted that the experience was like being a new boy on the first day of school. Although they might have known some of the younger officers either socially or from school, they were still expected to be seen and not heard:

> I think a young officer can easily be misled and think that he is better than he is when he comes out of Sandhurst. Like anyone who's completed some sort of training like university, or has been head boy at school, he might come to the battalion thinking he's the bee's knees and want to tell everybody about it as well, in which case the mess is a very good place for quietening him down a bit. Now it's not done by being rude to them noisily, it's done just by not talking to them directly. Some officers make a conscious decision not to speak to him and are not going to be really friendly until the young officer quietens down a bit. They soon get the message and the system works well.

Another captain who joined ten years ago recalls that joining the battalion was an awkward experience and the first three months were spent cautiously finding his way. People were friendly enough, he remembers, but distant and it was made perfectly clear to him that past achievements counted for little. He had to prove himself and ease himself into the mess before he could be finally accepted. Then one day he made a feeble joke by way of observation: because everyone laughed he knew that his apprenticeship was over and that at long last he belonged.

Twenty or so years ago and more there was a much stricter and more formalized attitude in the Welsh Guards. Newly commissioned officers were ignored as a matter of course for at least three months and as one older officer remembers it could be a terrible experience for naturally sociable young men:

> I joined the battalion in Aden, direct from Sandhurst, and it was obviously a very strange country; indeed, it was the first time I had actually been abroad. Instead of being welcomed into the Welsh Guards family – which I know happens now to any new officer – we were well and truly ignored for the first six months . . . I remember vividly sitting on the verandah of the Officers Mess after seven or eight months and very soberly and sombrely talking to the three fellow officers who had come out with me and acknowledging that we had made a great mistake, that we were in the wrong regiment and that when we got back to England we should bring about a change of battalion. Now, luckily this didn't happen and we became happier as the months went on, and I dare say we became probably more palatable to the battalion.

The Welsh Guards were in Aden in 1965 and 1966, a posting which many officers have admitted gave the mess a certain post-imperial stuffiness. It was also a much older regiment in those days – captains and lieutenants were often in their early thirties and they tended to believe that because they too had been ignored in their time that was the Welsh Guards way. One recalled a famous, and probably apocryphal, incident from the 1950s when an ensign found himself alone at breakfast in Chelsea Barracks, the only other officer in the dining room being an elderly major. 'Good morning,' said the ensign, sitting down. There was no response. 'Fine day,' he continued, oblivious of the frosty silence. Again there was no response. When the greeting was repeated the major called over the waiter. 'Mr – wants to discuss the weather,' he said angrily. 'Talk to him.' The same major was also reputed to have said 'Good morning' seven times in succession to another ensign who was rash enough to greet him and ended with the blunt warning, 'Now, I hope that will do you for the rest of the week.'

Nowadays such blimpishness would be laughed out of court mainly because it has disappeared from civilian life but also because most officers feel that it has no place in the modern army. It has to be said, too, that the officers of the Welsh Guards feel that they have been less regimental than other regiments of the Household Division and far more welcoming to outsiders.

There is, though, another group of officers who find that the transition to the officers mess can be a disconcerting passage: the three officers in the battalion who have commissioned from the ranks. By the time they have gained their commissions – initially a short service commission which can be upgraded to a special regular commission – they are experienced soldiers. Having held the post of Regimental Sergeant-Major or Superintending Clerk, they will be in their late thirties; yet one day they will be at the pinnacle of the non-commissioned ranks and the day after they receive their commissions they will be once more on the bottom rungs as a lieutenant. Moreover, they will have moved out of the vaguely comforting and familiar surroundings of the Sergeants' Mess into the unknown and perhaps awe-inspiring ambience of the Officers' Mess:

> I was extremely nervous. At one minute to twelve o'clock I'm still outside the Commanding Officer's door as a Regimental Sergeant-Major and at one minute past twelve I'm walking down the road with my soft hat on to go into the Officers' Mess. And instead of being the king of 150 people in the Sergeants' Mess up the road, all of a sudden I'm the most junior officer of thirty-six, all of them in a totally different age group to me. So you feel a little bit apprehensive of going in there and getting involved.

From being an RSM, one of the lucky ones who had enjoyed the 'tremendous bonus of doing a Trooping the Colour' he went on to become the battalion's quartermaster, one of the technical posts in the regiment that are open to officers commissioned from the ranks. The others are Families Officer and Transport Officer/Technical Officer.

There always have been army officers who gained their commissions from the ranks; in the past, true, they were a rarity and one hundred years ago they only made up 2.2 per cent of the cavalry and infantry officers. In 1922 steps were taken to encourage

suitable NCOs to apply for commissions with the introduction of
the 'Y' cadetships which enabled top soldiers with good educational
standards and military ability to pass through Sandhurst without
having to pay fees. Since then the trend to commission officers
from the ranks has increased and during the past forty years there
has been a steady rise in their number from one in fifty in 1950 to
one in three in 1980. None will ever reach the highest commands
partly because they lack experience in tactical concepts and partly
because they are too old; most will retire with the rank of major.
The process is understood within the Welsh Guards: the quartermaster does his job and the operations officer or intelligence officer his.
Are they then, all equal? 'Oh no,' said one, 'there's a great deal of
difference in experience and understanding between a young officer
and myself.' Many of the younger officers also remembered him
from his days as an instructor at the Guards Depot and 'their vision
of me was someone you avoided like the plague and they only said
hello to me from the other side of the room'. It took time, too, to
call his fellow officers by their Christian name and to hear his own
Christian name being used and after a lifetime of doing things at
the double he found that he 'couldn't be aggressive and thrusting
and grabbing people for minor disciplinary offences'. Losing the
RSM's touch, and adopting the relaxed style of command that
typifies the Welsh Guards officer, he admits, turned out to be as
difficult as coming to terms with the social niceties of the mess.
What did help was the kindness shown to him:

> The officers were very nice to me. One of the things I will admit is that
> when I was first commissioned I was worried about how I would be
> treated. But whether it's because the Welsh Guards is different from
> other regiments I don't know, but I've never met a nasty character in
> that place. I was accepted straightaway; they made a fuss of me, they
> looked after me and I found it extremely pleasant. So when people say
> to me, do you miss the Sergeants' Mess, I say, well no I don't because
> I've moved on from that.

An older ranker officer agreed, saying that it was just part of the
scheme of things, you went out of one room through a door and
into the next room which just happened to be slightly grander. You
remained the same person. Everyone accepted the system – he had
even rejected the possibility of an earlier commission in another

regiment because he wanted to remain a Welsh Guardsman – and there was no possibility of being taken for a regular officer. 'I was a captain at the age of a lieutenant-colonel. You can see the difference in the face!'

There are some differences, though, small enough not to matter perhaps but apparent nevertheless. On parade the ranker officer does not wear a bearskin but a cocked hat modelled on the staff officer's hat of Wellington's day and in the Distribution of Officers his name appears at the bottom of the list below the newest ensign. (In the tier of pigeon-holes in the Officers' Mess the ranker officers appear in the bottom rungs too.) The other feature that marks them out as being rather different is that all of them are demonstrably Welsh with Welsh surnames and Welsh accents.

They have also been brought up to believe that it is the Sergeants' Mess which runs the battalion and that the RSM is the final arbiter of how things should be done. With the shift of emphasis in the chain of command which has given additional responsibilities to the officers they now have to take on board the fact that the army and the regiment has changed in the twenty-odd years since they first joined up. 'Officers have become much more – for want of a better word – other-rankish. You'll find officers going round shouting and giving out orders. The whole thing has become much more aggressive and intense and they take a great deal more interest in running things like training programmes.' So, for the ranker officer the transition from the Sergeants' Mess seems to be as fraught with perils as the road to London is for the Pirbright based subaltern. What it boils down to, said one company commander, is whether or not the guys can metaphorically shed their chevrons and think of themselves as officers. If they can, they'll be all right, and after all, the mess is there to help them – and their wives:

> In all honesty the girls probably feel more uncomfortable in the Officers' Mess than we do, because we know them, we work with them every day, we have fun with them and we know their good points and their bad points . . . but the boys are very good. They meet them at the door, take them away, give them a few drinks, dance with them, this and that and the other, and make them feel at home. I think that in the main they probably feel it a little more than we do.

One of the things they discover is that social life in the Officers'

Mess is a more relaxed version of the equivalent social life outside the army and for the Welsh Guards that is quite normal. Unlike many other regiments or corps which have written rules about such arcane matters as when a Sam Browne belt might be worn or which uniform to put on at a particular time of day, the Officers' Mess have no formal rules at all:

> It's always amusing to watch people's faces when they come to our mess because they have all sorts of preconceived ideas about us being frightfully stiff and formal when in fact of all the messes I've been to in the army this is probably just about the most relaxed. We just don't have mess rules – at least not any that I can think of, and if there are any they're governed by common sense in the way you would behave at home. Therefore no one can see much point in writing them down – if you don't know them already you shouldn't be an officer.

This does not mean that the mess is a free-for-all. On the contrary, certain uses of vocabulary are frowned upon – London is London and not town – and officers are expected at an early stage to have grasped which uniform they should wear at any given time. The adjutant wears service dress with Sam Browne belt during the day, as does the picket officer and the captain of the week while during the day the other officers wear either combat dress or barrack dress – brown shiny shoes, service dress trousers, army issue jumper held in by the Household Division's blue and red stable belt. In the evening the picket officer wears mess dress which one officer described as 'British Rail waiters uniform, red coat and black trousers with waistcoat and black tie'. Sometimes, though, mistakes can be made. One Welsh Guards officer, invited to dine with the Queen while on Windsor guard, wore a soft shirt instead of the stiff shirt and collar demanded by convention. The Queen, who notices such things, asked him if it was not the custom in his regiment to wear a stiff collar. 'Oh, no, ma'am,' came the reply, 'only on special occasions.'

Not that the rules don't exist – they do, in elderly bound volumes which state in minute detail the Standing Orders of the Brigade of Guards – it's just that they have been overtaken by common sense and by the changing mores of the outside world. After all, one company commander reminded me, when he came into the Welsh Guards he brought with him certain standards of behaviour which he was sure are quite different from those which existed in his father's day. For the most part it's just a matter of employing discretion:

> There are a number of rules but people don't seem to know them or understand them now. I think there is a rule about when you wear your Brigade tie but nobody seems to know what it is. There are rules about public duties, though: for example, if you go to a Royal residence on a recce, to recce a future Guard of Honour or something, then you are expected to wear a stiff collar, but that is very much on the work front . . . it would look absurd and it would be discourteous to turn up at Buckingham Palace wearing jeans and a denim jacket. It would be totally and utterly inappropriate.

While they are stationed at Pirbright very few officers live in the mess. During the day the atmosphere there is relaxed and welcoming, almost jovial, a mixture of gentleman's club and country house weekend. After all, the officers insist, this is their home and they treat it as such. After the day's work, though, it is a quiet, somewhat forbidding place – apart from guest nights when jollifications can go on until late. This is because London is nearby and no one wants to stay in the wastelands of the Surrey commuter belt when there is a different kind of social life to be had elsewhere. ('I'd rather be tucked up in bed with a pretty girl in London than live here,' confided one young spark, or as another officer put it, 'you'd be paying psychiatric fees if you didn't get out on a regular basis'.) The other reason, also a sign of the times, is the preference to buy into the property market at an early stage in life: quite a few Welsh Guards officers own flats in London either singly or on a communal basis. This is in direct contrast to thirty years ago when young officers and unmarried older officers lived in the mess and led a routine, if monastic existence governed by arcane rules and regulations.

Today, the only people to be in the mess of an evening at Pirbright are the occasional officer or visitor and, invariably, the picket officer who dines wearing mess kit and who has to be on hand to deal with all routine duties. Often, this is a punishment awarded by the adjutant for minor indiscretions – one officer admitted that when he first joined the battalion he was awarded a month's worth of extra pickets and banned alcohol because he got drunk in another regiment's mess.

That was in Germany where the young unmarried officers were

forced, willy-nilly, to share one another's company in the mess. A period like that tests the 'fitting-in' policy to the hilt for when the Welsh Guards were in Hohne the officers were forced back on their own resources. 'Hohne is North Germany,' said one. 'North Germany is plain, fat and dull and the people are pretty fat and dull as well.' Most officers liked the work well enough – 'it's meant to be the zenith of our soldiering because that's where the threat is, that's the battle we'll have to fight' – but few had any kind words to say about their social life off-duty. Younger officers would be invited to have supper and watch televison with the families of the older officers just to escape the general tedium of mess life – although one mess servant confided that the subalterns still found excuses to let down their hair. 'I came back to the mess in the morning and found every single glass and coffee cup in pieces in the fireplace. They'd smashed everything. Anything that was breakable was broken.' Of course, he continued, they all owned up and paid for the damage.

Another senior warrant officer listening to the conversation said that once upon a time riotous behaviour like that would have been unremarkable. His memory went back to the days when it was considered *de rigueur* for the subalterns to beat up the mess once the Commanding Officer and company commanders had retired for the night. Curtains might be torn off the rails during mess mountaineering (attempts to circumnavigate the mess without touching the floor) or furniture might be smashed during games of high cockalorum (a team game in which one side attempts to break the other's line, formed up like a rugby scrum). All good fun, he said, the kind of high spirited behaviour expected of a Welsh Guards officer but punishable offences if committed by a guardsman!

Those were also the days when guardsmen were not permitted to address an officer directly; instead they had to make an application to the Company Clerk and thereafter face a grilling from the CSM who judged whether or not the request was in order. And that really is the great change that has taken place in the Welsh Guards in recent years. The men notice with approval that the officers are more approachable and are more willing to share the day-to-day responsibilities of army life. Gone are the days when a company commander would inspect his men in the morning and then disappear, leaving the men in the capable hands of his CSM. One or two of the older Welsh Guards officers look back on those days with a fair degree of nostalgia and will admit privately that the regiment offered an agreeable ambience for a young man who was not going to make the army his career. At the same time they acknowledge that there has been an important shift of responsibility in the chain of command that makes any return impossible:

> Over the years there has been a definite shift of power from the Sergeants' Mess to the Officers' Mess and I think this has been to the good. It hasn't been fast, it's been moderate and steady and is controllable. Whilst the Regimental Sergeant Major still holds very considerable sway, he is no longer the final arbiter of the execution of the Commanding Officer's wishes and I run this battalion very much more through my company commanders than I do through the Sergeants' Mess.

What this means in practice is that a company commander will work closely with his NCOs to ensure the smooth running of his company. Because the army is more professional in its approach to training there has to be more commitment and more reliance on the abilities of everybody in the team. And as every newly joined ensign discovers the management system begins from the day he joins the Welsh Guards. Sandhurst may have told him that he has to get out and lead his men but as the more experienced CSMs know, there is still much for the newly joined platoon commander to learn:

> It's not the same as being a new draft for them, they're on their own. When a new draft arrives he just slips in with twenty-five guys. When a platoon commander arrives brand new, he's out there on his own. He has to try and make the right decision with other people knowing that he's going to make mistakes – and they all do, just as a new draft makes mistakes. But they do learn and the likeable thing about most of our officers is that they will listen if they think they're being told the right thing.

At the start of their career the platoon commanders will enjoy fairly close contact with their men. After all, most of them will be much the same age as they are and it is noticeable that the guardsmen enjoy ribbing the younger officers and pulling their legs. 'It's easier when you're younger,' said a captain with ambitions to become a company commander, 'but as you go up the system then you have to make decisions that are not always pleasant. You might have to tell soldiers that their career is not possibly the guiding light they thought it might have been. It's up to you to have the moral courage to tell them.'

Getting the balance right is important in any command relationship whether it be in the office, on the factory floor or in the armed forces. A common Welsh characteristic is a desire to be liked and it is obvious from the way they behave in the barracks or on exercise that Welsh Guardsmen are talkative, even garrulous, and ask to be noticed. With their platoon commanders they can enjoy a reasonably close relationship, and this is encouraged, but further up the chain of command to their company commanders or to the Commanding Officer there is a distinct cooling off. The Commanding Officer on a company inspection might chaff an individual guardsman about his rugby-playing skills – or lack of them – in the way that a headmaster might stop to speak to a boy in the school corridor but, as two company commanders explain, that is the extent of a senior officer's cordiality:

> If everybody knows the framework within which they work it makes for a happier system; the guardsmen would be most surprised if I, as a company commander, went out and was over-friendly or familiar with them. They actually know how most officers are going to behave and they expect them to behave in a certain way. That probably sounds frightfully old-fashioned and blasé, but Welsh Guardsmen like their officers to be the bog-standard officer they know.

> Everybody knows exactly where they stand and as a result of that one can actually be much more relaxed and informal – because there's no danger that the gap is going to be bridged or that anyone is trying to bridge it. In some of the county regiments it's much less structured and therefore in many ways they have to be much more formal to keep up the barriers. Whereas our barriers are so well defined one can actually be extremely relaxed – the great advantage of calling Welsh Guardsmen by their last two numbers is that while it's not a Christian name, it's a much more informal way of doing things. When you want to give him a rollicking you revert to the use of his surname.

Some outsiders have likened the relationship between the Welsh Guards officers and the men they command to the squire and peasant alliance, with the NCOs playing the role of factor or bailiff. They will even say that the connection is cemented by the fact that the majority of the officers are English or Anglo-Welsh and the men are mainly Welsh. For the liberal-minded critic the observation has a comforting ring, smacking as it does of paternalism and it can be interpreted in a number of ways all of which have some validity. in Welsh social history – the simple peasantry in the servitude of their lords and masters, the nonconformist radical tenantry owing their allegiance to the Anglican Tory squirearchy, the miners and ironworkers in their uneasy industrial alliance with the Crawshays of Cyfarthfa or the Guests of Dowlais. Take the relationship one step further, they say, and it is easy enough to make the same comparisons between the Welsh Guardsmen and the predominantly English Welsh Guards officers. It is just like the Indian Army in the days of the raj.

Indeed, some Welsh intellectuals have interpreted their country's nationalism and sense of identity in those terms – the subjugation of a small country, Wales, by its larger neighbour, England and have drawn parallels with the old empire. The exploitation of Welsh natural resources, the imposition of English as the national tongue, the occasional use of the military to restore order as happened in Tonypandy, the indifference to Welsh culture and a general tendency to downgrade things Welsh: all these facts, all true at one stage or another in Welsh history, have been singled out to prove the point that Wales can be regarded as a fractious colony ruled over by the dominant English. One North Walian sergeant told me that Abersoch, a pretty seaside village in the Llyn Peninsula, had so many English bungalows that he imagined it must be like Simla in the days of Kipling's India.

The same man admitted that the one time he resented being in the Welsh Guards was the period he had spent as an officer's orderly – and were one to pinpoint the accuracy of the adage that the officer is the master and the guardsman the servant, then it is here. Orderlies are still employed in the regiment to help the officers with their ceremonial uniforms. For this they are paid an extra £3 a week, not a princely sum, but one which is generally supplemented by the officer if he is doing additional guards during that period. The British Army said goodbye to the officer's servant or batman in the egalitarian days of the 1960s but the tradition has remained in being in the Welsh Guards because of the regiment's ceremonial duties. Few guardsmen resent the duty and none regard it as an imposition unless the officer betrays the privilege by treating the orderly as his personal servant. Then, as in other things, the behaviour will be noticed, there will be a hint from the adjutant perhaps followed by an unexpected picket and the matter will be dropped. Young officers rarely fail to take the hint.

To utilize the instance of the officers' orderlies or to take the colonial view of history only and to apply it to Wales would be to tell only one part of the story. Even if it is convenient to see the officer-guardsman relationship in the Welsh Guards as an extension of the old squire-peasant alliance, it is a lazy reasoning. For a start, the squirearchy, as it is understood in England, disappeared in Wales after the First World War and had been long in decline before that. During the second half of the nineteenth century the Tory power of the landed gentry had been gradually eroded by the nonconformist liberal radicals of the chapels and by 1892 there were only three Conservative MPs in the whole of Wales. The landed gentry pulled out of their estates or mortgaged them, leaving their homes to become country house hotels, and the tenant farmers became small-holders. *Trech gwlad nag arglwydd* – 'the land is mightier than the lord' – said David Lloyd George during his election victory over Hugh Ellis-Nanney, the Squire of Llanystumdwy in 1890. 'The Tories have not yet realized that the day of the cottage-bred man has at last dawned!' Ellis-Nanney had thought himself to be an unchallenged Tory landowner, sure of his place in the world, yet here were his tenants casting their votes for a damned Liberal! As happened in Ireland, the landowners then threatened their tenants with eviction unless they voted their way, but to no avail. Already different from the squirearchy in language, customs and religion they turned to the Liberals and the day of the landed gentry passed into history. Unlike a few Scots regiments, including the Scots Guards, which number titled or landed gentlemen among their officers, the Welsh Guards are not dependent on a Welsh squirearchy because it no longer exists in a recognizable form.

That being said, many of the Welsh landed families who stayed on in Wales regard themselves as being Welsh, the Philipps of Picton Castle, for example, who fought so hard for the creation of a Welsh Regiment of Foot Guards in 1914. The officer rolls of the Welsh Guards, too, are rich with the names of prominent Welsh families – the Fox-Pitts of Anglesey, the Staniers of Ludlow, the Clives of Powys and Lloyd George's son was commissioned in the regiment during the Second World War. Even those families who are nominally English but live in Wales tend to regard themselves in some measure as being Welsh – 'My parents would be horrified if I said they were Welsh, but I would. In a rugby match I'd support Wales over England.' Being Welsh, it seems, can also be a matter of temperament and for many of the men that is enough:

> The majority of the officers are English – but it's never been held against them! They are still just as proud to be Welsh Guardsmen as we are and we all come from Wales. They always say they are officers in the *Welsh* Guards, not just *the* Guards. It doesn't make the slightest difference to us quite honestly. I don't mind if they're Scottish, Irish or whatever, as long as they're doing their job properly and they've got some pride in the regiment.

The sergeant, retired now, told a story which he felt typified the links which exist between the Welsh Guardsmen and their English officers. Shortly after the invasion of France in the summer of 1944 when the 1st Battalion were fighting in the bocage country in Normandy a group of twenty-five guardsmen were resting in a large barn. It was their first period of rest after some hard fighting and for some of the men it was the first time that they had been in the immediate company of the officer who commanded them. He started telling them about his family who, though English, had a home in Wales and he made much of the fact that they were fighting for the people at home, their families and friends in Wales. 'I would die for a Victoria Cross,' he suddenly said, 'not for me, but for the family, for the Welsh Guards, for Wales.' The men were profoundly impressed by his quiet outburst, until the silence was broken by a distinctive Welsh voice which said, 'Well, you can bloody well do it without my help!'

That mixture of fondness for the officer's courage and a need to pull him down to size seems to be typical of the Welsh Guards approach. In those latter stages of the Second World War it was a youngish regiment with young officers and the men who served in all three battalions have commented on the close links that grew up between them, the officers and the men. 'I had a friend in the RAF,' said one of their number at a reunion, 'and he couldn't understand why we could speak to our officers on equal terms. Not cheekily, mind you, and they in turn treated us with respect. "Come on boys," they'd say when we set off, "bags of swank." And of course, then we'd give it a swagger.'

Over their pints in the association they still remember with gratitude the names of the officers who led them in peace and war. 'Oh, he was one of the best,' said one sergeant of a company commander in the 3rd battalion in Italy. 'You'd follow him anywhere.' As the evening wore on the officer's virtues were repeated and perhaps embellished, almost as if he were one of the *Tylwyth Teg*, the Fair People of Welsh legend. Always looked after his men first he did, treated us fair and square, always ready with a joke and, of course, he was as brave as a lion. Do you remember that time we were advancing to San Marco on the high ground near Perugia? Tulip we called it . . .

No, he wasn't a Welsh man as a matter of fact, he was English, but he was a Welsh Guards officer and that made him one of us.

Chapter Seven

SOLDIERS OF THE QUEEN

THE WELSH GUARDS National Serviceman standing on Queen's Guard outside Buckingham Palace was coming to the end of his tether. It had been a long hot day, beneath his red tunic he was sweating heavily and unsociably and his bearskin cap was pressing vicelike into his skull. Not only did he feel physically uncomfortable after one and a half hours' sentry duty but the staring faces of the tourists were beginning to jangle his nerves. 'Look at those boots,' said an admiring matronly figure, 'they're beautifully polished.' Her husband was less impressed. 'He's just coated them with black gloss paint, that's all.' Earlier in the afternoon the cheekier ones, usually pretty girls, had tried to break his concentration, smiling coquettishly or pulling up their skirts to reveal stocking-topped thighs. There was nothing to do but think of other things – the CSM had warned them not to answer back. Ever. Just think of Pontypool and your mam's cooking, he had told them.

The guardsman's discomfort was interrupted by the sound of a rifle butt tapping twice in the neighbouring sentry box – the signal that an officer was approaching. He cut off a smart butt salute and after a decent interval stepped out on the patrols that every twelve minutes or so broke up his sentry duty. When he returned to his sentry box a singularly attractive woman was standing there looking intently in his direction. From the cut of her clothes she was American and there was a look of wonder on her face. 'Go on, ask him,' she whispered to her companion, a younger though no less glamorous companion. Plucking up her courage the girl stood four-square in front of the by now embarrassed guardsman. 'Know the Dorchester?' she asked. 'Nod if you do.' He nodded cautiously. 'Off duty tomorrow?' Another nod, 'Well, my name's ———. Be there at eight and bring a friend. And your uniforms.' It took all the guardsman's self control to stop his bearskin from falling off.

The next evening saw two conscript iron men leave Chelsea Barracks, their red tunics and bearskins packed, quite illegally, into a large suitcase, their imaginations working overtime with the possibilities that lay ahead. Ever since joining the battalion, at that time engaged on public duties, they had listened avidly to the old soldiers' stories about the sexual adventures awaiting the virile young men who guarded the Queen's palaces. Now it was happening to them.

And, sure enough, the girls were staying at the Dorchester Hotel. And, as they had anticipated, the guardsmen did have to change into their uniforms before anything happened. The girls seemed to enjoy themselves and their father, a businessman from the Mid West, was rightly pleased too: he got a fine photograph of his daughters proudly standing beside two slightly deflated young Welsh Guardsmen. Afterwards they all went out for supper and the evening ended as chastely as it had begun. Thirty years later the ex-National Serviceman could laugh at the memory. 'There we were, thinking ourselves real men, proper ladykillers, but as it turned out, we were just tourist bait, part of their collection of souvenirs from Merrie Olde Englande.'

Thirty years on not a few Welsh Guards ask much the same question. Are we serving our country or are we doing our bit for London's tourist industry? Not that the guardsmen of today have the same opportunities to meet the public. Following an unseemly incident in 1959 when a Coldstream Guardsman was forced to fight off the attentions of an over-amorous female tourist, the Queen's Guards stand inside the railings of Buckingham Palace, well out of reach of the general public. It is now only on some of the guards at the Royal residences of St James's and Windsor and at the Tower of London that they can come face to face with an inquisitive and frequently adoring audience.

The guards on the Royal palaces and on the Tower of London, all popular tourist traps, are an important part of the Welsh Guards' role when they are stationed in London District. Every Welsh Guardsman accepts that obligation when he joins the regiment, but as everyone acknowledges, both officers and men, a steady diet of public duties can lead to lethargy, boredom and restlessness. It is not a new phenomenon but in an army that is smaller, more cost-conscious and more professional than it was in the days of National Service, it is one that has to be watched:

16. A Welsh Guardsman on duty in Northern Ireland, 1971.

17. HRH The Prince of Wales and Guardsman Paul Thomas on Snowdon, 30 July 1976. Thomas lost both legs and an arm in the Guildford pub bombing.

18. The QE2 departs for the Falklands at the start of a three-week-long voyage in May 1982. The Welsh Guards were on board as part of 5 Brigade.

19. A guardsman mans a machine-gun position on board s.s. *Canberra*. These weapons were the last line of defence against enemy aircraft.

20. The *Sir Galahad* burns in Port Pleasant near Fitzroy after being attacked by Argentine aircraft. Forty-eight men lost their lives, thirty-two of them Welsh Guardsmen.

21. A section of the heavy machine-gun platoon in position on the Falklands.

22. Welshmen, like soldiers the world over, can rarely resist the children. A guardsman watches local girls doing their washing in Belize, 1989.

23. Jungle communications. Radio operators provide the vital links with patrols dispersed in the Belizean jungle.

24. 'Oh, it's very hot and sticky, I've never sweated so much in my life.' A patrol carrying the new SA-80 personal weapon.

25. 'We produce a marvellous product . . .' A squad of Scots, Irish and Welsh Guards recruits marches off the square at the Guards Depot, Pirbright.

26. 'Stevo'. W. Stevenson was the first Regimental Sergeant-Major of the Welsh Guards.

The first Queen's Guard was quite enjoyable because it was all so new, and there were lots of people taking photographs and making a fuss. By the time you were on to your fifth or sixth guard they were becoming a little bit tedious. You knew the system, you knew you were going to be woken up every four hours to stand outside the sentry box for two hours. This was probably the hardest thing that I've done in the Welsh Guards, just standing there for two hours all by myself.

The CSM who has sixteen years' service and two Trooping the Colour parades under his belt, was under no illusion about which side of soldiering the men preferred. 'The Marines go in by boat, the Paras by aeroplane but the Welsh Guards are infanteers at the end of the day and that is our prime role. The public duties side is just an offshoot. When we're in London District the public duties take on a stronger aspect than the pure infanteering because that is our dominant role. But in Germany our role was mechanized infantry and there wasn't a red tunic seen for four years.' Yet here was a conundrum. While he was the first to admit that public duties were 'a necessary evil', no sooner were his guardsmen away from them than they began to miss them. At the end of the Falklands War, on the day that the Argentine forces surrendered, he overheard a senior sergeant telling an officer, 'We'd better start rehearsing Queen's Guards again now, sir!'

As a spectacle, the daily Changing of the Guard in the Forecourt of Buckingham Palace is one of London's most popular summer tourist attractions. The traffic in the area comes to a halt, the air is filled with the sound of martial music and the red-tunicked guardsmen make a brave sight as they swing out of Wellington Barracks with the Colour to march the short distance to Buckingham Palace. For the thronging crowds who line the pavements it is all about pomp and circumstance, a pageant that seems to have stepped out of the history books. For the foot guards regiments the ceremony demands concentration, effort and discipline, all of which are supreme military virtues.

The Guard that is being changed is the Queen's Guard, the most prestigious and important of all the guards which the regiments mount when stationed on public duties in London District. It has its origins in the mid-eighteenth century when it was the duty of the three Guards regiments to mount the sovereign's guard on Horse Guards Parade and then to march to St James's Palace where the guard would be changed. The ceremony had much in common with the spectacle which the tourists watch today. The new guard would march to St James's Palace with their colours; the old guard would form up to receive them and the sentries having been posted, would then return to Horse Guards Parade, the principal military buildings in London housing the headquarters of the regiments of Horse and Foot Guards.

At that time, too, St James's Palace was the Royal residence in London. It was not until shortly after her accession in 1837 that Queen Victoria started to live for part of the year in the rebuilt Buckingham Palace, formerly Buckingham, or King's, House: although she professed to find it scarcely habitable and stopped living there after 1861, it was a Royal residence which required a detachment of guards. It was not until King Edward VII came to the throne in 1901 that Buckingham Palace became the principal London home for the sovereign, thus requiring a change in the Brigade of Guards' standing orders. Henceforth the King's Guard would be divided into the St James's Palace detachment and the Buckingham Palace detachment: both were required as St James's continued to be the official 'place' of the Court while it was in London. For the next sixty years the Foot Guards had to wrestle with the complicated rules of etiquette which governed the plans for mounting guards at Buckingham Palace and St James's, the numbers of men to be attached to each guard and the different procedures involved at various times of the year. In 1964, to the relief of every adjutant, the procedure was simplified to allow the Queen's Guard to mount 'at Buckingham Palace throughout the year with the exception of wet weather when detachments will mount separately'. This is the ceremony which so pleases the visitors to London today, and very impressive it is too:

> I would defy anybody to say that they don't enjoy it. It can be a drag at times but when you come round the 'birthday cake' at the top of Buckingham Palace Road or march out of Wellington Barracks when the band is playing and all the crowds are watching you and if you don't feel a sense of pride, then there's something wrong with you. You've got to have something missing in your make-up if you don't respond to that.

This former sergeant-major had taken part in three Troopings of the Colour and had mounted numberless Queen's Guards. Now commissioned, public duties are behind him but he still misses the swagger and the drama of it all. Having been a guardsman, though, what he does not miss is the bull that goes into producing the finished product:

> Come parade time our boots are better than any infantry regiment, or anyone else, and so is the rest of the kit. Beeswax plays a big part nowadays – the boots come with pimples on the leather and these have to be burned off before the polish and the beeswax can be applied to produce the high gloss. Once this has been done most guardsmen keep the polish with a Silvette diamond polishing cloth. It probably takes a good man fifteen to twenty minutes to do a pair of boots but it depends on the individual. Some people have a knack which they either develop or they don't.

He reckons that it can take the average Welsh Guardsman at least three hours to prepare his kit for Queen's Guard. The curb chain, the brass link with the bearskin, is the most difficult to keep clean but generations of guardsmen have learned which shortcuts can be taken without incurring the adjutant's wrath. It used to be considered difficult to maintain the shape of the bearskin cap, especially the men's which is made out of the coarser fur of a male Canadian bear – the officers' are made from the softer pelts of the female Siberian bear. After use it had to be wrapped round with damp towels but nowadays a discreet spray of hair lacquer can achieve the same result. But as one young lance-sergeant confided with a shudder, there have been times when lackadaisical preparations have been glaringly obvious in other – unnamed – Guards regiments. 'Not in the Welsh Guards,' he added, with understandable pride. 'We do everything with loving care and attention because we're Welsh and being Welsh we love being praised.'

Because ceremonial duties are so public it is not just the crowds who pay attention to what is happening. So, too, do senior officers and it is not unheard of for a Coldstream officer, for example, to complain to the adjutant of the Welsh Guards about some minor imperfection in dress or drill during the Changing of the Guard. It works both ways. One young guardsman – no more than nineteen – in The Prince of Wales's Company admitted that when he was on Queen's Guard 'you strike your weapon that little bit harder if the Grenadiers are there and you don't want to be shown up by them.'

That is one reason for the Welsh Guards wanting to make perfection perfect. Another is the very good reason that excellence at drill is a necessary prelude to learning other military skills. 'If a man looks good on parade, if he is smartly turned out, then he will feel good and he will believe in himself,' is the considered view of a retired sergeant who served in the Welsh Guards in peace and war. 'We found that drill made us more disciplined, yes, but more importantly it brought us together as a unit. And that helped a lot when we found ourselves under fire for the first time in 1940. Any old soldier will tell you that the man who cleans behind his brasses and looks after his uniform is unlikely to forget his ammunition in battle.'

To achieve the standards of perfection demanded by the adjutant the men who make up all the Guards found from the Welsh Guards put a great deal of time and effort into their preparations for public duties. The afternoon before the Queen's Guard mounts will be spent rehearsing the relevant drills. The guardsmen and their officers might look incongruous parading on the square at Pirbright in barrack dress and bearskins, a pole substituting for the Colour, but for the officer who will be the Captain of the Guard this is part of the 'mystique' – his word – of being in a Foot Guards regiment:

> I always tend to think that it's worth it on the day. It's a great feeling of I wouldn't say so much of importance, but a great privilege to wear the uniform. We do our bit not just for Her Majesty but for the country really because we are obviously very much in the public eye when visitors come here. I think we do provide a great public service. And it's tremendously exhilarating on the more important ceremonial occasions like the Queen's Birthday Parade or an important state visit. We did a Guard of Honour for President Reagan and that was very very special – every man in that company on that particular day felt, 'Well, I will never forget this day.'

For the men who form the Queen's Guard it can be a long and frequently exhausting duty. If the Welsh Guards are stationed at Pirbright the Queen's Guard rise early to leave the barracks by 7 a.m. in order to beat the London rush hour. At Wellington Barracks they will complete the finishing touches before starting to mount the guard at 10 a.m. The Changing of the Guard takes place at 11.30 a.m. in the Forecourt of Buckingham Palace and the guard will remain on duty for twenty-four hours in summer and forty-eight hours in winter. Whatever the season the routine for the guardsmen is two hours on duty and four hours off. They dismount the guard at around noon one day or two days later and can expect to be back at Pirbright at two o'clock in the afternoon. 'Having done that,' explained the Captain, 'they are jolly tired and for their pains they only get an afternoon off. For some the whole cycle can begin again the following week.'

During the day the Queen's Guard is mainly ceremonial and the Changing of the Guard is the high point as far as the tourists are concerned. Although the ceremony looks complicated it is, in fact, relatively simple. The new guard with its colours marches from Wellington Barracks to Buckingham Palace, forms up in lines and advances towards the old guard which has already formed up, facing north. They present arms, the Captain hands over the symbolic key to the new Captain and the sentries are posted. Once these formalities have been completed the old guard returns to Wellington Barracks and the new St James's detachment marches up the Mall taking with it the Colour which will be lodged in the guardroom at the palace. The crowds start to thin out, the military music recedes into a distant drumming and the roar of the traffic begins again: another picturesque and typically British ceremony has been performed to perfection.

The guards outside Buckingham Palace and St James's Palace will continue to attract attention from the curious and the in-quisitive, most of whom believe that they are simply a tourist attraction. They would be happy to see the Changing of the Guard performed twice daily – a suggestion that has been put to the Brigade of Guards by tourist companies in the past. With such a magnificent spectacle being performed daily at the height of the tourist season it can be difficult to get the message across that the Guards do have a serious function. Although they do not carry ammunition it is available in case of emergency and at night the men wear rubber-soled boots, carry two-way radios and wear peaked forage caps instead of the more cumbersome bearskin. The security of the Royal Family might be in the hands of the Metropoli-tan Police but the Guards can and do provide assistance and it is known that the Queen insists on their presence in the Royal palaces. Whenever suggestions are mooted to reduce the Queen's Guards the idea is always firmly quashed. For one Welsh Guards officer whose suspicion of ceremonial almost diverted him into another regiment while he was at Sandhurst, this was just as it should be. 'It's the rationale of what we do. People should regard it as an honour and a privilege and if they don't like doing ceremonial they shouldn't have joined a Household regiment.'

For the officers the privileges of doing Queen's Guard have some splendid advantages. Not the least of these is the Officers' Guardroom at St James's Palace which was built in 1793. Here the officers of the guard can entertain friends and relations in the discreet surroundings of their elegant mess. Here the silver sparkles, one of Marengo's many hooves adorns the table and a clutch of eminent Victorian generals smile benignly on a scene that has changed little since their day as Soldiers of the Queen. The food and wine are impeccably served and the conversation is witty and urbane: for the younger officers especially it can be a magnificent way of returning hospitality. 'Ah yes, it can be fabulous, if cripplingly expensive. It's just such a completely different way of life and your guests just love being invited to Queen's Guard, or the Tower, or Windsor,' admitted a young captain, a real outdoor type. 'I know a few Welsh Guards officers who have used the opportunity to entertain potential employers – as a sort of job-finding mission before they leave the army.'

Another privilege is the possibility of coming into contact with the Royal Family. The Captain of the Guard might be presented to the Queen at investitures or before state banquets and during evening receptions or he might be included in the guest list for dinner. Naturally such occasions are highly prized and obviously no Welsh Guards officer would want to talk about them for fear of being indiscreet or appearing boastful. Nevertheless, there is the well known story of the young ensign who found himself invited to dinner at Windsor where the after-dinner entertainment was a tour of St George's Chapel. The young man's confidence had been knocked slightly askew by the discovery of a torn button hole in his stiff shirt but it soared again later when the Queen Mother took a kindly interest in him:

So I sat down in a pew with her and had a lovely chat, about this and that, nothing in particular. And then we started walking around the Chapel again and Bach's Toccata broke out on the organ and the Queen came round the corner and said, 'Oh, Mummy, they're playing my tune.' And with that grabbed her mother by the hand and myself with the other and led us off to the back, with the Duke of Edinburgh following, and we all sat in a pew to listen to this lovely rendition of the Toccata. A magical moment. And then I realized how lucky I was to be a Welsh Guards officer.

In such agreeable surroundings the worries are few. For the Captain of the Queen's Guard there is an inspection at 11.15 p.m. and thereafter the Subaltern has to make his lonely way back to Buckingham Palace where he will sleep in the Guardroom. With both palaces made secure by the police the main concern is that the Guard will respond correctly if the Royal Family passes – the whole Guard turns out and presents arms only to the Queen, the Duke of Edinburgh, the Queen Mother and the Prince of Wales. It has been known for complaints to be made if the courtesies are forgotten and before he goes on Guard every guardsman will have spent time and trouble learning to recognize the members of the Royal family and their cars. It is, as a senior officer reminded me, all very pleasant and privileged. 'But do remember that while we sit upstairs enjoying ourselves, the boys are doing their two-hour stags throughout the night.'

For the guardsmen the prospect of those duties can be daunting. Although the guards are broken up by regular patrols – signalled by the senior man who will slap his rifle butt once to give the order to slope arms, turn about and march off – time can hang heavy after a while. 'It's like going on a fairground ride. Your stomach's turning over when you first go on. But after a time you just get bored. Really bored.' Like other Welsh Guards from South Wales the young man was happy that his home was so near and that his family could come to London to be photographed with him, but even that simple pleasure did not bear repetition. 'The summers are good,' he admitted, 'but the winters are a pain when you're standing there cold, your back's aching and worst of all, nobody's looking at you.' That was the worst part of the winter ordeal – the absence of spectators. On one memorable occasion Kylie Minogue appeared and stood beside him to be photographed – in exchange for a signed album, delivered later – but, famous or not, an audience does help to pass the time. For that reason the guardsmen tend to prefer St James's and Windsor to Buckingham Palace where 'you feel like a monkey in a cage. You can't get to the people and they can't get to you.'

There is a sizeable slice of exhibitionism involved in the performance of public duties. The guardsmen look good and know it and the tourists are suitably impressed. Small wonder that when the guardsmen are accessible the public – especially the girls – will try to make contact. To begin with they will try to catch the guardsman's eye or speak to him directly; then they will giggle and ask if he's a man or a model. Sometimes their flirtatiousness can go too far, sometimes they can be insulting or even aggressive, and all the while the guardsman has to keep his own counsel. Those are the orders but human nature being what it is guardsmen do break the rules and speak to the curious, usually to correct them on some irritating point of detail. 'You hear all the stupid things they say and it comes to the point when you have to put them right. They think that you stand there all day holding a wooden rifle with a plastic bayonet!'

There is also no shortage of exotic invitations but just as the Welsh Guards National Servicemen discovered, these are honoured more in the breach than the practice. 'Just fairy tales,' stated one CSM who gave the impression of having seen it all. 'Pirbright is a long way from London and very often the people talking to you come from too far away for a casual chat to develop into anything like the kind of relationship where the young guardsman will get his wicked way. I don't say it can't happen but the guy has to be determined.' And if he is, the guardsmen themselves are not slow to relate exploits which have quickly passed into company mythology. 'I heard that one guy in my platoon got a girl on five post at Windsor, didn't he?' enthused a young guardsman fresh out of the Depot. 'The only way you see the sentries is when you patrol. I mean you're supposed to patrol out, about turn and back in. But he managed to do a patrol, chat to her, go back, out again, chat to her and get an address out of her. He ended up going out with her for weeks. Got her out of her dress as well!' Everyone it seems, knows someone else who could tell you all about the incredible sexual adventures to be had on public duties. 'It always happens on Spur Guard at the Tower,' ventured another young guardsman. 'You get all sorts of propositions and I've been told that girls are always spending the night in the Guardroom. The worst are the homosexuals, though, I've been frightened to death by them.'

Stories about homosexuals and the Brigade of Guards are almost as old as the regiments themselves and many of the more celebrated accounts have passed into London folklore. In the 1860s the poet and critic John Addington Symonds, himself a homosexual, was able to note with some feeling the excitement caused by the numbers of guardsmen who stood in Hyde Park waiting 'to supplement their meagre pay with obliging gentlemen'. One hundred years later another writer, J. R. Ackerley, wrote about the scene that greeted him in the 1930s when he was a young man and still uncertain about his sexual preferences. For him, and others like him, solace could be found in the arms of the off-duty guardsmen 'perpetually short of cash, beer and leisure occupation' who waited in public houses in Knightsbridge and Victoria waiting for some kind gentlemen to buy them a drink 'in return for which and the subsequent tip – a pound was the recognized tarriff for the Foot Guards then, the Horse Guards cost rather more – they were perfectly agreeable to, and indeed often eager for, "a bit of fun".'

Some times the relationship could lead to disaster, as happened in the notorious 'Studio Murder' of 1906 when a young artist called Archibald Wakley was found murdered in his Bayswater studio, brutally bludgeoned to death. Wakley, a well-known homosexual, had been seen last with a Trooper of the Royal Horse Guards who was arrested and charged and then released. The jury found that Wakley had been murdered by persons unknown and the case was allowed to be dropped – it was said at the time that the Trooper owed his liberty to the influence of King Edward VII.

With the passing of more liberal laws concerning people's sexual behaviour many of the lingering homosexual fantasies about smart guardsmen have passed into oblivion. The last really sensational story was the discovery in 1967 of a homosexual prostitutes' ring which was operated by NCOs of the Household Division from the Tattersalls Tavern outside Knightsbridge Barracks. When it was broken up the police interviewed over sixty NCOs, guardsmen and troopers and the investigation was taken as far afield as the Channel Islands and France. Two soldiers were arrested, a trooper and a corporal who claimed to have earned £180 for introducing guardsmen and troopers to suitable clients. (In 1967 a private soldier's pay was £8 a week.) An interior designer was arrested and charged with procuring but he was considered to have been unlucky as others in the ring had already fled the country.

No such problems face the Welsh Guards today although the

guardsmen are sometimes amused to receive suggestive phone calls in the Guardroom of Buckingham Palace from a jovial old homosexual who has managed to get hold of this private number. 'Ah, he can't help it,' offered one young guardsman who admitted that he had never come across homosexuality until he came to London. 'It's our uniforms that do it, we look irresistible in them, I'm sure.' Most of the people, of both sexes, in the crowds outside the palaces would doubtless agree.

The other guards formed by the Welsh Guards when they are a public duties battalion are the Tower Guard and the Windsor Guard. Because these are smaller guards the men sometimes prefer them and there are few Welsh Guardsmen who do not admit to being moved by the impressive Ceremony of the Keys which takes place in the Tower of London each night shortly before ten o'clock. This is a very ancient ceremony, some seven hundred years old, which, while it has little to do with practical security, has everything to do with the British love of pageantry. And it is very dramatic. At ten minutes to ten four members of the guard, one carrying a lantern, form up under the Bloody Tower to escort the Chief Warder as he sets off on his rounds to lock the gates leading into the Tower. As he returns, he is challenged by the sentry, 'Halt, who comes there?' 'The Keys.' 'Whose Keys?' 'Queen Elizabeth's Keys.' 'Pass, Queen Elizabeth's Keys, all's well.' The escort then passes into the inner court where the complete guard has turned out; they present arms and the Chief Warder declares, 'God save the Queen!' to which the guard reply, 'Amen.' By then it is ten o'clock, the drummer sounds Last Post and the Chief Warder hands over the Keys to the Governor for safe keeping during the night.

To show that even in the best regiments things can go awry a sergeant admitted that the Ceremony of the Keys was once ruined by a none-too-bright North Walian who had begged to be allowed to do the challenge. 'No way, I told him. Your English isn't up to it. When he told me that he'd been practising, I relented but only on condition that he continued practising. When the great moment arrived, he said the whole thing himself, the answers as well – because that's what he had practised – all in a big hearty voice. It was all we could do to stop ourselves passing out with laughter.'

Fainting can ruin the most public of all the duties undertaken by the Welsh Guards – the Trooping of the Colour parade on the

Queen's Official Birthday. The sight of a red-tunicked guardsman keeling over is considered greatly amusing to the watching public and is almost a ritual in its own right. For the guardsmen themselves it's no laughing matter and until recently it could attract a charge for 'falling out on parade'. It is a point of honour among all Welsh Guardsmen to keep their lines intact longer than the other regiments on parade. Anyone in danger of fainting or showing signs of wilting will be held up by his waist belt until a guardsman from one of the other Guards regiments falls down; only then will he be allowed to drop. When he was RSM at the 1949 Troop Arthur Rees noticed that a man in the Prince of Wales Company was starting to waver like a tree in the wind. The main ceremony was over and the men were formed up in divisions to move off: it would have been an unfortunate ending to the day had the guardsman fainted, but Arthur Rees was not the kind of man to allow anyone to fall out prematurely. Acting quickly and unobstrusively he gripped the man by his waist belt and gave him a shake. 'We didn't lose a man on the ground that day,' he says, not without pride. 'If you do it nicely, if you do it properly and give them a shake, they appreciate it, because if that man had fallen out he'd most likely have gone before the Commanding Officer. Then he would have got eight days confined to barracks which was a Regimental Entry on your conduct sheet. It would spoil your record for the rest of your service and would practically debar you from getting any Long Service or Good Conduct Medal.'

By all accounts, both within and outwith the regiment, the 1949 Troop was one of the finest ever witnessed. It was only the second time in their history that the Welsh Guards had trooped their own colour and about a quarter of their number at that time were National Servicemen. It was also the first time since the war that the Foot Guards regiments wore their home service uniforms of red tunic and bearskin and many knowledgeable spectators noticed that this had changed from the pre-war days – the guardsmen had been relieved of their former burden of pouches, squared greatcoat and rolled cape and in their place wore a white waist belt. The other innovation was that, owing to his illness, King George VI drove to the parade in an open landau and mounted a dais to take the salute.

To celebrate the fiftieth anniversary of their foundation the Welsh Guards trooped their colour again in 1965 when the parade was almost cancelled due to bad weather. The night before had seen London hit by thunderstorms and heavy rain which continued almost to the start of the parade. Fortunately it stopped shortly before the Queen left Buckingham Palace and to everyone's surprise – but not the major-general who had asked for an accurate forecast from the RAF before allowing the ceremony to commence – it began again after the parade had dismounted two hours later. A mishap of another and more serious kind almost marred the 1981 ceremony when the Welsh Guards trooped the Colour for the fifth time. At the junction of the Mall and the approach to Horse Guards Parade a man in the crowd fired blank rounds from a starting-pistol at the Queen, an incident which demonstrated her vulnerability at public occasions and the inability of her Guards to do much to protect her. (The man was bundled forwards by the crowd and grabbed by a Scots Guards' street liner.) Later, the Welsh Guards wryly noted the date of that year's ceremony – 13 June.

The Welsh Guards first trooped the Colour in 1928 and will do so again in 1990, the year of their seventy-fifth anniversary celebrations. (They also trooped the Colour in 1973.) For everyone concerned it is a memorable occasion and a high point in the careers of the main protagonists – the Field Officer in Brigade Waiting who commands the parade, the officer commanding the Escort for the Colour, the Regimental Sergeant-Major who has the honour of handing over the Colour and the Ensign who has the honour of receiving it. For the Household Division it is also very much a family affair – the eight Guards are found from the Foot Guards regiments serving in the UK, the Queen's escort is provided by the Household Cavalry, the Massed Bands of the Foot Guards, the Corps of Drums and Pipes of the participating regiments and the Mounted Bands of the Household Cavalry are also on parade. Altogether, over one thousand men take part in the parade and several hundred more act as street liners. With the presence of the Royal Family and other distinguished guests, both on parade and as spectators, it is a day which no guardsman ever forgets:

I've done three Troops and I enjoyed them. I don't really enjoy the rehearsals because you do a lot of work beforehand but the actual Trooping of the Colour and the rehearsals in London are marvellous. For people to say they don't enjoy Trooping the Colour – well, they shouldn't be in the Welsh Guards in my eyes. I enjoy wearing the kit: I suppose I'm a bit of a show-off really, especially in tunic order. We are the bee's knees and I think we look the part. Anybody who doesn't enjoy it has definitely joined the wrong regiment.

The ceremony of Trooping the Colour, picturesque though it is, once had a vital military function: in the days when the flag was a rallying point in battle there was a real need for the men to be able to recognize their own Colours. For that reason the Colour was trooped regularly up and down the assembled lines of troops and this element is still an integral feature of the Queen's Birthday Parade. The actual ceremony which takes place on Horse Guards Parade today has its origins in the ceremony of mounting the sovereign's Guard and the first mention of a colour being trooped during the parade can be traced back to the Order Books of the Grenadier and Coldstream Guards in the middle of the eighteenth century. By 1805 it was recognized as an official celebration of the sovereign's birthday and apart from breaks during the Regency and the two world wars of this century it has continued ever since with appropriate variations continually being made to improve or simplify the ceremonial.

With good reason the Trooping of the Colour has been described as one of the world's great spectacles, a parade that combines military review with pageantry. It is one of the highlights of the London tourist season and through television it reaches a worldwide audience with the result that in many people's minds it is associated with all that is good about Britain and the British way of life. No one in the Welsh Guards objects to being a part of the machine which fosters this image; on the contrary, they are proud of their role as Household troops. What they will dispute is the unkind view, held by many, that they are pretty toy soldiers, fine for adding colour to a glamorous public occasion but dubious value when involved in ordinary operational duties. The CSM who admitted to a fierce joy in public duties is a Welsh Guardsman of seventeen years experience and his army career includes service in hot-spots as different as the Persian Gulf, Cyprus, Northern Ireland and the Falklands. His view is that people forget that ceremonial duties require stamina and discipline and that the Welsh Guards need the adaptability to change roles as required. 'I wouldn't like to do public duties day in and day out because you would get stale. But look at our recent service – we did four years in Germany as mechanized infantry, then back to public duties before going out to the jungle in Belize. I mean, we've got the best of both worlds, with operational duties on the one hand and public duties on the other.'

This is a theme to which the officers and men of the Welsh Guards return again and again. While they are one of the five Guards battalions stationed in London District their role as House-hold troops requires them to do their share of ceremonial duties. To do these properly they have to keep in shape, no easy matter, as a keen rugby-playing guardsman admitted. 'You're standing there for a solid two hours, your feet start to ache, your bearskin starts to feel tighter and tighter, your blood flow seems to slow down and yet you have to keep going.' If the regiment is stationed in London at Chelsea or Wellington barracks the opportunities for runs, games of football and other exercises are severely restricted and the guardsmen who are stationed there quickly earn the nickname of 'eggs on legs'. Pirbright is better for training but it involves wearisome early morning journeys by coach into London. For the company commanders, getting the mixture right can be a problem for at all times they have to keep up a decent level of enthusiasm:

> It's always good when you're doing public duties to do at least several other major things – like our tour of duty in Belize – or get back to serious training. First and foremost we are soldiers and as our record shows we do everything that every other regiment does. People still have the idea that we are just the men in red tunics, but it couldn't be further from the truth. There is obviously a period in the year when we do a hell of a lot, especially in the middle of the summer with the Queen's Birthday Parade and State Visits. Yes, we are in tunics the whole time but that is just one small part of the year and this year we're a public duties battalion yet we're spending six months in Central America. I do believe that people should start to recognize that we do many other things beside standing on the parade ground.

That the old order is changing could be seen in Belize. The battalion had spent a year doing public duties in London and would return to them after six months yet only a handful of the men had failed to adapt to operational duties in a hard and unforgiving climate. For the same company commander his men's ability to adapt and their good humour were the reasons why they were entitled to have a good conceit of themselves. While it was true that it took them time to get used to being in Belize their professionalism and enthusiasm had seen them through:

I think that field soldiering has to be important to anyone who's in the army. Gone are the days when Guards officers could regard themselves as foppish creatures about London who drift from one drinks party to another and appear at ten in the morning in a suit and have gone by eleven. If we're to pride ourselves that we are one of the Army's elite regiments – and we do – then we've got to prove that we are better than everybody else at the normal facets of soldiering as well as drill. I think we had a very good name for ourselves in Germany. We were described by the corps commander as his best infantry battalion by the time we left and in Northern Ireland we had a very good record on my last tour. I think Belize is the same. For a start it's proved to the men that they can do both jobs extremely well. They can do a Queen's Guard with the same skill and enthusiasm that they've brought to the jungle patrols. I wonder how many regiments can make the same claim?

The answer is probably not very many. The Welsh Guards are understandably proud of the fact that they are capable of performing two different roles, that they can appear immaculately on parade one day and as tough fighting soldiers the next. Occasionally, though, ceremonial duties in London are farmed out to the other regiments and corps of the British Army – kilted Highlanders are equally popular with the tourists – but this is not a trend which the senior members of the regiment would wish to be encouraged. While they were in Belize in 1989 they had been mildly surprised by the news that an English line regiment might be stationed at Chelsea Barracks – to put them into a traditional Guards residence, they argued, would be bad for morale and prestige. One of the older officers felt that it was another example of the steady erosion of the traditions and privileges associated with a Foot Guards regiment:

While I agree that the younger guardsman can easily become bored with ceremonial, it is an integral part of his military duties. I can see, too that it must be a tremendous thrill for a boy who has spent the better part of his life in a council housing estate or in a remote Welsh village and I can understand that the excitement might pall after doing a few Queen's Guards. What I cannot understand is the surprise and sometimes bitterness they feel after the first pleasure has died away. After all, our recruiting posters emphasize the regiment's ceremonial role and this has been drummed into them at the Depot. We are a Household regiment and we have to maintain standards of drill and discipline which set us apart from the rest of the army. We're not better than anyone else, just different.

Like others of his generation he would not like to see the privileges of the Welsh Guards being further cut back and the thought of surrendering them to other regiments is met with a polite shudder. What does upset the senior officers and NCOs is a recent tendency for those in authority to take the ceremonial duties for granted. For instance, it is not always appreciated that the duty of mounting guards places considerable strains on the manpower requirements of the Guards regiments. When the Welsh Guards provide a Queen's Guard this amounts to three officers, two senior NCOs, two junior NCOs, four lance corporals, one drummer and thirty guardsmen for a large guard when the Queen is in residence. A Tower Guard requires one officer, one senior NCO, two junior NCOs, three lance corporals, one drummer and fifteen guardsmen while a Windsor Guard's requirements are one officer, one senior NCO, one junior NCO, three lance corporals and twenty-one guardsmen. Because a public duties battalion is classed as a Type B infantry battalion numbering 538 men, of which 498 are Welsh Guards capped, public duties can swallow up some twenty per cent of the strength at any one time. 'During the busy season public duties come round quickly and repetitively,' explained a former company commander. 'The gloss soon wears off and the boys get bored and want to do other things.'

And that is not the end of the problem. Men can also be absent on promotion courses, whole platoons and companies have regular training schedules, men are encouraged to do adventurous training courses, there is always a small quota of men absent without leave and with so many people doing guards these shortfalls in manpower have to be made good by those left behind. The Welsh Guards have to concentrate on public duties while stationed in London District, but they ignore at their peril basic operational training. The difficulties are neatly summarized by a company commander, a graduate who has made the army his career. Once upon a time, he says, the Welsh Guards did public duties but very little else, apart from one or two weeks training. When the officers and men came off Queen's Guard, for example, it was understood that they should be given a certain amount of free time. The system might have been unsatisfactory from the point of view of military efficiency but it was appreciated by the men who had been on duty for a forty-eight hour period. Nowadays, such a routine would not only be impossible but impractical for the Welsh Guards, like any other

infantry regiment in the British Army, have a hefty training schedule which has to be kept if standards are to remain high. While he
admitted that the Welsh Guards had learned to live with the
pressures the company commander agreed that his regiment would
not be human if it did not look for a greater understanding of its
unique dual role.

One practical consideration would be the release of additional
funds to help replace the expensive uniforms which are worn on
public duties. 'After all, because the tourists come to see us, we
make a contribution to the nation's economy,' argued a CSM,
fingering his somewhat faded blue-grey overcoat which is worn in
place of the red tunic during the winter months. 'I can't see why
we don't get a spin-off from some of that money to help with our
uniforms.' Although every guardsman is given his own home
service uniform when the battalion is stationed in London District
– bearskin, tunic, tweeds, greatcoat and cape – there have been
shortages in recent years and the patched up blue-grey Argyll
greatcoats in the Master Tailor's office are both a testimony to his
skills and an indictment of army parsimony. They are in such short
supply that they have to be shared among the battalions doing
public duties, with the inevitable result that some fall apart in the
hands of successive owners. Bearskins, too, present problems, said
the same warrant-officer:

> They come to the guardsman in a brand new condition which means
> that they're all stiff and hard. After a time they form to the shape of the
> head by the need for constant grooming: they're just like a head of hair
> and have to be brushed and combed. Sometimes, though, the sun
> affects the fur and it turns orange, or the cane frame inside breaks up
> and then the bearskin has to be written off. It's an expensive business
> because it takes two and a half bears to make one bearskin – the long
> hairs needed for the cap only grow on the shoulders and rump. There
> have been threats to use artificial fibres but I'm sure that would be a
> poor substitute.

While those sentiments might not endear the Welsh Guards to the
animal conservationist lobby, the bearskin is much more than an
expensive piece of ornamentation. Since the middle of the nineteenth century the tall bearskin cap has been regarded as the
Guards regiments' ceremonial headgear while on parade and like
other subtle distinctions of uniform its use is jealously guarded.
The Master Tailor of the Welsh Guards goes to great lengths to

maintain the battalion's bearskins and all the other items of uniform which are worn by the men when they are in the public eye.

In fact, few facets of the regiment excite so much curiosity as the number and complexity of their uniforms. Some of the distinctive touches relate to the regiment's role as Household troops; the RSM, for example, wears a larger than average Royal Coat of Arms upon his sleeve to signify the Welsh Guards' Royal connection. The battalion's three field officers all wear tight trousers and spurs with their mess kit and on parade wear the elegant dark blue frock coat which harks back to the Victorian army commanded by the Duke of Cambridge. A crimson sash is worn over the officer's sword belt on public duties but this will be replaced by a gold sash when in the presence of the Queen. The home service uniforms for the officers and senior NCOs are individually fitted and sumptuously decorated. It would be a strange fellow, argued a newly joined ensign, who did not feel like a king wearing such clothes. Girl-friends are fairly partial to them too, he added, but it is an expensive way of impressing them. Standing on parade when Royalty is present he will be wearing £3,500 on his back but fortunately for him the uniform and accoutrements are provided by the government. Like every other officer fresh out of Sandhurst he received a uniform allowance to purchase his service dress, blues and mess kit plus the relevant headwear; if he grows out of any of these items it is up to him to replace them.

And yet for all their peacock finery it is endearingly noticeable that in barracks the officers and men of the Welsh Guards tend to dress in a way that could be called relaxed if it were not also slightly scruffy. 'Very rarely if you walk along the camp will you see guardsmen or NCOs with pressed shoulder pads on their heavy duty pullovers,' confided a company quartermaster-sergeant, the acme of smartness on parade. 'You'd be very likely to find a wrinkled mass which is more or less straight out of the washing machine and you wouldn't find that in most other regiments. But come parade time our boots are far better than any other infantry regiments and so is the rest of the kit.

'We seem to go from one extreme to the other. When we put on our bearskins and tunics we're the best but when we go into lightweight trousers and DMS boots, it seems that anything will do.' While there is a slight element of exaggeration in his self-deprecation, it is true that in barracks the Welsh Guards look much like any other unit in the British Army, but on parade they are transformed utterly. This is not so much the myth of the ugly duckling but further proof, perhaps, of the Welsh Guards' personality being split between their ceremonial and operational selves.

If there is one constant factor in the ever changing world of the Welsh Guards it is provided by the regimental band. Cutbacks in defence expenditure might have reduced its strength to one director of music and thirty-nine musicians but it still remains a vital part of the regimental ceremonial role. It was formed in October 1915 shortly after the Welsh Guards came into being and its first bandmaster was Major Andrew Harris who had previously been with the South Lancashire Regiment. Under his direction the regimental band made its first appearance on public duties on St David's Day 1916; later in the year it went to France on a three months tour of duty to entertain the Guards Division and at the end of the war it had the honour of playing the Colour Party of the British Army through the Arc de Triomphe during the Great Victory Parade in Paris. In the inter-war years the size of the band was increased to sixty to conform with the other Foot Guards regiments and like them it settled down to a busy routine of providing music at civilian and military occasions. It has fulfilled the same function ever since, one noticeable change being that the musician of today does not enjoy the same chance of moonlighting with the large dance bands which enlivened London's hotels in the 1930s.

Unlike the line infantry regiments which have battalion military bands the Welsh Guards has a regimental military band whose activities are quite separate. The Welsh Guards' band could find itself formed up with a Queen's Guard found from the Irish Guards, for example, because the rotas of the bands and the public duties battalions do not always coincide. The musicians at the disposal of the battalion belong to the Corps of Drums which is in fact a band of drums and fifes. They will play at all battalion occasions from Pirbright, where they also provide the bugle calls, to Belize where one of their most colourful appearances was at the Belmopan Agricultural Show dressed in full home service uniform. Whenever the Welsh Guards are represented in a Trooping of the Colour the Corps of Drums will be on parade, too, massed with the other bands of the Foot Guards; otherwise they are very much the battalion's own means of making music. The men who make up the

Corps of Drums – and the musicians in the band – are all trained soldiers who act as stretcher bearers in time of war. That they can fulfill that function could be seen when they provided cover during the ambulancemen's strike in 1979.

It is the regimental band, though, which attracts the most public interest. Almost an organization in its own right it has a hectic annual programme of public appearances, from providing the music at guard mounting to playing at social occasions as different as the Royal Tournament and Royal Ascot. The band also accepts invitations to play abroad: under the auspices of the Boeing Aircraft Corporation it played in Seattle to mark the retirement of the Chairman and then continued on to Australia to play for Boeing at an international air show. The choice of music is always important and it is left to the discretion of the director of music to make the appropriate selections. If the band is formed up with 3 Company when it mounts Queen's Guard he will choose 'Happy Wanderer', the march associated with the little iron men. If the Welsh Guards provide a Guard of Honour during a state visit he will put together a programme of music reflecting the tastes of the country concerned. The bandsmen are all skilled musicians, some having begun their training as junior musicians at the Guards Depot in a fifty-six week long course which includes basic infantry training. Afterwards they are sent to the army's school of music at Kneller Hall. In fact the bandsmen have to practise their weapons training annually and when the battalion is abroad they always visit them, both to make public appearances and to experience soldiering under conditions which are sometimes very different from their comfortable civilian engagements. When the battalion was in Belfast in 1986 they were visited by the band who played in the city centre and gave three more public concerts. As well as showing the flag the visit had other equally important side effects. 'After seeing the conditions that the guardsmen had to work in,' admitted the director of music, 'our respect for their professionalism was considerably enhanced. During the two week stay we were given opportunities to join patrols in their armoured carriers, "Pigs" and visited all companies giving concerts wherever possible.'

When the Welsh Guards troop their colour on Horse Guards Parade in June 1990 they will find themselves at the centre of a good deal of critical attention. The Number One Guard, or Escort to the Colour, will be found from the regiment, the new colour will be trooped and the parade will come under the direction of a senior Welsh Guards officer. The music will have a Welsh flavour too with a medley of airs being played during the Inspection of the Lines, the moment when the Queen inspects the Guards and the Sovereign's Escort.

For the admiring crowds and the even larger audience who will watch the parade on television it will be a ceremony whose pageantry and colour never fail to impress. To the Welsh Guards, though, the ceremony has a more profound significance. The Colour they will be trooping will be their new Queen's Colour presented to them a few weeks earlier by the Queen. This will only be their sixth Queen's Colour but in the words of Sammy Stanier who was the adjutant when the second set was presented in 1925, 'the new Colours will be not only the rallying point for the Regiment, but having been consecrated and presented they will continue to represent the living spirit of the Regiment, as the other Colours have done in the past, which we recognize when we salute or stand and remove our hats as they pass'. In that sense the Trooping of the Colour becomes less of a military or ceremonial parade and more of a public demonstration of the loyalty of the Welsh Regiment of Foot Guards to the person of Her Majesty the Queen.

Chapter Eight

BULLISH IN BELIZE, BEARISH IN GERMANY

THERE WAS NO doubt about it, the Boy Scouts were by far the most colourful detachment in the Queen's Birthday Parade. In their old-fashioned khaki shirts and shorts they seemed to have sprung from a bygone age, shades from the Edwardian past; yet there was something endearingly symbolic about their presence among the serried ranks of soldiers. It was a scene which many an elderly empire-builder would have recognized immediately: the celebration of a Royal occasion in the heat and dust of a far-off colony many thousands of miles away from home. True, some of the younger Cubs let down the side when they looked in the wrong direction as they passed the Governor-General's saluting base; and, true, they threw themselves on to the ground in undignified confusion when the British gunners fired a twenty-one gun salute, but they did add a delightful, and not inappropriate, touch as they marched behind the other elements on parade – the National Fire Service, the Prison Service, the Police Force, the Defence Force and the men of The Prince of Wales's Company, 1st Battalion Welsh Guards.

It was half-past eight in the morning and already the temperature was climbing into the high nineties. The Colours limped in the hot air, the Welsh Guards Corps of Drums bravely played their tunes of glory, the Governor-General graciously inspected the parade, the national anthems were saluted and the spectators looked on approvingly. The proudly named MCC Grounds at Belize City may only have been a dusty football pitch which would have disgraced many a Welsh village, the surroundings were tawdry and washed out by the tropical sun, but the men of The Prince of Wales's Company were carrying out their duties to perfection, wheeling round the goalposts with a precision that attracted murmurs of approval from the army officers in the crowd watching the parade. (Contrary to a belief which has some currency among civilians, soldiers in general like drill and take a good deal of critical interest in its proper execution.) Horse Guards and guard mounting were five thousand miles away and the Welsh Guards were entirely in their element.

Having the Welsh Guards on parade was something of a bonus for the Governor-General of Belize, a formidable lady of ample proportions who obviously values her country's long-standing relationship with Britain. Even if the guardsmen wore ordinary combat dress instead of the expected red tunics and bearskins, their presence on parade was a definite plus because in an indefinable sense the regiment's connections with the Royal Family meant that London seemed nearer in spirit. Indeed, the Belizean authorities treated the ceremony with a dignity and respect that has been forgotten in many parts of Britain – as well they might for it was a solemn reminder of the military and political ties that still bind Belize to her old colonial masters.

Formerly known as British Honduras, Belize was first settled by British seamen in 1638 and the right of settlement was ceded to Britain by Spain thirty years later. Although Spain, the main European colonial power in Central America, attacked the British settlement on numerous occasions during the eighteenth century British Honduras was finally recognized a British colony in 1802. The Spanish territorial claims, though, were inherited by Mexico and Guatemala and the latter country was especially vociferous in pushing its right to possess Belize, largely, it has to be said, because it wanted a ready access to the Caribbean Sea. The first threat of invasion came in 1948 and as a result Britain deployed two cruisers and an infantry battalion (2nd Glosters) in the country. These forces were eventually withdrawn but in the interests of securing a British presence a company of infantry drawn from the Jamaica garrison was posted to Belize. The country became self-governing in 1963 and talks began with Guatemala to resolve the territorial claims, talks which dragged on until the end of the decade. There were further flare-ups along the border in 1972 and 1975 necessitating the deployment of further British forces which have remained there ever since.

Belize, though granted independence in 1981, is still very much a British military enclave: there are approximately 1,600 British servicemen in the country occupying one major garrison (Airport

Camp) near Belize City and three military camps, one in the west (Holdfast) and two in the south (Rideau and Salamanca). In 1989 the army alone provided one infantry battalion, an armoured reconnaisance troop, an artillery battery, an engineer squadron and a helicopter flight; for their part the RAF operated four Harriers, four Puma helicopters and a Rapier missile detachment of the RAF Regiment. In addition, there is the Royal Navy's West Indies Guard Ship, normally a Type 42 destroyer which is never more than seven days sailing away from Belize. Opposing them in Guatemala is a much larger armed force, made up mainly of conscripts but in recent years much of its energy has been concentrated on fighting an internal guerrilla war. It is also lacking essential equipment, especially transport and combat aircraft, but the military threat is still taken very seriously by the local British commanders.

That the Welsh Guards should have found themselves in surroundings which owe more to Kipling's India than to Aldershot or the Lüneberg Plain is due to the army planning system which keeps the regiments of the British Army on the move in the different operational areas available to them. In 1989 it was the Welsh Guards' turn to be in Belize for six months doing the kind of job which their forebears had done in Egypt in 1929 and 1953 – guarding the country's interests in a hot and frequently disagreeable climate. By long-standing tradition Guards regiments rarely served abroad except in time of war, their peacetime role as Household troops denying them the service in India, Africa or the Far East which the line regiments and corps enjoyed during the heyday of the British Empire. After the First World War the Welsh Guards became the first Household regiment to serve in the Mediterranean theatre of operations, considered so vital for guarding the sea route to India and the precious oil deposits in the Gulf.

When the Welsh Guards went to Egypt in 1929 they arrived in Cairo to find themselves 'at the beginning of the fiercest heatwave the city had known since the days of the great Pharoahs'. Moreover, the famous Kasr-el-Nil barracks offered only the most primitive living conditions – but despite the poor accommodation the battalion excelled at sport during the two-year tour of duty, winning the rugby and boxing cups and reaching the finals of the cricket cup. Almost a quarter of a century later Welsh Guardsmen of a younger generation found that little had changed when the 1st

Battalion returned to its old stamping ground on the Nile. Although some of the younger men enjoyed the prevailing 'Desert Rats' atmosphere while engaged on exercises, for the most part it was a trying time in which the Quartermaster's energy and ability to improvise were stretched to the utmost. The solidly built barracks at Moascar provided a glimpse of civilization near the end of the tour but before that happy day the battalion had to endure Wolseley Camp at El Ballah which one observer described as 'a somewhat dilapidated collection of sunken marquees and small, broken-down outhouses, the whole surrounded by barbed wire'.

Fortunately the same kind of conditions did not prevail when the 1st Welsh Guards arrived in Belize during April 1989. The army might have been in the country since the days of British Honduras – the Nissen huts and examples of elderly equipment proved that – but the recent build-up of British military strength meant that living conditions are, on the whole, quite good. The first surprise for every Welsh Guardsman was the intense heat. Belize, it must be admitted, does not enjoy an agreeable climate. It is either very hot and very dry or, in the rainy season, very hot and very wet. Stepping off the RAF VC10 troop transport at the incongruously named Belize International Airport, the first impression is of heat, a wall of suffocating aridity that takes the breath away. For one of the platoon sergeants from Cardiff it was his first experience of the tropics and what he found he did not enjoy:

> I don't like the heat and I don't like Belize. It hit me as soon as we arrived at the international airport – and that's a bit of a joke, isn't it? I really thought my head was going to explode. No wonder the people sit around all day doing nothing, wouldn't you? You can drink gallons here and still be thirsty. What a dump.

During the hot season the temperature rarely strays from the 95–105° range and the heat and humidity does cause problems for guardsmen who have never strayed from South Wales or the London area. ('It's not like this down Aberdare way, I can promise you!') Inevitably in a Third World country the other shock was the low standard of living found everywhere. Belize is not a wealthy country – being the size of Wales with the population of Swansea and surrounded by cantankerous neighbours it is difficult to see how it could be. Agriculture and fishing are staple industries but the export of mahogany which brought wealth to British Honduras has largely evaporated due to lack of demand and shameful over-exploitation of that important national resource. Everywhere they went during the first few impressionable days the Welsh Guardsmen found numberless examples of the country's poverty, not just of things material but also, seemingly, of spirit. The same platoon sergeant who objected to the heat disliked the country for similar reasons, because it offended his sensibilities:

> Oh Belize, it's a poor country. The way the people live – a dog shouldn't live the way they do. Terrible, stinking, absolutely stinking – they don't look after the place at all. They pollute all the rivers, blatantly pouring rubbish into them, open sewers, trucks dumping toxic waste – they don't give a damn.

Other guardsmen made the same complaint. The country was too hot, too filthy and too far away from home. If the Guatemalans wanted it so much then they were welcome to it. Now, while soldiers are liable to grouse – or 'purge' as the Welsh Guards say – at the slightest provocation it is not difficult to understand the younger guardsmen's perplexed response to Belize and its way of life. Whereas their grandfathers were probably immune from such sights during the days of the British Empire nothing could have prepared these Welsh soldiers of today for a posting in the tropics. A young lieutenant, trying to jolly along his men, told them that at least Belize was better than Hohne, a posting which was not generally liked by the officers in the regiment. 'Maybe,' cracked a lance-sergeant, 'but at least the Germans had cut down the jungle before we arrived!'

And therein lay the heart of the matter. Between their last tour of duty abroad, in Germany, the battalion had spent a year doing public duties in London, with most guardsmen able to spend their weekends at home in Wales. The lance-sergeant had no sooner finished his last Queen's Guard at St James's Palace than he was on pre-embarkation leave before the long VC10 flight out to Belize. Ahead lay six months in an environment which at first encounter seemed to be unfamiliar at best, hostile at worst. He admitted – cheerfully enough – that the Welsh made bad travellers and pined for home when they were far away in a strange and alien land. For the first few days the homesickness was almost unbearable:

We started off very unsure of the country and the heat and I know that most people were homesick. Most Welsh Guards like going home for the weekend: that's the reason why the boys were so apprehensive. They were so far away from home.

The Commanding Officer agreed that the most familiar phrase on people's lips during the early days was, 'Oh, I don't like this Belize much, sir.' Heads went down for the simple reason that the average guardsman did not like what he saw when he first arrived in the country:

It's a definite culture shock when you first come out here. You begin to appreciate what you've got and what they haven't got and you do feel sorry for them. But frankly half of them are lazy bastards – you see it, they just lie there and can't be bothered to do anything.

It's not difficult to understand the reasons for the sergeant's sense of culture shock. Belize has only two metalled roads that resemble anything found in Europe – the Northern Highway leading to the Mexican border and the Western Highway which connects Belize City to the new capital Belmopan, a sorry collection of ugly concrete buildings built in the middle of the central plain to house the administration and government. Otherwise the roads are little more than rough tracks which provide heavy going and slow journey times even for solid military Land Rovers or Bedford four-tonne trucks. The only practical way to get around the country in any comfort is by helicopter.

On the ground the most common form of building is made of wood and built on stilts, both precautions against the hurricanes which frequent the area – Belize was devastated by one in 1961 and the decision was taken to rebuild the capital at Belmopan. Most of the houses are small and from the outside look cramped and squalid with whole families living in conditions which shock even the most cynical Welsh Guardsman. 'Unbelievable,' said a young ensign newly arrived from Sandhurst. 'I mean, you just have to put aside all notions of what you'd expect to find in Britain. We went out for a drink last night to a bar that was nothing more than a ghastly dive.' He shuddered with the same polite disgust that his platoon sergeant had shown earlier. 'It's impossible to understand how people can live like that. Perhaps the heat makes them too lazy to bother!'

It has to be said that there is an element of racial arrogance in the British soldiers' attitudes towards Belize. While they tend to like the fine-looking Mayan Indians who live in the south and the people of Spanish extraction in the north, there is a definite tension between most soldiers and the Afro-Caribbeans, especially the Rastafarians. The feelings are reciprocated. Two paratroopers were attacked with machetes in Belize City and there is a standing order that men can only go out of camp in parties of three or more. For Welsh Guardsmen who have served in Northern Ireland the precaution makes sense. Some of the younger boys 'purge' about the restriction and place the blame firmly on the 'boons'; others, the older NCOs, take a more detached view:

> I don't think we should be here and I don't really understand why we are here. I don't mind the country but the Belizean people I don't like at all. I don't like the way they live here – besides everyone wants to rip you off. Always. I think I can understand it though – if this was my country and soldiers armed with more money than me, well clothed and with money to spend, turned up, I'd be bitter. So on that level I can see why they don't like us much.

The same company sergeant-major likened it to any other colonial posting in the dying days of the British Empire, Cyprus or Aden for example, when the troops had to hold the peace while the politicians argued about what was to be done. Though comforting, the comparison is not altogether apt. The Welsh Guards were in Aden between 1965 and 1966, during the long-drawn out state of emergency which saw rival Arab nationalist groups jockeying for power before Britain decided to finally pull out from the colony in 1967. This was a real shooting war in which lives were lost – the British forces had forty-four killed and 325 wounded – with British soldiers acting as an internal security force. The situation was also exacerbated by the decision to take punitive action against the Radfan tribesmen who were causing trouble by acting more like medieval brigands than modern guerrillas. Those Welsh Guardsmen who served in Aden are agreed that it was a dirty and untidy campaign which could never be won because the British forces were limited by the political constraints of a 'no-shoot first' policy.

Belize, though, cannot stand any direct comparison with the operations which accompanied Britain's withdrawal from empire.

Despite the occasional, and not unexpected, antagonism of the Rastafarians there is no internal guerrilla warfare of the kind that infects neighbouring countries like Honduras and El Salvador and at present the military threat from Guatemala seems unlikely to be translated into action. It is also true that the Welsh Guards are hardly part of an army of occupation – they are in the country at the invitation of the Belizean government who no doubt welcome both the sense of security and the spending power provided by the British troops.

While this is a good thing politically the low state of alert does cause problems for the men in the British garrison – not a few guardsmen complained about the lack of 'drama' in Belize and seemed unimpressed by the fact that their very presence was the reason for this low-key state of affairs. ('It's so quiet on the front it makes you wonder if it's worthwhile being here.') To counteract any boredom the guardsmen have to be kept busy and here the Welsh Guards are helped by the army's command structure which divides the country into two separate battle groups – north, commanded by the second-in-command, and south, commanded by the Commanding Officer. While Airport Camp, the amorphous tri-service garrison, might be the nerve centre of British Forces Belize, the sharp ends are definitely to be found in three outlying camps which come under the command of a Welsh Guards company commander. And it is in these romantically named camps – Holdfast, Rideau and Salamanca – that the true nature of the British presence in Belize is to be found. With their barrel-shaped Nissen huts, their neat palm-tree lined avenues and their Union Flags flying proudly from the flagpole they look like the last remnants of an empire that might have passed into the history books in other parts of the world but which has remained obstinately alive in Belize. Here the company commanders reign supreme over their own Welsh Guardsmen and the men of the supporting arms – armour, artillery, engineers – in a style that found its zenith in the days of Kipling's India:

I can honestly think of no more satisfying job for any company commander. Here I've got two hundred and thirty men of all arms under my command; I'm three hours away from anyone to tell me I'm doing anything wrong and what I make of the place is entirely up to myself. Quite honestly this is what I joined the army for.

It is obvious why the company commander felt so cock-a-hoop about his command in Belize. His camp is strategically important – guarding the direct route from the Guatemalan border to the capital of Belmopan – and it is from here that the Welsh Guards provide the northern foot patrols and the men who run the observation posts overlooking the border crossings. There is, too, a certain raffish frontier atmosphere to the place. Sitting in the midst of the hot and dusty central plain it is a British bastion, a bulwark against whatever savagery lies outside it. Everything about the camp is solidly – and for the guardsmen, satisfyingly – British. Scorpion tanks are repaired under large palm-branched workshops which remind the casual observer of another time and another place, the 14th Army in Burma perhaps. Land Rovers and trucks stand throbbing in a heat which can reach the upper nineties and the Welsh Guardsmen are dressed in T-shirts and shorts which make Birdcage Walk seem like a distant mirage. Several of the men I had last seen in the early morning winter light of Pirbright before setting off to mount Queen's Guard in London. They took part in the Queen's Birthday Parade in Belize City but for them it was only a Mickey Mouse version, not the real thing. Said one, 'It doesn't seem like the Queen's Birthday Parade. It's a Belize Birthday parade. It's for them, it's not for us and it's not right. I didn't think I would be doing drill out here in Belize!' There is a homely smell of frying food drifting out of the cookhouse, the NAAFI provides cold drinks and the CSM's office is as busy as it would be in Pirbright. Outside in the Friday heat a party of guardsmen are repairing the perimeter fence which gives the camp its security: they curse the previous occupants for the mess they have left behind and wish they were at home. 'Oh, for a pint of lager, man. They'll be down at the social by now at home . . .'

Keeping homesickness and boredom at bay is a prerequisite for the company commander and here he is helped by the fact that it is a fully operational camp. Patrols are sent regularly into the jungle, a standing requirement of British tactics in Belize, and these can be arduous exercises remarkably similar to the warfare in Burma during the Second World War or the counter-insurgency operations against Communist terrorists in Malaya during the emergency of the 1950s. It is very much a young man's game: the jungle may well be neutral but to survive in it the Welsh Guards patrols have to be fit and tenacious. After a year's worth of public duties they soon find that Windsor is not always the best preparation for the terrain they will discover in the badlands of Belize:

> The easiest way to describe it is it's like an overgrown allotment. You fight your way through the undergrowth and the thing is you have to walk through it even if there's a fallen tree in the way because you've got to keep on a bearing. It's pretty hard going. You can be talking about forty minutes to cover a kilometre.
>
> You always camp up before last light. What you do is reach your objective at least by half-past four and radio in. Then you set up your hammock, your mossie net and your poncho because you never know when it's going to rain. One of the things I don't like about the jungle is that it could be sunny one minute and the next it could be tipping it down.

The jungle which has become the patrols' habitat for five days is a dirty place, overgrown, desperately hot and humid. Although most of the patrolling goes along recognized tracks the need to keep on a bearing means that the guardsmen have to use machetes to hack their way through the deep and unyielding undergrowth. At night, if they are lucky, they will have reached a village and will be invited to sleep there; if not, it is a case of setting up camp and settling into the pitch-black night that always falls at about six o'clock.

Had the terrain all been flat, progress during the day might have been simpler but the Belizean jungle has layered itself over hills and into river valleys, up creeks and through ravines. The first thing that struck most young Welsh Guardsmen on entering it for the first time was its scale. The attap trees, often rising forty feet up into the sky, formed an airy canopy while down below their roots snaked out into the vegetation, thus providing traps for the unwary. Added to this hardship were dangers of its denizens who regarded the jungle as their home and resented man's intrusion – the scorpions, tarantulas and, most feared of all, lethal reptiles like the coral snake and the dreaded fer de lance. One Welsh Guards sergeant was bitten by a pit viper on his first day in the jungle – luckily for him only one of its fangs struck home but his mates were still badly shaken by the incident. 'Basically, everything wants to bite you or sting you,' said one. 'That's Belize all over.'

If the jungle patrols are often unwelcome intrusions into a guardsman's otherwise well-ordered life they do at least provide a solid basis for some real soldiering and are understandably popular with the more senior officers:

The beauty of the posting for the Welsh Guards is that it's ideal for the young commanders. They're the people who will either sink or swim here – the good ones shine out like beacons while the poor ones are overshadowed. It's just so obvious. It's also a good thing for us coming from the materialistic south of England to a place which is very simple. It does all of us good to lead a much simpler life.

His thoughts may not strike the same chord in the hearts of the men who actually do the patrols. They have to face the slog of cutting their way through the undergrowth or lengthy journeys by bumpy Land Rover to reach their objectives while they see their senior officers swanning around the country by helicopter. ('You have to remember what it's like for a guardsman,' one officer had already warned. 'They have less opportunity to see the country and their views are bound to be coloured.') Hardly surprisingly, the men's reactions tend to be somewhat ambivalent. Although most of them rather enjoyed the idea of cutting their way through the jungle and preferred it to the tedium of guarding a camp, they could not always understand the reasons for their presence. For a start there is no enemy as such and the chances of being involved in the kind of ambush encountered in the Malayan jungle during the emergency are remote. Without a perceivable enemy the only opposition is the jungle and its reptilian inhabitants and these dangers soon pall – patrols make so much noise moving through the jungle that the snakes quickly get of the way. That the men are a deterrent is fine in theory but the practice quickly loses its glamour. Even winning the hearts and minds of the natives can be a losing battle due to difficulties with the language although, being fond of children, the Welshmen, like soldiers the world over, can rarely resist them when they ask for biscuits and sweets. Instead, they tend to dwell on the debit side – 'Oh, it's very hot and very sticky. I've never sweated so much in my life. And you do smell, you smell like a rat after five days out there.'

Not every guardsman is called upon to do jungle patrols – no more than eighty in any company according to one of the company commanders – and others have to man the observation posts which overlook the Guatemalan border, another less than popular task because the OPs offer fairly basic living conditions. At all times, the patrols and the OP parties are accompanied by one or more soldiers of the Belize Defence Force, the country's standing army.

(It also has a naval and air section.) One day, it is hoped, these men will take over responsibility for the defence and internal security of their native country – soon, but not just yet.

Few Welsh Guardsmen had good words to say about the performance of the BDF. One reason for the guarded view may have been language problems, another the differences in culture which are bound to emerge when the men are forced to live together in the close proximity of an observation post or a patrol camp. There are contrasting standards of personal hygiene and divergent attitudes to discipline – Welsh Guardsmen take it for granted that they are expected to clean up after a meal and do not resent being ordered to do so if they forget. And there is a suspicion that the BDF soldiers, for all their smart uniforms and keen appearance, feel inferior in the company of the organized and well-equipped Welsh Guardsmen, for the BDF is hopelessly underfunded. One of the sadder moments of the Welsh Guards tour of duty was the Quartermaster's discreet transfer of toilet paper to the BDF's stores: the Belizeans, a battalion-strong, had been issued twelve rolls for the week. Some of the guardsmen compared the position to the relationship they have with the Ulster Defence Regiment in Northern Ireland. There they can rely totally on the local force; in Belize they are not so sure.

A story told by an experienced platoon sergeant with twelve years service, part of which has been spent in Northern Ireland and Germany, illustrates the point. While engaged on a vehicle patrol in the north of Belize he came across certain evidence of drugs trafficking. The road had been sealed off to allow an aircraft to land, a number of armed gangsters were in the area and the local policeman was directing operations. Like the rest of the British Forces in Belize the Welsh Guards patrol was powerless to interfere and could only report the matter, but to their disgust the BDF soldier accompanying them refused to do anything and cowered in the bottom of the Land Rover. His excuse was that he only had a few months left to serve and wanted to avoid trouble.

With its rich fields of marijuana and the proximity of the country to the southern states of the USA, Belize is a substantial contributor to the international drugs market but only the BDF and the Belizean police are enabled to make arrests. (If Welsh Guardsmen come across covert marijuana fields in the jungle they note the position and a crop-spraying aircraft flies in to destroy the harvest.)

Although the platoon sergeant was enraged at the time and felt that the BDF soldier had behaved dishonourably, in the cold light of day he could see that British interference would only have caused more problems: 'Personally I don't intend dying for no drugs dealers over here because it's not my country and it's not my problem.' Besides, there was the very real fear that his men would come off worst in the ambush. 'I didn't fancy getting into a fire fight with the drugs dealers because we could see that they had big weapons.' His Commanding Officer was thankful that nothing untoward had happened: 'We're not here to act in aid of the civil power,' he explained, 'unless we're specifically asked. I shouldn't think that we'd be particularly sharp if we had to deal with drug trafficking. We'd only get in a muddle.'

So, without an enemy to face, other than the jungle's sweats and snakes, what good would come from the Welsh Guards' tour of duty in Belize? Their Celtic cousins, the Irish Guards, are no strangers to the country, being denied service in Northern Ireland, and they have come to like this hot and humid part of the world. Would the same hold true for the Welsh Guards, a regiment which in its short history had not built up the same traditions of being frequently posted abroad? It was a worry which had settled in the mind of the commander of the British Forces Belize, a no-nonsense brigadier. At the beginning of their tour he felt that the Welsh Guards were unhappy and withdrawn, demonstrating too obviously the feelings of homesickness which Welshmen tend to fall into when they are far from home in a strange land. Many of the younger guardsmen had hated the initial jungle training – the snake bite had not helped to calm nerves – and their acclimatization, both to the weather and to the rougher standards of living, had taken time. Then, one day, it all changed. The sun, once the enemy, was a welcome friend, there was life beyond the camps, mail began to arrive and, wonder of wonders, they found that they could telephone home to Wales. In short *hwyl* was restored. 'Let's make the most of this,' advised the more senior NCOs and officers. 'It's like everything in life: you have to put a lot into it to get anything in return.' After two months morale was sky-high and despite the moans which soldiers will always make when life is unfamiliar, the battalion was wheezing and banging like a firework cracker.

For all that the men disliked being in Belize and for all that they believed the patrols and observation post duties to be pointless, a change had taken place in the battalion since it left winter Pirbright. One of the younger company commanders operating from a southern jungle camp had seen the changes begin as soon as his men got down to work, to the real business of soldiering. Yes, he admitted, it was a difficult country but the men had to adapt to the conditions because the jungle would not adapt to them:

Overall the benefits are obvious – we've come to a greater understanding of working in difficult conditions and we've learned the ability to survive in the jungle. Individuals have benefited too – we'll be able to see how a soldier has performed; we'll be able to take a closer look at his character, his mental build and make-up and be able to pick out the future leaders. It's much easier to see what a man is made of in the jungle where he's left on his own and faced with a problem.

What this means in the day-to-day management of the battalion is a temporary shift of emphasis in the power structure. Whereas in Pirbright authority is normally in the hands of the company commanders and their senior NCOs, power has been devolved further down the chain of command while the battalion is in Belize. It begins with the company commanders – whose authority has in fact been increased in the outlying camps – and continues to the junior leaders, the lance-corporals and lance-sergeants who take the patrols out into the jungle:

If you have a young section commander, say nineteen or twenty, he has command of a patrol of five or six people. He goes into the jungle some sixty or seventy kilometres from his base camp; there might not be any tracks, there might not be any water. He gets put in by helicopter and told that he'll be extracted in seven day's time. He has a medic and a radio operator but neither of these things might work. It's quite a responsibility for the chap and for someone who's just been on guard outside Buckingham Palace he has to up the ante quite quickly.

For the officers, then, Belize will help the Welsh Guards to become a better battalion. Men who have been promoted beyond their abilities will be found out and some men who have sunk in the organized anonymity of Pirbright will come through to win positions of responsibility. 'This is what a lot of people joined the army for – travel, adventure, excitement, different experiences,' enthused one of the battalion's more senior officers. 'We're doing things which would normally take three or four years to do back in England, or even in Germany. Yes, it's very good training especially at junior leader and young officer level.' One of the young ensigns, Welsh and fresh out of Sandhurst, was quick to agree, not out of deference to the older officer but because he felt that Belize was giving him a head's start over his contemporaries. Whereas most went on leave after the Sovereign's Parade, he found himself on the weekly VC10 to Belize. 'It's giving me a lot of practice in basic skills like map reading. Obviously coming from Sandhurst I know the theory but I haven't had the experience of doing it for real and that's invaluable. Also I think I've got an insight into the minds of the soldiers – going out into the jungle on patrol with four men, you get to know them quite well.'

Small wonder that the Commanding Officer revealed at a briefing that his officers were being bullish about the posting to Belize. As an experience it was doing great things for the battalion's confidence, especially after the year they had spent doing public duties in London. 'I think we needed this in a big way,' claimed an enthusiastic subaltern, one of the stalwarts of the rugby XV. 'We needed a break from ceremonial – I think that when the boys get back to London District they'll look back and say that Belize was bloody good. Welshmen always complain when they're in the place but afterwards they'll say it was great.'

That may be so but it was the officers who were making the claims on behalf of their guardsmen. Now, it is true that they are supposed to take a wider view while the men only see the components of the scene, but it was difficult to avoid the impression that Belize is perhaps too much of a training ground, a useful laboratory in which to test the potential of the future leaders. 'Nothing wrong with that,' countered the Commanding Officer, 'I'll be taking back a battalion that'll be fit, much more confident, particularly the commanders. And I'll be much more confident myself that I know who is really worth his salt.' As is the case with most of his colleagues he actually likes Belize both for the simplicity of life there and for the challenge it offers his battalion. 'Could we handle that dumb thing or would it handle us?' he wondered, echoing Marlow in Conrad's *Heart of Darkness*. 'I felt how big, how confoundedly big was the thing that couldn't talk and perhaps was deaf as well.' During the early days of their tour the struggle for mastery of the country was an all-absorbing factor in the lives of the Welsh Guards officers. Physically and emotionally draining, it seemed that Belize might overwhelm them and many admitted that they had to fight to stop their own truths and moral definitions blurring and diffusing themselves into meaninglessness. Faced by a country and a climate that could reduce utterly they had fallen back on the inner certainties which come from being members of a closely knit regiment. 'That's why we're one of the best regiments, because we can adapt,' said a fit young captain, not without pride. 'We can come straight from the discipline of ceremonial into this role and then go back to Queen's Guard six months later as if we had never been away.'

It was rather different in Germany where the Welsh Guards had been stationed at Hohne in a large military complex containing different elements of the British Army. There the battalion had earned high praise for its operational skills as a mechanized infantry formation but the officers had not cared particularly for the posting. It is perhaps easy to understand why because Hohne is hardly attractive. For a start it is situated in the middle of BAOR-land, the Lüneberg Plain in Lower Saxony. Not only is this a military landscape dominated by the necessary excrescences of the army's architecture but it is also flat, monotonous heath and rolling moorland. Then, to the dismay of many, Hohne is a neighbour of Belsen, the infamous Nazi concentration camp. Neither the pretty town of Celle nor bustling Hanover helped matters: as one of the younger officers remarked, 'Hohne is just too brutal, too much of a garrison, to be much fun.' True, the soldiering was busy enough with the BAOR 'roller coaster' of exercises and a brisk timetable of training cycles but the social life for the young unmarried officers was dull:

> It is satisfying soldiering there and, after all, you have joined the army to do just that. It's fun and it's very quick moving because you're in armoured vehicles and you have to move fast and think on your feet. It's a challenge but from a personal point of view – or, rather, from a family point of view, I could thoroughly do without it . . . we lived in pretty ghastly quarters for a very long time and having returned from three weeks on exercises for example, you would come back to a rather dissatisfied wife and screaming children. It didn't actually mount up to a terribly happy period of one's life.

For the same company commander, though, Belize was completely

different, a world apart. There he had his personal autonomous
command – but there was another side to his satisfaction. Whereas
Germany had been flat and amorphous Belize was a kaleidoscope of
different sensations and experiences. For him it was the opportunity
to drive along empty tracks with colourful birds chasing the sunlight
in the bordering jungle, or the sudden sight of whole families of
villagers washing themselves and their clothes in a brown river,
oblivious of the passing patrol, or a chance meeting with one of the
Mennonite families who settled in the country as farmers earlier in
the century. His family was far away and he missed them but as
another officer, similar to him in outlook and temperament,
remarked, Belize had taught them the important lesson that they
could tame the conditions and survive. It was as if they had tasted
the salt of life and its savour would never leave them:

> I find it a beautiful country because it's totally unspoiled by the things
> that I hate about western Europe. It lacks traffic jams, it lacks aggres-
> sion. There's a wonderful charm about the countryside and the people
> who seem to have been untouched by western capitalist aggression. I
> think that the compensation of being in a great climate far outweighs
> the cons.

Men serving in the outposts of empire felt much the same way
about the lives they led, the animal pleasures of being at the
extremities of life, of being in charge of their own destiny and of
giving service to a great ideal. When asked why most of the officers
had adapted easily and had shaken off so quickly the garb of
ceremony the answer came back to the familiar Welsh Guards
concepts of the loyalties inherent in the regimental family, to the
well-ordered *esprit de corps* and to the hierarchical structure which
demanded that they all pull together.

This sense of separateness and self-confidence is not to be
confused with aloofness for the officers were hardly a beleaguered
band of brothers in Belize herded together in blind opposition to
the rest of the world, conscious of their own vulnerability. It was
most noticeable at Airport Camp where the large tri-service mess is
most un-Welsh-Guards-like on first inspection. A radio blared out
pop music from behind the bar, the dining room was run like a
canteen and the overall impression was more students common
room than officers' mess. 'Worse than that,' whispered one Welsh

Guards officer in mock horror, *'they have rules.'* What these amounted to was the absolute necessity of knowing what to wear at any given hour of the day, particularly in the evening when it was 'planter's order' – slacks, shirt and tie, with sleeves buttoned at the wrist. If this smacked of sahibs dressing for dinner in the jungle it was nonetheless a sensible and comfortable idea to change after a day's work in the hot sun. What the major resented was being ordered to do something he accepted as a matter of course. Was this a further test of the policy of fitting in?

> In an oblique way, yes it is. It's certainly a test of whether or not we all get on well together for if we do then we'll tend to get on well with the others. For example, if we can fit into a set-up like this the odds are that we'll enjoy life in the army. An officer who couldn't, or wouldn't, adapt or dug in his heels because he didn't like the conditions would let down the side. We're very hot on that score – obviously we have to put up with a certain amount of ragging because of it but I'm sure the others find that we're just as human as they are.

The major in question was a great believer in the policy of 'fitting in'. It's easy enough to work the system in Pirbright, he claimed, because there the officers rarely lived in mess and went home in the evenings. Here in Belize, especially at Airport Camp, they not only lived on top of one another but they had to get on with other officers from the other arms and services. Even in the outlying camps which came under Welsh Guards command, officers from different military backgrounds shared the same mess. For most of them it was a novel experience. 'When I was told I would be stuck with a Guards regiment for six months I thought, ye Gods, how on earth will I manage? Will it come to blows?' said a young gunner officer with a regional accent. 'All that saluting and stamping . . . actually it's turned out to be rather unexpected and different. They're a good bunch, quite normal in fact, and so far no one's worn his cap at breakfast.' Being a Marine, of course, he knew the famous story.

At the same camp the Welsh Guards CSM had been equally surprised by the ease with which all the NCOs had gelled together. Perversely, he added, the problem of fitting in had been felt most acutely by the guardsmen at Airport Camp. There had been several fights with men of the Parachute Squadron (RE) which provided the engineering elements in Belize. The Falklands factor was one reason, regimental pride another but the real cause seems to have been drink and boredom – as a result of one brawl an insalubrious drinking den near the main gate had to be put off-limits to join a long list of dubious drinking haunts banned by British Forces Belize. While most of the guardsmen admitted that a bottle of Beliken, the local beer, was reasonably drinkable it was not the same as a pint in the pub or the social club back home. The bars in Belize City were hardly congenial either, being little more than dives offering drink but little else. (Some entertainment was provided by a jovial bar owner in the southern town of Punta Gorda whose speciality was to take the boys out in his boat and then dive overboard to tease the resident nurse sharks. The bite marks on his back proved that he rarely failed to humour the troops.)

Not so long ago, girls, or more precisely the lack of them, did cause problems for the British Army in Belize. There are still a number of brothels in Belize City and elsewhere and sexual relationships are possible with the local girls but since the advent of AIDS the soldiers have become cautious. The Welsh Guards were given a thorough and sufficiently graphic briefing on the dangers of sexually transmitted diseases before they left Britain. Service medical personnel in Belize also adopt a pragmatic approach towards any girl in the local brothels who requested screening. The army in India had the same problem during the days of empire, a senior doctor admitted, and they adopted much the same solution. Two Welsh Guards subalterns confided that they had dropped their girl-friends before coming out to Belize and regarded the six-month posting as a season in a monastery.

At weekends, though, when the guardsmen were off-duty, time could hang heavy. For some this was not too much of a problem, they stayed in camp and saved money; others could become increasingly demoralized as the time passed ever more slowly. 'You just have to go without mail for a week, then have a few days off and suddenly you're in trouble,' explained an experienced and avuncular CSM. 'The boys start getting upset, especially those with wives or girl-friends, and then they want to phone home – which can be an expensive business.' While the Welsh Guards are sensitive to problems of that kind – two guardsmen were on my flight home because their wives were ill – the officers believe that prevention of melancholia is better than its cure. For one of the company commanders in the south, far removed from the questionable delights of Belize City, this was very much a Welsh characteristic, one he had noticed before.

No one particularly wants to be out here. They'd like to be in Wales, they'd like to be with their wives or girl-friends and they miss what you might call the comforts of life. However, there's a large proportion who joined the army to travel, to do different things, have a bit of excitement and that is a good base to start at. The biggest problem with the place is not the work, it's the off-duty hours.

Down in the south it's much more limited what we can do. Punta Gorda is pretty basic, nigh as primitive as to what we're used to in Wales and there are definite limits to what entertainment you can expect to have here … It's a different environment and also when you've been to Punta Gorda a couple of evenings, well you've still got another one hundred and seventy-eight or whatever to while away. It's not a particularly flashy place.

It's a matter of getting out and doing it: it's not going to fall in your lap.

Part of his responsibility, he maintains, is to make sure that his guardsmen are fully occupied, that they do not fall into the trap of feeling sorry for themselves. But even in pursuit of this worthy aim he admits to some failures: a party of North Walians who had spent an idyllic weekend on the cayes – the atolls on the Belizean coral reef – returned complaining that there had been too much sun, too much rum and too much relaxation. Not at all like Pwllheli.

The trips to the cayes should in fact be the highlight of any posting to Belize for it is there in the protected shallow waters of the barrier reef that the country is seen to its best Caribbean advantage. The sea shines azure and turquoise, the sand on the atolls gleams white, a cool sea breeze is always blowing and the sun is like an oven: 'As far as this goes,' said a corporal from Cardiff, 'the place is brilliant. I mean we're being paid for doing things – like swimming and snorkling – that civvies would have to pay thousands for.' Indeed. Forget the mainland's stinks and humidity, the furious attacks by mosquitoes and sand flies, the dangers of the fer de lance and other crawling things and on the cayes Belize is a paradise. Each caye generally has at least one bar and a rudimentary hotel with rooms opening out on to the shimmering beach; the only thing missing say the guardsmen are girls. The other trouble said one is that when he sends the photographs back to my wife she says, 'Why do you complain if life's that good? Anyway, why don't you take me on holidays like that?'

The difficulty for the officers and NCOs lies in encouraging the younger guardsmen to make the trip to the cayes. 'Welshmen tend to be conservative – I don't mean that politically – but they are cautious about doing anything new,' said one of the older officers with family connections in Wales. 'Whereas an Englishman will generally plod along with the crowd fairly uncomplainingly, unlike the Scots who will make a lot of noise but will do it nonetheless, the Welsh prefer to hold themselves back. Partly it's because they're naturally polite and partly it's because they're rather shy about doing something new and different. They also prefer doing things in a crowd – a bunch of boys going to watch a rugby match. We've had the devil of a job getting them out and about. Why, some of them are going back home to Pirbright for their leave instead of spending it on this side of the Atlantic. You know, I think some of them would rather be in Germany.'

He was not far wrong. When asked, most Welsh Guardsmen do prefer Germany and not just because it gave them the opportunity of having their families with them. 'Germany?' said an ambitious young lance-sergeant, already marked down for early promotion. 'Those were the best four years I've spent in the army. I love the way the Germans live, everything is clean and the people there have got a really nice way of life. As for myself I hope we're given our next posting there. It's brilliant.' The other men in his company are quick to agree, one had married a German girl and felt that he might settle in the country once he left the army. They like the country for its modern efficiency and for the opportunities it offers. One guardsman who had been brought up with a large family in a council house in South Wales admitted that Germany had given him a vision of what life could be like. The people, too, had been to his liking. Being a married man he had met several German families socially and although his wife had occasionally railed against the petty local rules which allowed washing to be hung outside one day but not on the next, they had felt accepted by the local community. 'And why not?' he added. 'After all we're supposed to be defending them against the Soviets aren't we?'

The Welsh Guards had last been in Germany between 1984 and 1988 when they took on the role of a mechanized infantry battalion with 22 Armoured Brigade. The tenor of their tour was determined by the BAOR training schedule which involved not only local exercises at Soltau, a place that was to become a second home for the battalion, but also live firing exercises in Canada with elements of 1st Royal Tank Regiment. It was a busy period for the whole battalion – 'hectic but also varied and interesting' according to the Commanding Officer – with the men being pushed to their limits. Whether skiing in Bavaria, taking part in field firing at Sennelager, adventure training on the Baltic coast or participating in larger-scale exercises with NATO troops, the battalion had rarely had its hands so full. It was also during this period that they were involved in their last four-month emergency tour of West Belfast. Most married guardsmen admitted that they were often away from their wives and families for at least four months of each year while they had been stationed in Germany but such inconveniences had been more than compensated by the better living standards and increased overseas allowances. Unmarried guardsmen might have missed the weekend leaves in Wales which they claimed as a right while stationed in London District but with the Channel ports within easy reach of northern Germany getting home was not the problem it would be in Hong Kong or Belize.

There was another reason why the men tended to like Germany while their officers felt more diffident about the place. Apart from taking part in local parades there were no ceremonial duties to be performed – other than a much-valued trip to Brussels to provide a Guard of Honour for the fortieth anniversary of the Welsh Guards' liberation of the city – and a guardsman joining the battalion in 1984 on a three-year tour of duty could have spent his time in the regiment without ever donning red tunic and bearskin cap. For some this might have been a cause for regret but others were charmed by the idea. 'Give me a hot and stuffy APC any day,' claimed one group from The Prince of Wales's Company while they were sweating beneath the stifling Belizean sun. 'At least you're going places and you don't know what'll happen when you get there. Real soldiering that is.'

Coming back to Pirbright from Germany, to what the Commanding Officer described as 'the crunch of boot on tarmac' and the square resounding with 'demonic yells' was quite a shock to the

younger guardsmen, many of whom had not experienced public
duties before. 'The worst thing was the first Queen's Guard.
Commanding Officer took it but it was as hot as hell, even in April.
You sweat like a pig in those tunics and they're bastards to clean
up afterwards.' 'That first guard was all right,' countered another,
'but after that I soon got bored.' He was taking part in the Queen's
Birthday Parade the next day and with his mates had got up at four
o'clock in the morning for the long drive into Belize City for the
rehearsal: for all that, like his commanding officer, he was still
feeling bullish about Belize. 'I reckon it'll bring the company much
closer together because in Britain doing Queen's Guard we never
seem to mix. But here everyone's got to know each other much
better. And that's good, isn't it?'

The heavy timetable of public duties in London District might
have been far ahead of them but they still managed to weigh
heavily on the small group sitting beside the swimming pool at
Holdfast Camp. How will they keep the boys down at Pirbright
now that they've seen Belize? As the Commanding Officer admits,
it will not be easy. 'I am fearful for our numbers. We could be
seventy men below normal strength when we go home. All my
management team have trouble keeping the men under twenty-five
motivated. After that they tend to develop the love of the regiment
which keeps us older ones in.'

By mid-tour the younger guardsmen were keeping their options
open about their next step. Many were waiting to see where the
battalion would go next before they made up their minds. For them
Berlin or BAOR were favourites, London District less so and an
accompanied two-year tour to Northern Ireland definitely at the
bottom of the list. The upturn in the Welsh economy is another
factor: not a few were toying with the idea of returning to civilian
employment with its promise of high wages. For one of the
company commanders, though, the most unsettling factor might
well have been Belize itself. While he had been the first to admit
that many of his men had disliked the country initially it had still
been an unrepeatable experience, one which could become a yard-
stick for the remainder of their army careers. For those who had
been given positions of authority it had been a taste of things to
come and it would be difficult to return to London District where
everyone had to work to an immediate boss and mistakes were less
easy to conceal. Moreover, London District meant public duties:

There is nothing which kills a battalion more than doing a hell of a lot of public duties. They come round rapidly and repetitively. For the soldiers it's nothing more than standing about on guard in uniform for six hours, perhaps eight hours a day. Unless it's the height of the tourist season and you happen to have got one of the nice spots where there's a lot of interest, where there's a lot of activity – perhaps pretty girls eyeing you up or giving you a hard time by flashing their tits, which has happened – it can be very boring and that's what they can see themselves doing for the next year.

While all the officers and men in the battalion would agree that public duties were part and parcel of their lives as Welsh Guardsmen, the thought of them were unlikely to send spirits soaring in mid-tour Belize. This is the eternal conundrum of being a soldier in the Welsh Guards. The regiment takes a fierce pride in the fact that it can switch from operational to ceremonial duties at the drop of a hat, but there is little doubt in the minds of the senior officers that, given the chance, most guardsmen would prefer field soldiering. Belize had given them just that:

At the end of the day we've all got to know each other much better. Operationally and training wise we've improved enormously. Friendships will have been formed and that's really important for the well-being of the regiment. The other good thing is that in this sort of setting you find out people who you didn't think were particularly good suddenly coming to the fore.

The Welsh Guards came home from Belize at the end of October 1989. By common consent they were fitter than they had been six months previously. The jungle patrols, the field firing exercises, the adventure training on beautiful St George's Caye and the hard unyielding climate had seen to that. Also, the fact that they had been forced to fall back on their reserves and their inner strengths, both mental and physical, meant that a new feeling of togetherness – part camaraderie, part *esprit de corps* – had been built up. If anything the battalion was more of a cohesive unit than it had ever been in London District.

And Belize? For all its heat and stinks and creeping things, and for all that the men had found a poor third world country so different from the homeliness of Wales, they were agreed that it had been an experience. 'Oh yes,' agreed the lance-sergeant who had driven me from the country lanes of Thetford to the rough tracks of Belize, 'it's an experience all right, one to put in the back pack like Kenya, Cyprus or the Falklands. It'll be something to talk about during the winter months but the fact of the matter is that I'll never want to come back here again. Ever.'

Chapter Nine

FALKLANDS

DURING THEIR THREE-WEEK long voyage to the Falkland Islands in May 1982 the men of the Welsh Guards grew accustomed to reading regular issues of the 5 Brigade Broadsheet which was published on board the *Queen Elizabeth 2* by the brigade's education centre. Partly a digest of information and partly a morale booster, this simple Roneoed broadsheet contained a summary of international news culled from the BBC World Service, a 'thought for the day from the Padre' ('For the Christian the spiritual watchword must be "Forwards,"') and a selection of feeble jokes ('Confucius says he who cooks beans and peas in the same water is unhygienic'). The broadsheet also published elementary details about the Argentine weaponry under the title 'Know your Enemy': the issue of 21 May provided some facts about the McDonnell Douglas A-4 Skyhawk which was described as a single-seat land and carrier based light attack bomber with a combat range of 400 miles. Among the recognition features which distinguished it from other Argentine aircraft such as the Mirage and Super-Etendard were the squat bulge housing upgraded avionics to the rear of the cockpit and the half-moon shaped air intakes on either side of the fuselage.

Had the authors of the description taken that basic information a stage further they would have informed the men of 5 Brigade that the Skyhawk had been developed in 1954, delivered to the US Navy two years later and that by 1979 2,960 models had been built by the McDonnell Douglas aircraft corporation. In its time the Skyhawk had held the world airspeed record by flying a 500 km circuit at over 695 m.p.h. and that it had proved itself in combat during the Vietnam War where US Navy and US Marine Corps pilots had given it the affectionate nickname of 'The Scooter'. By the late 1970s it had become a second line of defence aircraft and many had been sold by the US government to other friendly countries. Argentina had been among the customers and in May 1982 the aircraft, in two different models, equipped the 3rd Naval Fighter and Attack Squadron and the air force's 4th and 5th Fighter Groups. All told the Argentines operated some sixty-eight Skyhawks during the war and despite their age the aircraft distinguished themselves as reliable attack systems which scored a number of notable successes against British targets. Among these would be the attack made on the LSL *Sir Galahad* by Skyhawks of the 5th Fighter Group on 8 June 1982.

Most Welsh Guardsmen admitted later that the information about the Skyhawk was just another piece of information which had to be learned as they went to war – like the requirement to speak a few words of Spanish to deal with prisoners, or knowing that the Argentine Army operated Panhard Lynx armoured cars armed with a 90mm gun. At the time of being told these facts it was understandable that the Welsh Guards did not make much of them; they were assimilated and put to the back of the mind, to be recalled as required. As it turned out, though, there would be no need for the Welsh Guards to recognize the aircraft which inflicted such grievous damage on them three weeks later. By the time the men knew they were under attack from the air the Argentine Skyhawks had dropped their bombs and were out of range of any possible retribution. As it turned out, too, the Argentine attack on the *Sir Galahad* was to be the most serious British setback of the whole conflict.

That the Welsh Guards should have found themselves on board a luxury liner like the *QE2* ('luxury not dreamed of, food fit for a banquet') heading for a war zone in the South Atlantic owed everything to an escalation of diplomatic blunders, political misunderstanding and hasty military improvisation. The background events which led to the outbreak of hostilities between Britain and Argentina on 2 April 1982 are now well enough known not to require any elaborate reiteration: the basic issue at stake was the sovereignty of the 1,800 people who lived in the Falkland Islands, a small and rocky British outpost less than four hundred miles to the east of the Argentine mainland. Also part of the diplomatic equation were the even more remote South Sandwich Islands and the island of South Georgia which lay further to the south-east in the near vicinity of Antarctica. The Falklands and their dependencies had enjoyed British sovereignty since 1833 when a British warship, HMS *Clio*, commanded by Captain John Onslow arrived at the islands and ousted the small Argentine garrison which had been there since 1820. Prior to that the islands had been variously occupied by the British, French and the Spanish and the Argentine claim to the Malvinas, as they call the islands, is based on the Spanish possession which lasted from 1774 to 1811. When the Spanish South American empire was overthrown in 1816 Argentina laid claim to the former Spanish possessions in its area and it is on that point that they claim sovereignty over the Malvinas. There had been numerous, mostly desultory, attempts to settle the issue but *de facto* the Falklands were British, their inhabitants wanted to remain so and succeeding British governments showed no immediate desire to quit the South Atlantic. By the same token the Argentines continued to hold a passionately nationalistic feeling for the Malvinas and in 1981, spurred on by signs that Britain might be losing interest in her possession – the decision had been taken to reduce the British garrison and to scrap the ageing ice patrol ship *Endurance* – the military junta headed by General Galtieri began to lay plans to retake the islands by force. The decision to invade was taken on 23 March and over a week later, on 2 April, the first Argentine units had landed in the Falklands.

'Most Welsh Guardsmen didn't even know where the Falklands were and not a few thought they might be somewhere to the north, off the Scottish coast,' remarked a Welsh Guards officer who was a platoon commander during the conflict. 'But I had no cause to feel superior – I had to look up the place in the atlas myself.' For him, as for others in the battalion, the outbreak of hostilities had come as a complete surprise. The battalion had recently returned from a six-week training trip to Kenya and in mid-February had taken over the army's Spearhead commitment which required them to be ready for service in any part of the world, including Northern Ireland. This called for training in street patrolling at Lydd and Hythe in Kent and further training on the army's ranges at Senny-bridge in Wales and on Salisbury Plain. By March, with the Major-General's inspection completed and the summer season of public duties beckoning, 'everyone started talking about the Falklands, it came on television and within a few days, at the beginning of April, we thought that we might be taken too. We were all very excited.'

There was good reason for the subaltern to feel that he was living on the verge of momentous events. As soon as the news broke that a British task force was being assembled to re-possess the Falklands the Commanding Officer, Johnny Rickett, had phoned the Brigadier at UKLF Wilton and offered the Welsh Guards' services. 'Look here,' he told him, 'if you're looking for another battalion we are ready and willing to go. Our boxes are packed – we've just come off Spearhead – it obviously makes sense, we're as trained as we can be: do ask.' The Brigadier thanked the Commanding Officer for his 'interesting' offer: he would see how events progressed.

The land force component of Operation Corporate – the name given to the British plans to retake the Falklands by force – was entrusted to 3 Commando Brigade which was commanded by a Royal Marine officer, Brigadier Julian Thompson. An independent brigade group, it had been conceived as a formation which would travel to war by sea with its own supporting arms and stores. Although primarily a Royal Marine force it had been strengthened by the addition of two infantry battalions, 2nd and 3rd Parachute Regiment both of which formed 5 Infantry Brigade with the 7th Duke of Edinburgh's Own Gurkha Rifles. As 5 Brigade was the British Army's main 'out of NATO theatre' formation it would have to be reinforced and after much lobbying it was decided to find the additional battalions from London District. The Commanding Officer of the Welsh Guards was on the telephone again and the Welsh Guards were selected together with 2nd Scots Guards who were stationed at Chelsea Barracks. 'Everyone wanted to go,' he remembered. 'It was part of the jingo feeling, part of the big push. Let's go.' One of the subalterns recalled later that the announcement arrived at the best of all possible times:

> I remember sitting down after lunch and everyone happened to be grouped round the television and we all learned about it at the same time. Our Commanding Officer had been up early to make a number of calls and then it was confirmed that we would be going – if we weren't setting sail the next day, at least we would be going and in some capacity. And when this announcement was made there was that wonderful feeling of togetherness, of being amongst a whole lot of brother officers.

It still had to be decided that 5 Brigade would definitely join the task force but they seemed to be the obvious choice should the land forces require reinforcements. The Ministry of Defence had already decided not to weaken the Rhine army by extracting any infantry battalion from Germany and the only alternative would have been to send 1 Infantry Brigade, Britain's 'ACE Mobile Force' (Allied Command Europe), one of whose battalions, 1st Queen's Own Highlanders, was specially trained in winter warfare. This proposal was rejected on the grounds that it was a NATO-designated formation containing elements of the Territorial Army. That left the newly reinforced 5 Infantry Brigade which had started training in Wales.

There was a certain amount of criticism within the army about the selection of the two Guards battalions in the reconstituted brigade; most of it was either ill-informed or malicious but the echoes have continued to this day. It was argued that neither battalion was 'match fit' for winter warfare and that a diet of Queen's Guards was hardly conducive to fighting a hard war over one of the bleakest terrains in the world. Moreover, it seemed to those critics that the Guards had made use of their privileged positions and that lobbying in high places had won them selection over the claims of other regiments like the Queen's Own Highlanders. There is some truth here, the Welsh Guards' Commanding Officer had promoted his regiment's cause but he was not the first Welsh Guard to have done so. In 1919 Murray-Threipland had volunteered the Welsh Guards for service in North Russia during the ill-conceived British intervention to support the White Russians against what Winston Churchill, then Secretary of State for War, had called 'the foul baboonery of Bolshevism':

I have the honour to request [he wrote to HQ London District on 9 April 1919] that you will forward this my application to volunteer for the Relief Force being formed for service in North Russia in accordance with the War Office notice appearing in the press.

Further, may I be granted permission to call for volunteers from the 1st Battalion of the Regiment under my command and also through the Welsh press for demobilised and discharged Guardsmen of the regiment to form a battalion for the above named relief force.

The offer was not taken up by the War Office and the Welsh Guards may be thankful that their Lieutenant-Colonel's letter was turned down. By October 1919 the British had finally faced up to the unpalatable truth that they could not shore up an ideologically bankrupt opposition with men and arms and the 18,000 strong remnants of the British force were withdrawn in some disgrace from Murmansk and Archangel.

In April and May 1982 no one believed that the same fate would await the British task force in the Falklands. Indeed, as the ships sailed south and as the diplomatic attempts to solve the crisis continued, few servicemen thought that it would come to a shooting match. Although the logistical problems of fighting a campaign 8,000 miles away from home base were horrendous, the British forces were surely too well equipped and better trained than the largely conscript opposition? That was one of the feelings which ran through the Welsh Guards when they joined 5 Infantry Brigade and began two week's intensive training in Wales. As remembered by Simon Weston, Exercise Welsh Falcon was an unforgettable experience and the battalion had no reason to doubt why they had been selected. They had trained together in Kenya, they had just come off Spearhead duties and they were all in a high state of fitness and readiness:

> To a humble guardsman used to government cutbacks and tightfisted quartermasters, Welsh Falcon was unbelievable. It suddenly seemed that we could have any stores we wanted, and any facilities. We practised with our mortars on ranges that normally we would never have been able to get on to, with ammunition that we would never have been able to procure. I'd never seen so many helicopters in all my life. It was like something out of Vietnam. I can still remember the constant 'wop-wop' sound as they swooped and hovered over the Welsh hills, and the hot, eye-watering blast of Avtur aviation fuel-exhaust that hit you every time you jumped on or off.

It was not until 25 April that the decision was taken to send 5 Infantry Brigade to reinforce the task force in the South Atlantic; they had only been with the brigade a mere three weeks but there was little doubt in the minds of the Welsh Guards that they at least were fit and ready for the task that lay ahead. Of course, there were still those who doubted that a battalion fresh from ceremonial duties could exchange red tunics for camouflage cream – as if to counter the critics the Welsh Guards showed something of their versatility by reversing the procedure, interrupting their training on 30 April to accept the Freedom of Carmarthen wearing full home service dress. One of the officers who took part in the ceremony remarked that the unexpected change of style reminded him that he 'was also a member of a regiment of the Household Division . . . it was a lovely moment in the middle of an exhausting time.'

During the course of the Falklands campaign, the battalion would encounter many difficulties, some of which they could not over- come; there were even those in the Ministry of Defence who excused the hasty creation of the reconstituted 5 Infantry Brigade with the thought that the war might have finished before the reinforcements arrived, but when the Welsh Guards went to war in the spring of 1982 their confidence and morale were sky-high. No one knew what the future might hold but as the Commanding Officer told his officers and men it was now up to them to uphold the traditions of the regiment:

> In case you didn't know, the first Welsh settlers gave the bird the penguin its name; it is Welsh for white head. I am sure that there will be other Welsh words floating around the South Atlantic by the time we come home. We sail south quietly confident that we have the capability of undertaking any task that our country requires us to do. I know that we will live up to the high standard of our regimental traditions, whatever lies ahead. Everybody in Wales and those who know us within the UK generally will be looking at us. Let us ensure that we carry out our duty to the best of our ability. Go to it; may God bless us. Good luck to you all.

Some of the Welsh Guardsmen to whom he spoke were men who had been absent without leave earlier in the year but had quickly rejoined after learning that the Welsh Guards had been tasked to join 5 Infantry Brigade.

Having finished Exercise Welsh Falcon the battalion was given a short leave before reassembling on 12 May for the journey by bus to Southampton and embarkation on *QE2* which the government had requisitioned from Cunard. The cost was reputed to be in the order of £1 million a week but as the advance party of the Welsh Guards discovered it was money well spent – 'gradually swimming pools disappeared under ingeniously constructed flight decks, the trappings of timelessness and ease were removed and plywood hid the deep pile of carpeted corridors.' *QE2* was one of the STUFT (ships taken up from trade) vessels used during the war and its transformation, plus the scale of the military and naval reinforcements which accompanied it, were further signs of the British resolve to retake the Falklands. As had happened during the recent exercise, items of equipment which had taken months to arrive in the past were suddenly there for the asking. The voyage south was to take three weeks, half the time taken by 3 Commando Brigade; but it was still uncertain whether the Welsh Guards would see action despite the escalation of hostilities between the opposing naval and air forces in the Falklands area.

For most Welsh Guardsmen the war had suddenly become real while they were on leave on 4 May when an air-launched Exocet missile hit the Type 42 destroyer HMS *Sheffield*, killing twenty men and injuring twenty-four. It was the first serious British setback of the war and although it was obvious that in an operation of this kind losses to ships would be inevitable it had a sobering effect on the battalion's officers and men. 'I remember sitting flanked by my stepfather and mother and my mother looking round rather worried,' said a subaltern who heard the news on television while at home with his family. 'I said, "Don't worry, I'm an infantryman. That's what I joined the infantry for, and you know I won't be caught." I remember being rather rude about the cooks as well. The majority of the casualties on the *Sheffield* were the cooks and I just thought that they were probably rather badly trained – but in fact we all know now that they were just in the place that was badly hit.' Privately he admitted that the greatest shock of all was the stark image of a modern British warship being disabled by a single guided missile.

The *QE2* left Southampton on 13 May carrying the 1st Welsh Guards, 2nd Scots Guards, 7th Gurkha Rifles and the supporting arms and services of 5 Brigade.* As recorded by the world's television cameras, it was one of the highly emotional leave-takings which helped to transform the Falklands War into a public event. As remembered by the Welsh Guards themselves it was a curious yet solemn mixture of pride and sadness; not a few thanked the stiff eye-watering sea breeze which helped to disguise emotions for to their surprise many were able to pick out loved ones in the crowds which had thronged into the dockyard area.

---

*Ninety-seven Battery Royal Artillery, HQ 4 Field Regiment Royal Artillery, 656 Squadron Army Air Corps, 10 Field Workshop REME, 16 Field Ambulance RAMC, 81 Ordnance Company REME, Tactical Air Control Party.

The Major-General came to say goodbye to his men and Rickett remarked wryly that had another Guards battalion been included in the brigade then he too might have found himself going to war. It was not an idle thought: after the war some Welsh Guardsmen admitted that they felt uneasy about the brigade structure from the very outset and would have preferred an all-Guards brigade, headed by a Guards' officer and with a Guards HQ staff. This idea revived memories of the wartime 1st Guards Brigade and of the formation of independent Guards Brigades in the post-war years. The suggestion did not impugn the ability of the Brigadier, Tony Wilson, an experienced and well-liked former commanding officer of 1st Light Infantry, but the feeling persisted that the brigade was too much of a heterogeneous mixture to withstand the stresses and strains imposed by war.

Life on board the *QE2* was a curious blend of barracks discipline and cruise-ship comfort. There was a hefty daily training schedule but even though the more obvious luxuries had been hidden away for the duration of the war there was no denying that this was a modern luxury liner and not a simple troopship. 'On the *QE2* there was a certain amount of apprehensiveness which was understandable,' admitted one of the company commanders. 'But it was mildly unreal. It's quite difficult in a luxury liner where the waiters still wear black ties to get into the frame of mind that you were going to war.'

Although the training was hard – it began with a dozen laps of the upper deck, each lap being equivalent to a quarter of a mile – the general mood on board ship encouraged a tendency to indulge in mock heroics. The favourite film was *The Exterminator* and over pints of beer there was much talk of zapping Argies; for the younger officers and men in particular it was difficult to believe that the voyage south was for real and that, looking back on the experience, they were quite happy to play up the image of the gung-ho, devil-may-care guardsman:

We were anticipating a great heroic time . . . there were lovely dinners each night, Chablis was around £2 a bottle and we took advantage of that. I remember sitting down one night and the recce platoon commander and a platoon commander from 3 Company both joined me and one said, 'My God, I've just taken on board the fact that I've got to patrol the other side of the battalion area and there are mines and all

sorts of nasties out there. You know, it's all a bit frightening.' And I –
surely through ignorance – said, 'My God, that'll be fun,' thinking you
were in command at last. They both turned and looked at me as if I
were mad and I think told me words to that effect too.

The other dominant feeling, shared mainly by the older men, was
that they should not miss out on this opportunity to see war for the
first and perhaps the only time in their lives. It was rather like a
dark hidden monster, said one CSM, you felt afraid of it but at the
same time you knew your life would be incomplete unless you faced
it. Johnny Rickett, not much older than his warrant officer, echoed
the sentiment which he felt was held by most of the senior men in
the battalion:

> If you're a soldier you want to be part of the big show and all of us
> were very keen to be so. As the marines yomped and yomped further,
> and as we got further and further south, we thought well, goodness me,
> are we going to get there in time?

The news that a beachhead had been established by 3 Commando
Brigade at San Carlos on 21 May removed any lingering doubts
about whether or not the Welsh Guards would see action. Away
flew ideas that the battalion would only be required to pick up
spent cartridges or form the post-war garrison and in came a new
and much more sobre feeling. There was a brief flurry of real fear
when it was rumoured that the Argentines would be using
napalm. 'My God,' admitted a shaken young officer to his colleagues, 'I don't want to die by fire, not in a pile of napalm.' He
was one of the officers who survived the bombing of the *Galahad*.

From the very outset of *QE2's* requisition it had been agreed that
she should not be allowed to enter the immediate war zone. The
same rule had applied to the other large liner, the *Canberra*, before
the first D-Day landings at San Carlos – the British feared heavy
casualties should she be bombed – but by the time that the Welsh
Guards arrived in the war zone the rule had been relaxed for the
smaller liner. *QE2* dropped anchor at Grytviken Bay in South
Georgia after last light on 27 May and four hours later the first
elements of 5 Brigade found themselves being cross-decked by
trawler to exchange the comforts of a Cunarder for the refinements

of a P & O luxury liner. (South Georgia had been retaken by the
British on Sunday 25 April.) Life on board the smaller ship was
more cramped for the three-day journey but the crew – who had
been to 'bomb alley' in San Carlos Water and had seen war at first
hand – soon let the men of 5 Brigade know that they considered
themselves second to none:

> There was a completely different atmosphere on board that ship. When
> we were on the *QE2* we all thought, what a grand ship, how suitable for
> the Welsh and Scots Guards. Great. And then we went on the *Canberra*
> and were very snooty about it – the crew didn't like that impression at
> all so we had to be slightly more diplomatic. With good reason the
> *Canberra* regards itself as good as the *QE2*, if not better, especially after
> its war record.

On 2 June the Welsh Guards landed at Port San Carlos to find a
BBC camera team already working on the jetty – 'This must mean
that we really are at war!' joked one of the officers to his men. Once
the morning fog and drizzle had dispersed, revealing the rocky and
boggy open ground of San Carlos Settlement, the Welsh Guardsmen
were immediately and sentimentally reminded of home. 'Just like
Brecon,' said some while others saw echoes of Pembrokeshire in the
green-brown coastline with its sandy inlets ringed by small white-
washed houses. Unfortunately there the comparison ended: the
terrain might have been picturesque but it was not ideal for digging
in and making a temporary habitation. Trenches quickly filled with
water, the boggy ground and the thick clumps of heather – the
never-to-be-forgotten 'diddle-dee' – made the going difficult, it was
numbingly cold and there were fourteen hours of darkness. There
was little in the way of reliable ground transport and helicopters
were at a premium following the sinking of the *Atlantic Conveyor*
with the loss of three Chinook and five Wessex helicopters on 24
May. The low cloud which hung over the nearby Sussex Mountains
also kept remaining helicopter operations to a minimum.

At that stage in the war the British were rapidly gaining the
upper hand even if that superiority was not always apparent to the
men on the ground. The navy had lost a number of valuable ships
– on 21 May the frigate *Ardent* had been hit and abandoned, the
destroyer *Antrim* had also been hit, as had been the frigates
Argonaut, *Broadsword* and *Brilliant*; three days later the frigate

Antelope was sunk, to be followed by the destroyer *Coventry* on the same day as the *Atlantic Conveyor* – but the British had established their beachhead at San Carlos and the Argentine air power had been substantially weakened. Second Parachute Regiment had fought the first successful land battle of the campaign at Goose Green on 28 May and Brigadier Thompson had begun moving the bulk of his brigade across the north of East Falklands to begin the investment of Stanley. For 45 Commando and 3rd Parachute Regiment this entailed a hard cross-country march, yomping (the Marine word) across boggy heather-tufted land, and two days earlier, on 31 May, 42 Commando had been moved by helicopter to Mount Kent, twelve miles short of Stanley. This left 40 Commando at San Carlos to guard the Force Maintenance Area, a task they disliked but one which they hoped to relinquish once the army reinforcements had arrived.

Meanwhile 5 Brigade had started arriving at San Carlos. Major-General Jeremy Moore had landed ahead of the brigade with his staff and a small advance party to take overall command of the land forces in the Falklands. He arrived to find a favourable position with 3 Brigade headquarters established at Teal Inlet within striking distance of Stanley and a secure beachhead at San Carlos. With his troops established in the northern sector of the East Falklands the way was open to exploit the southern flank for a pincer attack on Stanley – a classic infantry strategy.

During the voyage south with the new land forces commander it is reasonable to suppose that Wilson advanced his brigade's claims to be given an equal chance of seeing action. (His last message to his men in the Brigade Broadsheet had starkly warned: 'we shall start earning our pay as a team shortly, and we are in this game to win.') Also, as an army man, Wilson would not have been human had he not wanted his service to take part in the final victory – Operation Corporate was, after all, a naval operation and the land forces were headed by a Royal Marine. Inter-service rivalry was not a new factor in this war, or in any other war: as Johnny Rickett remembered it was certainly present in the Falklands. 'I mean if you have the elites of the British armed forces – the Marines, the Paras, the Gurkhas and the Guards – there's bound to be rivalry.' It takes little guesswork to imagine, therefore, that Wilson and his battalion commanders wanted 5 Brigade to see action, that they did not want them to be kept in reserve or as guards to the San Carlos Force Maintenance Area.

With the arrival of Moore the land forces in the East Falklands were rearranged to take account of the new tactical situation. Thompson moved his headquarters up to Teal Inlet and Wilson established his brigade headquarters at Darwin which had been won after the Battle of Goose Green. Second Parachute Regiment and 29 Battery RA reverted to the control of 5 Brigade and the Gurkhas were tasked to guard the large number of Argentinian prisoners of war at Goose Green.

A tall laconic man with a fine service record – he had won the Military Cross in Northern Ireland – Wilson was in a bullish mood. From Moore he had won agreement that his brigade should have 'parity of resources' with 3 Brigade and that it should play an equal part in the final attack on Stanley. To do this he had to move his men quickly along the thirty-five mile southern flank, no easy matter as it was harder going than the terrain experienced by the Marines and Paratroops during their epic yomp a few days earlier. For one Welsh Guards subaltern though, the news of the special forces' exploit only acted as a spur: if they could do it, then so could his regiment:

> As a company we wanted to have a go, dying to get going we were, and we thought, 'If the paras and the marines have done their stuff, then let us get through now.' And so we all packed up our defensive positions, thought right that's the end of that hole – and grateful we were to get out of them because they were beginning to fill up with water. So we set off after dark to move over the mountains to meet up with the recce platoon which had already moved forward. But we soon realised that it was going to take a hell of a long time to move the battalion over that wet and dank terrain.

That first experience of the Falklands' energy-sapping arena came when the battalion was ordered to march over the Sussex Mountains towards Goose Green. Knowing that other units had suffered badly from weather casualties, and knowing that helicopter lifts were at a premium, they took as much kit with them as they possibly could – in most cases this amounted to approximately 100 lbs per man all packed into large unwieldy bergens (rucksacks). Two tractors were called up to carry the mortars and the .50 Browning machine-guns, plus ammunition, but they quickly became stuck in the boggy soil. The promised snowcats never materialized and unable to continue without these vital assets the battalion was ordered back to the defensive positions at San Carlos. Although Moore had warned his men that they would have to rely on the LPC (Leather Personnel Carrier, or boot) as their main means of transport, it was obvious that the two Guards battalions would experience grave difficulty in moving to either Bluff Cove or Fitzroy, now designated as 5 Brigade's headquarters. Surely in the late twentieth century, there must be some other means of moving troops, mused one of the platoon commanders who had seen his men struggling with the boggy moor and stumbling over the thick heather-tufted ground which makes up most of the land in the East Falklands.

To this day the Welsh Guards insist that they would have marched the southern flank – whatever the cost. One of the senior officers in 3 Company pointed out that they were probably fitter than any other infantry battalion at that time – 'We'd been to Kenya just before Christmas for six weeks and had done a lot of physical training there; we'd been on Spearhead and had trained for that, then as soon as we knew we were going to the Falklands we'd taken steps to increase our level of fitness.' His argument is backed by others in the battalion: an older NCO who used physical stamina as a barometer of his own military abilities confirmed that he had never seen the battalion as fit as it was when it left for the Falklands. Besides, he said, he had spoken to older Welsh Guardsmen, veterans of the 3rd Battalion who had served in Italy during the winter of 1943–44. 'To be fair, you could say that we weren't fit in the last war,' they had told him. 'We weren't toughened up to march in the mountains of Italy, especially in the conditions we encountered. We weren't tough. We had to get used to it.' As had happened in every war in history, it had taken them time to acclimatize – and they were experienced and highly motivated infantrymen, many of whom had served in North Africa.

Nevertheless, the feeling persists in some quarters that the Welsh Guards were not properly trained to fight a campaign in such a hostile environment as the Falklands and that they cannot be compared to the Marines or to the Parachute Regiment. On one level it is difficult to see how an infantry regiment could ever measure up exactly to commando or airborne troops, both of which are trained as special forces possessing the motivation and the equipment for service in difficult areas. On another, and perhaps more basic level, the criticism was ill-informed or based on hearsay and unfortunately for the Welsh Guards it gained a common currency once the fighting was over. The crew of the *Canberra* complained to the press that the Welsh Guards (and the Scots Guards) had done little physical training during the voyage from South Georgia to East Falkland but at that stage the seas were extremely rough and the only form of physical exercise possible was the famous 'guardrail dash'. Similarly, at San Carlos, the marines had taken considerable pleasure at the sight of guardsmen landing with plastic dustbin liners covering their boots – how like the Guards to keep up the standards of the parade ground, they thought – but as a lance-sergeant in 2 Company admitted, not without pride, any soldier can get his feet wet, but it takes a sensible infantryman to keep them dry. Then there were stories of Welsh Guardsmen breaking into tears and collapsing during the trek into the Sussex Mountains but this, too, seems to be another taradiddle, a myth that was given greater weight by some of the war correspondents attached to the special forces.

The biggest problem facing Moore was the lack of helicopters after the sinking of the *Atlantic Conveyor*. Without them it would be difficult to move 5 Brigade along the southern flank and by that stage in the conflict the helicopter had established itself as *the* essential weapon. Marching round was one solution but that would take time and the Welsh Guards' experience in the Sussex Mountains showed that a long tramp would result in exhausted men unfit for immediate battle; in any case their heavy equipment, mortars, machine-guns and ammunition would still have to be moved by other means. Wilson, though, was determined to push forward and, ironically, it was the unexpected availability of helicopters which provided him with the initiative. On 2 June Major Chris Keeble, now commanding 2nd Parachute Regiment after the death of the Commanding Officer (Lieutenant-Colonel H. Jones) at Goose Green, persuaded Wilson to move forward an element of his men to Swan Inlet House, half-way between Goose Green and Fitzroy. Five Scout helicopters of 656 Squadron AAC were made available and when the paratroops arrived at the house they found that the telephone connection to Fitzroy was still open. Grasping the opportunity the senior officer, Major John Crosland, telephoned the families at Fitzroy and was told that the settlement and nearby Bluff Cove were free of Argentine troops. The way was open for 2nd Parachute Regiment to dash forward by helicopter – a Chinook also took part in the operation – and by 4 June a jubilant Wilson was able to tell the correspondent of *The Times* 'I'm moving people forward as fast as I can with stocks of ammunition to launch what I suppose could be called the final offensive. I've grabbed fifty-five kilometres in this great jump forward and I want to consolidate it.'

Thus began a series of moves which would lead directly to the tragedy on board the *Sir Galahad* four days later. Wilson was anxious to keep the upper hand and to ensure that there was no slackening of effort within the brigade – no commander in his position would have wanted to do otherwise. The bold initiative which had taken his men forward had to be maintained yet the move was fraught with dangers. Second Parachute Regiment were in an exposed position and without the reinforcement of air defences, artillery and more men they were prone to retaliation from Argentine aircraft or to counter-attack by the ground forces. It was imperative, therefore, to move the rest of the brigade round to Fitzroy and Bluff Cove and on 5 June it was agreed that the two Guards' battalions should be transported by sea.

This would involve the use of the navy's two 11,500 tonne assault ships *Fearless* and *Intrepid* which had been designed in the mid-1960s specifically for amphibious operations. Large and unwieldy vessels, their efficiency lies in their unlovely design – landing-craft capable of carrying heavy tanks are stored in their large dock and landed from the open stern above which there is a huge helicopter deck. The trouble was that *Fearless* carried Moore's headquarters and the Royal Navy, aware of the possibility of Argentine air assault, were unwilling to risk the two ships in exposed positions off the southern coast. Not only would they be within range of shore-based attack aircraft but it was known that the Argentines had positioned land-launched Exocet missiles at Stanley. Both were sufficient reasons to make the navy cautious.

After considerable discussions, which involved the task force's expert in amphibious operations in the Falklands, Major Ewan Southby-Tailyour RM, it was agreed that *Intrepid* would take 2nd Scots Guards half-way to Bluff Cove, to Lively Island on the night of 5/6 June; there they would be met by Southby-Tailyour's landing craft and transported to their destination. The following night *Fearless* would take the Welsh Guards as far as Direction Island and the operation would be repeated. It was a compromise plan but it did have the twin virtues of employing the available resources and safeguarding two vital capital ships. On hearing the plan the Welsh Guards were happy to be on the move and delighted to find themselves in relatively comfortable surroundings.

They could leave their wet trenches at San Carlos and dry out in the warmth and cheer of the large assault ship. For the first time in many days there was the benison of hot showers, clean clothes and the chance to reorganize kit. The officers and NCOs were invited into the respective wardrooms and invited to sign for drinks – which would be charged to them at the war's end. The fighting ashore began to seem quite remote although there were men who felt uneasy aboard the ship: this was not their natural environment and one of the senior warrant officers remembers worrying that his men had not been trained for amphibious operations:

> I had been in the regiment for fifteen years and I thought that I'd done most things but all of a sudden I was stuck in a ship which was completely alien for someone like me. They were used to carry marines and the terminology and the rules on board were difficult for infanteers like us. It really was unfamiliar – once we were on land, OK, there was no problem – but it was the unfamiliar environment of the ship that caught most of us out, with the confined space, the restrictions and the naval terminology.

His fears seemed to be confirmed by the experience of the 2nd Scots Guards who had a dreadful journey, tossed around for hours in the frail landing craft which eventually landed them at Bluff Cove on 6 June. That night saw *Fearless* meet the same sea conditions when she hove to off Direction Island: due to the weather Southby-Tailyour's landing craft were unable to make the rendezvous and it was decided instead to use the assault ship's two remaining landing craft to take ashore half of the battalion – 2 Company, machine-gun platoon, anti-tank platoon, recce platoon and HQ staff. The remainder – Prince of Wales's Company, 3 Company, the mortar platoon and half of A echelon – were ordered to remain on *Fearless* where they thanked their lucky stars that they were still safe and warm while their mates braved the elements outside. Johnny Rickett went on with the leading half of the battalion by landing craft and he was later to remember his parting words to the force commander. 'General?' he asked Moore. 'You must promise me that you'll look after my men, because I can't do so.'

Back at San Carlos the last hopes of using *Intrepid* or *Fearless* again vanished when Admiral Fieldhouse, the task force commander, banned the big ships from being risked once more. Instead it was agreed to take the rump of the Welsh Guards round to Bluff Cove by the LSL *Sir Galahad* which was being loaded with a Rapier detachment and a field ambulance bound for Fitzroy. It would surely be an easy matter to load the Welsh Guards too, deliver them to Bluff Cove under cover of darkness and then for the ship to proceed to Fitzroy with the rest of its complement. Both company commanders knew exactly what the plan was and their orders from the Commanding Officer were plain enough: 'they had a clear-cut order from me; to get their men to join us at best possible speed'. Travelling at night on *Sir Galahad* seemed sensible enough too; there was less danger of Argentine air attack and a combat air patrol had been ordered for the following morning to cover the landings. It was then that events began to get out of joint because problems with the signal network meant that 5 Brigade headquarters thought that the Welsh Guards were at Bluff Cove, having already disembarked from *Fearless*.

The Welsh Guards had already encountered the squat shape of the Landing Ship Logistic *Sir Galahad* when they were sent to Northern Ireland and many guardsmen had unpleasant memories of her flat-bottomed inability to ride heavy seas. The big compensation was that she would take them all the way to Bluff Cove: at midday on 7 June the remaining companies of Welsh Guards crossdecked to the *Sir Galahad* to be greeted by its largely Chinese crew, many of whom were surprised to find themselves in the Falklands. (When they went to war, they told some of the guardsmen, they thought they were bound for Cyprus.) In some respects the *Sir Galahad* was more like a cross-Channel ferry than a naval vessel: it had ramps at bow and stern and like a civilian ship it had ample accommodation. The Welsh Guards settled in and began waiting due to a lengthy delay while 16 Field Ambulance was loaded. Instead of sailing at last light, as planned, the unexpected hitch meant that there was the very real danger of the LSL reaching her destination at daylight – this was bad news for the captain and for the Welsh Guards' company commanders:

When we got on board the *Galahad* at San Carlos we were under the impression that we were going to be taken to Bluff Cove or that we would be met by landing craft and taken there ... the night before.

When it was quite clear that we weren't going to sail until one o'clock and thereby not arrive until it was light, the captain of *Galahad* [Captain Philip Roberts] summoned me to the bridge and said, did I agree that we should signal *Fearless* to say that we weren't going to sail? Which we did because it seemed sensible not to arrive in daylight. However, the *Fearless* ordered the ship to sail . . . I think it was a fair arrangement.

The new orders from *Fearless* also told Captain Roberts to sail only as far as Fitzroy where the Rapier detachment and the Field Ambulance would be off-loaded as planned. A further decision would be taken about the Welsh Guards, regarded now as a low priority, once the availability of landing craft became known – but this information was not passed on to either of the company commanders who went to bed thinking that their destination was still Bluff Cove.

The following morning, 8 June, the *Sir Galahad* arrived as dawn was breaking at Fitzroy and the men began assembling their weapons and equipment for the day ahead. By 11 a.m. it was fully light, revealing a scene from a picture postcard – 'the sea was still, like a mirror,' recalled a young guardsman in 3 Company 'and the sky was blue and cold and there was a superb view across the moorland to the hills beyond. It was just like the Highlands of Scotland.' Idyllic the view might have been for the passengers but when the *Sir Galahad* arrived at Port Pleasant near Fitzroy it had sailed into potential trouble. The clear skies revived the possibility of Argentine air attack and the area was as yet undefended: unknown to the task force the Argentines were in fact planning such a raid having heard from their observers on Mount Harriet ten miles away that *Galahad's* sister ship *Sir Tristram* had arrived at the anchorage the previous day. The attack would be made by eight Skyhawks and six Daggers of the 5th and 6th Fighter Groups while four Mirages of the 8th Fighter Group would make a decoy attack to the north in order to lure away the Sea Harrier combat air patrol.

Meanwhile the Welsh Guards company commanders were having to wrestle with the problem of being in the wrong place at the wrong time. They had expected to find themselves at Bluff Cove; instead they were at Fitzroy without any fresh orders. Also, they were without the means to continue the journey because there was only one landing-craft and a Mexeflote pontoon raft working at

Fitzroy and they were both engaged in unloading the *Sir Tristram*. It was an unwelcome situation for the senior officers:

> When we got to Fitzroy in the first hour it wasn't a question of who got off first – no one could have because there were no means of getting off, there weren't any landing craft available. Then one appeared and I was told by the First Officer to disembark – as simple as that, we were told to get off. So I refused, I said no. About half an hour later the Captain asked me to go to the bridge and said, 'Are you saying you're not prepared to get off?' And I said, 'It's not a question of not being prepared to get off. I'll take them all ashore provided I get some orders what to do, either from my battalion or from brigade.' It was a little bit frosty to begin with. Inevitably everybody was fairly fraught – everybody had their own priorities.

While this was happening the Sea King helicopter which had accompanied the *Sir Galahad* had begun unloading the Rapier detachment which would supply the headquarters area with an air defence system: this was accomplished in eighteen trips. Then would follow 16 Field Ambulance, the other unit which was due to disembark at Fitzroy. It appeared that the plan was for the Welsh Guards to get off too and then march to Bluff Cove, no easy matter as recent intelligence reports suggested that one of the bridges over an inlet had been blown up.*

The reasons why the Welsh Guards stayed on board are simple enough. Assuming, as they had to, that the bridge was impassable, the distance to Bluff Cove was a good eighteen miles over particularly difficult country. While the men were capable of tackling such a march it would have taken at least thirty hours to complete and they would have arrived in the afternoon of 9 June, several hours after the time they had been given for the start of the second phase of 5 Brigade's advance. Communications, too, were causing problems with frequencies changing and new instructions failing to get through to the company commanders. Moreover, a forced march would mean leaving behind all the heavy equipment plus the front-line ammunition for the mortars and the machine-guns. (No unit going into action would ever agree to be separated from its reserves of ammunition; stealing was rife throughout the war and there was the real danger that unguarded supplies might 'disappear' or be 'borrowed' by others.)

---

* It was only after hostilities ceased that this information was found to be wrong.

To disembark the men on a Mexeflote which was still unloading brigade ammunition and to leave their heavy equipment at Fitzroy were risks that the company commanders were not prepared to take. There was also the added irritation that the arrival of *Sir Galahad* at Fitzroy gave brigade headquarters the first inkling that the entire battalion of Welsh Guards was not at Bluff Cove as planned. To the company commanders on the spot it seemed 'to be unwise to go wandering off into the battle area with apparently no means of communicating and without a clear picture of where the other units were and what they were doing and on a journey the majority of which would be completed in the dark.'

The next solution was to take the Welsh Guards round to Bluff Cove by the solitary landing-craft that was working at Fitzroy – four others had returned to their mother ship, the *Intrepid*. It was thought that this landing-craft, *Foxtrot One* (17 Port Regiment, RCT), could take them round in relays:

> About an hour after I'd seen the Captain he called me back to the bridge and also there were a couple of officers from the staff of Commodore Amphibious Warfare. He said there was a new plan: the Mexeflote would off-load the field ambulance and an LCU – which had appeared half-full of ammunition but had gone to off-load it – would take us round in shifts to Bluff Cove. That was about four hours before we were actually bombed and it was rather like going into an airport to wait for an aeroplane and the take-off time gets delayed.

Despite the inevitable delay this seemed to be a fair proposal. 'Short of swimming – which I suppose some people might say we should have done – at that time there were no means of getting off.'

Then there was another delay. The leading echelon of the field ambulance had priority use of the landing-craft but during the operation its ramp was damaged and it was discovered that it could not link up with *Galahad*'s stern ramp. Repairs were tried but there were no spare parts. The time was 12.30 p.m.; another change of plan was ordered. The landing-craft was brought alongside the *Galahad* so that the LSL's crane could transfer the heavy equipment while the men would disembark by scrambling nets. One of the officers in 3 Company, Lieutenant Hilarian Roberts told his men that the operation would not be completed until nightfall. 'The men of both Companies were either helping with the winching, filing out of the tank deck to scramble down into the boat or merely waiting to get off,' he wrote later in the *Guards Magazine*. 'Some were still up in the main superstructure in the canteen and television rooms.' They could have been day-trippers on their way to Boulogne.

It was then that disaster struck. The Argentine aircraft, having left Rio Gallegos in the late morning, arrived in Falklands airspace and their presence became known to the British forces at San Carlos – by then three Skyhawks and one Dagger had been forced to turn back due to technical problems. The faster Daggers were the first to arrive and would have attacked *Galahad* and *Tristram* from the west had they not sighted the elderly frigate *Plymouth* alone in Falklands Sound. The British ship was attacked and badly damaged but it replied with heavy defensive fire and, running short of fuel, the Daggers were forced to return to the mainland.

No such problems awaited the five Skyhawks, although as their commander, First Lieutenant Cachón, was to remember later, they too had to rely on luck. While heading towards Fitzroy they flew through a rain squall and finding the bay deserted, turned right to begin the flight home. Below them they could see formations of soldiers – men of 2nd Scots Guards – who put up a curtain of small arms fire. It was while they were winging over the area that Cachón's wing man noticed the ships in Port Pleasant. The Skyhawks straightened up, banked to the left and pressed home their attack. One of the company commanders saw the planes before he heard the scream of their turbojets:

> The first I realized what was happening was when I looked up and saw the bottom of the Argentine aircraft and the bombs coming off them. One disappeared into the hold. The attack came from the starboard side and we were on the port side. Another hit the *Galahad* and bounced off above our heads and hit the water twenty feet away.

By then the headquarters of Prince of Wales's Company were aboard the landing craft and the rest of the platoons were lined up awaiting their turn to complete the cross-decking. (The prearranged order of march was Prince of Wales's Company, 3 Company, HQ Company, 350 men in all.) One of the platoon commanders still on board the *Galahad* had hung back and told another platoon to go in his place as he was unsure where to go next. For him, as for everyone else on the tank deck the attack was a complete and utter shock:

> I heard a loud roar of jets going ahead – and I remembered that the last time I had heard such a roar was when I was taken to the Farnborough Air Show by my father when I was aged seven. Rather embarrassingly, I had hit the deck then because I was so frightened and, of course, everyone else did nothing. But this time I'd become used to the noise and I didn't hit the deck for about a second. So did fifty other people and we all suddenly said 'Get down!' together. So we got down and I could see one of the jets going overhead through the gap in the top deck where the crane had been operating.

Three Skyhawks attacked the *Galahad* and three bombs scored direct hits – one exploded in the engine room, another in the empty officers' quarters but the one which did the most damage hurtled through the hold into the open tank deck where the bulk of the Welsh Guards were waiting to disembark. A fourth bomb, noticed by the men on the landing-craft, bounced off the ship harmlessly into the sea. The remaining Skyhawks also hit *Tristram* twice killing two Chinese crewmen. Because the Argentine pilots were able to press home their attack from a fair height their bombs' fuses were correctly timed to do the most damage. No sooner had his men shouted at him to get down than Hilarian Roberts felt the full force of the blast:

> There was a bang, a flash, and a big bang. I sensed the fireball rush past me and I saw my hands turn as if to grey rubber gloves. Then I became aware of my hair frizzling and I put up my hands to rub out the flames because I felt that I might suffocate if the oxygen was burnt from my face, but the flame died away as quickly as it came and I realised, very strongly, that I was alive but burnt and I knew that I would not now die.

Those, like Roberts, who had survived the initial blast were then faced with the appalling problem of getting out of the tank deck which had exploded into an inferno. Thick black smoke filled the area and the intense heat threatened to explode the piles of ammunition and the fuel drums for the field ambulance's Land Rovers. Roberts could hear his CQMS telling everyone to 'keep calm' and as if it were a mantra he found himself repeating the words over and over again as he and a dozen others were led through a narrow hatch up to the deck and safety. He had suffered terrible burns to his hands and face. Behind him came another platoon commander who had taken shelter behind a full fuel drum and had lived to tell the tale. A lucky escape, but he had witnessed the full horror of the blast – 'a lot of the men had fire on their backs or their hair was on fire and everyone was screaming, and then there was the gathering smoke and the gathering suffocation.' Simon Weston, who was waiting with the rest of the mortar platoon near the stern, has provided a graphic and horrifying account of what happened on the other side of the blast:

> Men were mutilated and burning, and fought to rip off their clothing or douse the flames and beat at their faces, arms, legs, hair. They rushed around in circles in the roadway, screaming like pigs. A human fireball crumpled just ten feet in front of me like a disintegrating Guy Fawkes, blistered hands outstretched as he called for his mum. He fell flat and horribly still; in the heat of the flames all around me I watched transfixed for a second or two as he died. Black, choking smoke engulfed the area and I heard the voices of men I knew, friends who were crying out for help as they died in unimaginable pain. It was the sound of hell.

Incredibly, Weston fought his way through to the stairwell where CSM Brian Neck of 3 Company was calmly guiding the survivors to safety. By then the ammunition and the spare fuel had started to explode and the tank deck had become a living hell: in all thirty-two Welsh Guardsmen, four Army Catering Corps men, three members of the RAMC and two each from 9th Parachute Squadron (RE) and REME were to die on *Sir Galahad*. Also killed were three ships officers and two Chinese crewmen. At least a further 150 men were to suffer from wounds and burns, including Simon Weston who was to make an extraordinary and much publicized recovery.

The aftermath of the attack on the *Sir Galahad* was captured by television cameras and the footage was shown on British television news on 24 June 1982. Few viewers will ever be able to forget the uncanny sight of the fires raging aboard the ship and the thick pall of dense black smoke which hung over it, grim testimony to the carnage below decks. Few will forget the courage and the tenacity of the rescuers, especially the helicopter crews who flew mission after mission to pick up survivors or to fan the life-rafts to safety, like collies carefully marshalling their flock. And who will be able to erase the memory of a Welsh Guardsman victoriously holding the stump of his shattered leg as he was carried gently ashore by his mates? Smile, the wounded had been told, there are television cameras on the beach.

That so many men survived the incident says much for the efficiency of the men of the RAMC who held to the view that the late twentieth-century warrior should not expect to be left to die of his wounds on the battlefield. The medics of 16th Field Ambulance performed wonders providing first aid to the shattered guardsmen both on board the ship and on shore where they were given tremendous support by the medics of 2nd Parachute Regiment. The helicopter crews of 825 Squadron Fleet Air Arm and 656 Squadron Army Air Corps shuttled to and from the *Galahad* to bring out the casualties, flying without the benefit of any ground control. Within minutes of the attack a huge and entirely un-orchestrated rescue operation was at work and the worst of the wounded were hurried over to the task force's medical centre at Ajax Bay, the home of Surgeon Commander Rick Jolly's celebrated Red and Green Life Machine:

> For each patient there is one attendant, sometimes two. It's a heartening sight. The fused and charred clothing is cut away and the total percentage of burned skin area assessed and recorded. Where necessary an intravenous infusion is set up. Then carefully and lovingly, Flamazine is spread thickly over the afflicted areas. The cool white cream contains a silver and sulpha drug mixture which is pain-killing, antiseptic and promotes healing.

From Ajax Bay the wounded were transferred to *Fearless* and *Intrepid* and later to the hospital ship *Uganda*. For many of them it would be a long and painful journey to Britain through Montevideo and onwards by RAF VC10 to Brize Norton and the services' specialist hospitals.

Another factor which helped the Welsh Guards that day was discipline. While it was hardly Horse Guards Parade on the tank deck, men kept calm and reacted well to the accustomed and familiar voices of command which kept them going when everything around seemed strange and uncharted. For one of the officers in 3 Company this was the ultimate test of army training:

> Oh yes, initially it was confused. Why? Well the lights went out. A big bang had happened. Heard people screaming. Of course it was confused,

I mean you don't know what the hell's happening . . . however, when we got on to the flight deck people were going about their business as one would expect. A man was injured there, someone was trying to look after him. If he was trying to get off the ship people were trying to do something about it. Things like that went on pretty well like clockwork.

And then there was the nobility of the men who discovered reserves of stamina and courage which astonished those who witnessed their actions. Hilarian Roberts told friends later that he knew something was wrong when one of his men appeared in front of him, saluted and said, 'I think we ought to get off this ship, sir.' Forgetting his own pain Roberts looked at the guardsman incredulously and saw that the skin on his face was melting. Another platoon commander had a similar experience when one of his men approached him on the upper deck to report that there seemed to be something wrong with his foot. 'Sure enough, when I picked up his boot and examined it I found that a bullet had lodged itself in his foot.' Minutes earlier another guardsman, his skin hanging lifelessly from his chin, 'looking awful', merely confirmed that he was 'fine' and could wait. Pride and common human decency also played their part in helping the Welsh Guards through that awful South Atlantic afternoon.

The remainder of the battalion had seen the five Skyhawks flash overhead and had opened up with their small arms in a vain attempt to hit the aircraft. Earlier in the day some of the men had noticed the LSL at Fitzroy and the pall of smoke which now hung over the bay was an ominous sign that the Argentine air attack had been successful – but they still did not know that their friends and comrades had been at the receiving end. 'I didn't know they were there, nobody at brigade HQ knew they were on that ship,' remembered Johnny Rickett. 'Nobody had any information, any news about it at all.' Like wildfire, though, the bad news spread rapidly from Fitzroy and Rickett himself heard it on a small portable radio while visiting 2 Company. ' "Welsh Guards casualties down at Fitzroy. Get yourself down there." Well, it was a ghastly shock quite frankly and I don't mind admitting that the tears streamed down my face as I rode the motor-bike down to the helipad.' The scene that greeted him and the RSM was one of organized chaos, one that he has never been able to forget:

If one gets a hold of oneself it's easier to lead people. The important thing was to turn the battalion round, to forget what had happened and get everyone to look forward. The survivors were struggling back, all the casualties without their equipment. They were in a state of shock – and we were under Argentine air attack at the time – they were like a lot of sheep wanting help, wanting guidance. And the cry was 'Sir, what shall we do?' And I said, 'Stick close to me because I'm lucky, I haven't been hit by anything yet.' Somehow that steadied them and it was all right. I remember, too, that one of the company commanders was frightfully upset about it all and when I said that I had to get back to commanding the battalion because we've still got two companies and we're on our way to Stanley, the cry was 'You're not going to leave us now?' I then realised at that stage that the system would look after them, the system would re-equip them and I was confident that the best would be done for them.

In fact it was to take at least a fortnight before the two companies were to be properly kitted out again. Three Company was evacuated that night to San Carlos while Prince of Wales's Company spent the night in a sheep shed at Fitzroy where they were taken under the wing of 2nd Parachute Regiment. The following day, to the dismay of men who never wanted to go on board a ship again, they were taken back to *Fearless* by helicopter. Bereft of all their kit and equipment their war was over and they would spend the rest of the war guarding the Force Maintenance Area at San Carlos. Even at that stage it was not possible to gauge their losses and it was not until a few days later, after the fall of Stanley, that the full extent of the tragedy could be computed. The shortage of sophisticated communications systems, the confusion of the attack itself (it was followed an hour later by another Argentine air raid) and the fact that the war was still in progress inevitably caused delays in getting accurate information back to Britain and there were to be many anxious Welsh Guards families waiting for news in the immediate aftermath of the initial announcement.

The bombing of the *Sir Galahad* at Fitzroy was a serious blow to the British war effort. It deprived 5 Brigade of half a battalion of well trained troops and a good deal of much-needed ammunition, transport and supplies were also lost. For a while, too, it also dented task force morale and because it was a public and well reported tragedy it sparked off lively interest in its causes. To the layman at home it seemed inconceivable that two unarmed ships, one full of troops, should have been left unprotected for so long, especially when the extent of the Argentine air threat was so well known. The plan seemed to smack of negligence and as so often happens after a public disaster a search was made for a scapegoat. It was felt, both within and without the services, that someone should be blamed for allowing the Welsh Guards to remain on board ships which were sitting ducks in the open waters of Port Pleasant. One candidate was Brigadier Tony Wilson who as brigade commander had to shoulder part of the responsibility – shortly after the war's end he retired from the army and although his battalions had done well it was noticeable that he did not receive the stock CBE awarded to other senior commanders in the Falklands. The other contenders were the Welsh Guards company commanders on board the *Galahad* at the time of the attack. In particular it was alleged that they had refused to take their men ashore at Fitzroy and that they had chosen to ignore the advice given to them by the task force's experts on amphibious warfare.

The claim was made by Major Ewan Southby-Tailyour in the Yorkshire Television documentary *The Falklands War: The Untold Story* which was broadcast in 1987. Southby-Tailyour, a keen sailor, had been stationed in the Falklands in 1978–79 and had acquired a detailed knowledge of the islands' coastline; as such he was held in high respect as one of the key planners for the amphibious operations which would retake the Falklands. When the Welsh Guards arrived at Fitzroy he was helping to off-load ammunition from the *Tristram* and was deeply troubled that both ships were in danger of air attack – he had been a witness to the abilities of the Argentine bomber pilots in San Carlos airspace.

It was his view that the sooner the Welsh Guards disembarked, the safer they would be. Unfortunately his wishes were in direct contradiction to the orders held by the Welsh Guards – to get to Bluff Cove to rejoin the battalion at best possible speed. 'It wasn't a question of any order of getting off – if we weren't meant to be there in the first place,' insists one of the Welsh Guards company commanders. Even had he agreed to move he points out there were no means available and that the Rapier battery and the field ambulance had priority because Fitzroy was their destination. Also, it would take time to off-load the ammunition from the landing craft and the Mexeflote which were the only craft able to transport men and the Welsh Guards were insistent that they would not be separated from their heavy equipment. Once it was agreed to shuttle them round to Bluff Cove the correct solution had been found – but the delay had eaten into the valuable hours of daylight.

Southby-Tailyour also spoke of angry words being exchanged with the Welsh Guards company commanders and the whole tone of his televised evidence was that they should take some of the blame for the tragedy. At the time of the broadcast the Welsh Guards refused to make any comment but other officers who were on board the *Sir Galahad* at the time have denied that there was a major disagreement about whether or not the Welsh Guards should disembark. Having argued their case after the Captain's first order to leave the ship, it was agreed that ways and means should be found to transport the 350 men round to Bluff Cove, their original destination. Those were their orders and amid the chaos they found at Fitzroy they were determined to stick to them.

The sad reality of the attack on the *Galahad* is in fact beyond petty quarrels about individual blame. It happened, as indeed do most accidents, by a steady accumulation of mistakes, errors of judgement and plain bad luck. The first faulty link in the chain of misfortune was the *ad hoc* nature of 5 Brigade's administrative arrangements and the inability of headquarters to assimilate essential information about the movements of one of its battalions. No one knew that Welsh Guardsmen were in that ship at Fitzroy which is hardly surprising given that Wilson's priority was to get his men into position for what everyone hoped would be the final battle of the war. Many of the men who served in the Falklands – not all of them Welsh Guardsmen – have described the shambles which existed within 5 Brigade, the lack of co-ordination, the constant shortages of supplies and rations which resulted in units stealing from one another and the absence of any administrative back-up. For these shortcomings it is hardly fair to blame Wilson and his staff. Five Brigade was a hastily improvised formation which had been given little time to work itself up for the demands of a war in which its ultimate role was only known at the last minute. Small wonder that its administrative machinery was so creaky. On the communications front, too, the brigade was badly handicapped. Its signals system was less sophisticated than 3 Brigade's and there were problems in relaying signals to the forward positions at Fitzroy and Bluff Cove. The problem had been exacerbated by the accidental shooting down of a Gazelle helicopter by missiles fired from HMS *Cardiff* on the night of 5/6 June. Among the passengers were two Royal Signals personnel who had been flying to the newly established relay station on the slopes of Mount Wickham. Wilson had also been stymied by the shortage of helicopters to move forward troops and supplies in order to maintain the tactical breakthrough made by 2nd Parachute Regiment. Against that background the plan to move the two Guards battalions to Bluff Cove by sea was always going to be a risk – just as any bold plan has to be in time of war.

Had all the guardsmen been able to land from *Intrepid* on the night of 6/7 June all would have been well, but even the revised plan, to use the *Sir Galahad*, was sound enough – the men would be landed during the hours of darkness and at first light there would be a combat air patrol to neutralize the threat from the air. The plan, though, did not make any allowance for the delays and hesitations which began almost as soon as the Welsh Guards boarded the *Galahad* in the afternoon of 7 June. The loading of the field ambulance caused the first hold-up; nevertheless, *Fearless* ordered the LSL to proceed as far as Fitzroy. At Port Pleasant – where the Welsh Guards did not want to be – there was another delay while the Rapier detachment and field ambulance were off-loaded, and the final hitch was the malfunction of the landing craft's ramp.

While all these curbs on the Welsh Guards' movements were accumulating the communications failure meant that no one knew what was happening – even Johnny Rickett was not aware that his men were on one of the ships anchored in Port Pleasant. And then there were the other accidental factors which contributed to the tragedy – 8 June was a clear, sunny day, ideal for flying, and there were no air defences at Fitzroy. Even though the Rapier units had been landed and set up, their electronics had not settled down and the unit which covered Port Pleasant was inoperational due to a damaged tracker optic. (The hand-held Blowpipe missiles proved to be ineffective.) Also, by early afternoon the Harrier combat air patrol had flown off to chase the decoy Mirage attack to the north and it was not until after the Argentine attack that they were back in the area. (To their credit, later in the day, they shot down three Skyhawks which had sunk the landing-craft *Foxtrot Four* which was carrying 5 Brigade signals equipment from Goose Green.)

In any war errors will be made, there will be an overdose of bad luck and lives will be lost, perhaps unnecessarily. Usually in a long campaign such drawbacks can be weighed against what happened elsewhere and can be seen later in perspective as incidents on a wider canvas. The Argentine air attack at Fitzroy came near the end of a short sharp war which was going Britain's way and which was within a week of coming to an end. Because a large number of lives were lost in circumstances which seemed controversial at the time the Welsh Guards found themselves caught up in an un-welcome incident which was not solely of their making and for which they should not be blamed. It was, admitted an experienced CQMS, one of the misfortunes of the hellish business of war. 'In fact, it didn't take us long to get over it once we came home, even though we'd had a tremendous blow and suffered casualties. I like to think it's something we'll never forget – inevitably it's something which will always be there.'

With the Prince of Wales's Company and 3 Company having to be re-equipped – a task greatly helped by the Master Tailor who joined that gallant band of men who went to war armed with a sewing machine – the battalion was reinforced by two companies of 40 Commando. Their first task was to act as reserve for the attack on Mount Harriet on the night of 11/12 June. There was a spirit of revenge in the air and even though the men were not to take a direct part in the action, they did have the satisfaction of destroying an Argentine machine-gun position with a well-aimed MILAN anti-tank missile fired by a section of the anti-tank platoon. Once again, though, as Johnny Rickett remembers, the physical conditions were extremely difficult and dangerous for a night attack:

> Moving up to get ourselves into position was a most unpleasant business. Two marines lost their feet on mines which seemed to have been scattered indiscriminately everywhere, totally against the Geneva Convention. We were being shelled heavily and could not move quickly enough to get out of the minefield. In addition we had to negotiate yet once more these ghastly 'stone runs', stretches of lichen-covered slippery rocks. These were very difficult to cover even in daylight. At night they were a perfect nightmare. It was one of the most frightening experiences that I can remember.

Before the attack the recce platoon secured the start line on the south-eastern slopes where another mix-up in communications led to Marine allegations that the Welsh Guards had let them down. The commando company complained that the guardsmen were in the wrong place, but this was not so: the recce platoon had been in the correct position two hours before the attack began. According to a sergeant who was there, the commandos 'arrived from the wrong direction, disgruntled and thoroughly pissed off and the word I got from one officer was that he felt like killing his company commander for cocking it up . . . the problem was that we should have been told to change frequencies and to send the code word that we were in position. We were given neither frequency nor code: I took the orders for that operation and I still have them written down.'

On a happier note, Johnny Rickett ruefully admitted to an accompanying correspondent that, under normal circumstances, his battalion should have been on Horse Guards Parade that morning instead of lying in the Falklands' bogs. Like others, he had picked up a broadcast of the Queen's Birthday Parade on the radio. The following day, 13 June, the battalion acted as reserves for the 2nd Scots Guards victorious assault on Mount Tumbledown. Next day they were tasked to attack Sapper Hill in daylight; this would be the final phase of the brigade attack, the feature closest to Stanley and the key to its downfall. Because the ground between Sapper Hill and Mount William – over which the assault would be made – had been mined heavily the men would be lifted forward by helicopter to the start point. This should have been the Welsh Guards' compensation for all the hardships they had to endure but no sooner were the first units in position than a message came over the air announcing an imminent ceasefire. The war was over: the Welsh Guards had only been in the Falklands a mere twelve days, although for most of them it had felt like a lifetime.

Over a month was to pass before the battalion left the Falklands on board the Sealink ferry *St Edmund* bound for Ascension Island and the onward flight by four RAF VC10s to Brize Norton. Before that happy day there were to be further trials and setbacks, all of which threatened to dent further the battalion's already battered pride. On 13 July, while clearing the runway at Stanley, a party of men including six Welsh Guardsmen were seriously wounded when a Sidewinder missile was accidentally discharged from a Harrier: coming on top of the *Galahad* incident and the loss of Lance-Corporal Thomas (03) who was killed by artillery fire on Mount Harriet, it seemed that the gods had temporarily deserted the Welsh Guards.

Once settled in Stanley the men began the massive task of clearing up; according to the Commanding Officer it was an unglamorous though 'difficult, dangerous and time-consuming job with the ever present risk of booby traps and unexploded ordnance.' The Argentinian prisoners of war also had to be dealt with and 2 Company were tasked to provide the guards which accompanied the Argentines back to Puerto Madryn. This could have been a disconcerting task, guarding the military representatives of a power which had wreaked so much havoc on their friends, but needless to say, 'the guardsmen carried out their duties with faultless humanity, sense and good humour.' The Commanding Officer also admitted that the men's experience of Northern Ireland helped them to cope with what could have been an explosive situation. Even more enthralling was their voyage to the same port in Argentina – by chance 'Madryn' is a Welsh name – with the last load of prisoners which included General Menendez, the commander of the Argentine forces in the Falklands. They had been kept longer in British captivity until mid-July as hostages against an outbreak of further hostilities.

And so, after a short eleven weeks of winter war, the men of the task force went back to Britain to meet a rapturous welcome from the British public. The Welsh Guards returned on 29 July to be met by a crowd 5,000 strong which included their Colonel, the Prince of Wales. All were thankful to be home, all regretted the loss of comrades and friends and as happens in time of conflict, all felt deeply united by the experience of war. 'Tell the captain to take us back again,' quipped a guardsman as his VC10 began its approach into Brize Norton, but he said it only half in jest. Many men admitted later to 'a slight reluctance to walk down the steps of the aircraft', and others said that they were taken aback and slightly embarrassed by the warmth of their reception – however well meant it was:

I remember coming up through the Guards Depot at Pirbright on the buses from Brize Norton and the recruits had all been turned out as street liners. And I thought, God, what the hell is happening? I don't want this. I just want to go home to my wife and children and just forget about it. Just let's forget it, get back into civilian clothes, go back to the normal job and put it all to one side.

Later, as the Falklands War became part of history, to be analysed
and re-fought by the experts, the Welsh Guards, too, allowed it to
slip into the past. Everyone who fought there felt transformed in
some small measure by an experience which for one guardsman had
seemed like 'a real solid exercise' until he saw men falling in battle
or being accidentally killed in live minefields. It had been a test –
perhaps the only real test for any soldier – and despite the battalion's
setbacks, the men had come through it older, wiser and more
experienced. In retrospect some began to believe that the war was
unnecessary and that in modern times a diplomatic solution should
have been found before the shooting started. 'All war is hell,'
admitted a young subaltern, echoing Sherman, 'and this just showed
us how hellish it can be. It's not glorious and it's not heroic; nasty
things happen and people get hurt.' There was, too, the enduring
hurt of the *Galahad* and the sudden sight of scar tissue on the limbs
of the survivors would never let men forget what had happened. 'In
a major conflict people have more time to get used to setbacks,' said
one of the company commanders who had served in the Falklands.
'That was denied us and we had to find out the hard way that it is
much easier to win a battle than it is to lose it.'

Of the badly burned men on *Sir Galahad* Simon Weston recovered, retired from the army and after a number of setbacks
established a charity in Liverpool to help unemployed teenagers.
His triumphant experience was told in three BBC television documentaries and later in his autobiography, *Walking Tall*. Hilarian
Roberts, the son of a distinguished Welsh Guards Brigadier J. M.
H. Roberts, returned to the battalion but was sadly killed later in a
motoring accident. The *Sir Galahad* was declared a war grave and
towed out to her final resting place in San Carlos Deep. Out of the
stones of the Falklands the officers and men of 3 Company built a
simple effective monument in the shape of a Welsh Guards leek;
later, in November 1983 it was joined by a more lasting memorial
to the valour of many ordinary men. A ten feet high Celtic Cross
sculpted from good Welsh stone stands above the eastern pro-
montory at Port Pleasant and looks across the waters to where the
Welsh Guards had to face the unimaginable horror and confusion
of war. Its inscription reveals the simple truth: *Yn angof ni chant
fod*. ('We will remember them.')

Chapter Ten

LOOKING BACK: LOOKING FORWARD

IT WAS TO take many months before the Welsh Guards could put behind them the terrible experience of the Falklands War. Although the Commanding Officer could claim at the end of 1982 that 'the extraordinary days of May and June have already acquired a strange and almost dreamlike remoteness', the memory was still too recent to be relegated entirely to the bottom of men's minds. This was especially true for the men who had been wounded on board the *Sir Galahad*. For them the path to recovery was to be long and painful, entailing for some a succession of operations to graft new skin on to badly burned bodies. Simon Weston alone underwent thirty-five operations before he was allowed to leave hospital with his body looking like 'a pink and white chessboard'. As he was to discover, though, he might have won the battle for physical recovery but he still had to wage a war to overcome his mental torment. Two years later, at the end of 1984, he was discharged from the army.

Around one hundred and fifty Welsh Guardsmen were wounded or burned on board the *Sir Galahad*, some less seriously than others, and all made full recoveries. Those who were not severely incapacitated eventually went back to the battalion which had returned to what one officer was moved to describe as 'real soldiering on the barrack square'. After six weeks' block leave the men had reassembled at Pirbright in September to pick up again the timetable of public duties which had been so rudely interrupted three months earlier. A tour of Wales, also postponed from the early summer, took place in October, the battalion dividing in two to visit the northern and southern halves of the country before joining up again to lay up the old colours in Swansea. 'As so often happens,' reported the Commanding Officer 'the people of Wales took the battalion to their hearts and it was a happy and successful tour.' Two months earlier, on 12 July, had seen other members of the regiment in Llandaff Cathedral for a sombre service of thanksgiving for the men of the Welsh Guards and the attached soldiers who had given their lives in the Falklands War. The service was taken by the Dean of Llandaff in the presence of the Colonel of the Regiment, the Prince of Wales, and the address was given by a former chaplain to the Welsh Guards who took as his text St Paul's first lesson to the Corinthians on the resurrection of Christ:

> Those we remember today did their duty – they were called to set out across the wide ocean to a wild windswept speck on the map – to do their duty, just as the Welsh Guards have always done their duty in two World Wars, in Aden, Cyprus and Northern Ireland.
>
> How much criticism is often levelled at the youth of today, let us not forget how many young lives set out, willing to defend everything our country has stood for – the youth of today!

The battalion also found a detachment to take part in the Falklands Parade which took place in London in mid-October but welcome though these public demonstrations of gratitude were, the senior officers in the regiment were understandably anxious to put the past behind them and look only to the future. This was not an easy task for although the wounds had healed the mental scars remained. A sergeant in 3 Company who had been on the tank deck of *Sir Galahad* when the bomb exploded, admitted that he would find himself weeping uncontrollably months afterwards if he unexpectedly thought about a dead friend. A tough no-nonsense individual with ten years service behind him at the time of the Falklands War, he thought that he was alone in his feelings, that it must be due to a terrible weakness, until he discovered that similar feelings haunted other men in his company. It took another year for the sadness to fade away but at the time he admits that it was a painful and dislocating experience. But he was lucky, he adds, some never got over it:

> One lad who lives not far from me at home, who went to school with my wife's brother, he never recovered. I don't think he can live with the fact that so many friends died in such a short space of time and I think that's one of the problems with the army nowadays, and possibly

with society in general. People can't accept death as part of life. I think a lot of people can't accept that you can die at twenty or twenty-two. And if you're a soldier and you go to war, as we did, you've got to expect that people are not going to come back and people are going to die.

Death and wounds in battle are inseparable clauses in the soldier's unwritten contract but no Welsh Guardsman could have expected to honour them in the type of battles fought during the Falklands campaign. The war was too short to allow the men to come to terms with the inevitable and hellish sights that face soldiers in the field of battle and it was difficult to accept the heavy casualties at Fitzroy. At the beginning of the campaign the war seemed more like an exercise than a life or death affair in which lives might be lost. Digging in at San Carlos had an unreal quality and as one officer admitted later, amid the rain and the mud 'no one could say when ENDEX might be'. Even the march into the Sussex Mountains seemed more like the Brecon Beacons writ large than a tactical move in real war. Few were prepared, therefore, for the bizarre and awful effects of modern weapons on suddenly frail and unprotected human bodies, for in addition to the more immediate enemies of the infantryman – the high velocity bullet and the anti-personnel mine – the battalion had to confront the infinitely more complex suffering on board the *Sir Galahad*. 'I didn't reckon with burns when I joined up,' claimed a former guardsman. 'When you enlist in the army you accept that you might be sent to Northern Ireland and be shot or blown up. But I didn't think that I would end up on board a ship in the South Atlantic and see my mates being burned alive.' He has now left the army and admits to being 'a bit of a pacifist'.

Closely associated with the numbness caused by the loss of close friends in unpleasant circumstances was a hollow feeling of personal unworthiness. A few of the men in 3 Company who survived the fire on the tank deck felt unreasonably guilty that they were still alive while their friends were dead. 'Why me? Why was I the lucky one?' was a typical question asked by those who had witnessed the worst effects of the explosion. This is a common enough post-battle syndrome and it has been experienced by front-line soldiers throughout history. It is also more profoundly felt by soldiers in closely knit units. Having lived through a catastrophic experience they start to believe that it is wrong for them to go on living after so

many others have died. At its most obvious it is the regret still felt
by a sergeant who was left behind in an administrative post when
the battalion joined 5 Brigade for the voyage south. 'Most of my
platoon were killed on the *Galahad* so if I had gone it's unlikely
that I would be sitting here now. I should class myself as lucky but
at the time I was really upset that I didn't go with them. The
feeling still gets to me.' Or it can be the lingering grief still felt by a
close friend of Simon Weston who saw the horror on the tank deck.
'No, I can't forget it and I can't forget the boys who died. For a
time I wished that I'd died too – we were such a close group, all
from South Wales – but that feeling soon passed. I just had to get
on with the rest of my life.' Like many others in the same company
he finds that he dislikes the smell of burning meat and while in
Belize he was slightly astonished to find himself shaking after a
Harrier had made a high-speed low-level pass over his camp.

Another, and perhaps more unexpected, aspect of the regiment's
repression of war experience was the belief that the Welsh Guards
had not really performed to the best of their abilities during the
Falklands war:

> In my heart of hearts, no, I don't think that we did acquit ourselves
> well. But not through any fault of our own, through circumstances.
> Once the ship was hit we ceased to exist as a fighting unit. We did have
> the commandos with us for a bit but we weren't committed to a major
> offensive like Tumbledown which the Scots Guards did. Now, seven
> years later, I don't really care but at the time and immediately afterwards
> it did hurt that we were never given the chance to prove ourselves in a
> proper battle.

The sergeant, another older soldier with experience of service in
the border country of Northern Ireland, acknowledged that the loss
of two rifle companies plus all their kit was the reason for any
shortcomings – which are, in any case, entirely imaginary. The
campaign was short: the San Carlos landings began on 21 May and
the surrender was accepted on 14 June and the longest battle,
Goose Green, only lasted twenty-four hours. In such a brief and
tense period men could not react quickly to setbacks: it has to be
remembered that the Welsh Guards lost not only a high proportion
of men at Fitzroy but also their kit, heavy equipment and ammunition. 'I think it would be sad if the rest of the army thought we

weren't up to it,' was the opinion of an older officer, now no longer with the battalion, 'because, having been there, I think that we were in top form. We would have been on Tumbledown had it not been for the *Galahad* and as the Scots Guards proved, that was a remarkably heroic achievement and victory.' As is the case with every other Welsh Guardsman who was in the Falklands he regrets the comments, made by some of the accompanying war correspondents that the battalion could not cope with the conditions. At the time these angered him and they embittered others, especially those singled out for blame, but seven years later he is inclined to the view that they were ill-informed and published before a more reasoned view could be taken of what happened.

Like a ship leaving a strange and fearful island, the Welsh Guards have left the Falklands War far behind them in their wake. There are guardsmen in the battalion for whom it is now ancient history – they might only have been ten years old at the time – and many senior NCOs and officers have passed further up the army's ladder of promotion. The voyage of recovery has been assisted by several cathartic interludes. The pilgrimage made by the bereaved families in 1983 was one, the presence of the Welsh Guards at the launching of the replacement *Sir Galahad* was another. The noble example of Simon Weston also helped the healing process. Horribly burned on board the *Sir Galahad* he underwent a transformation that was both physical and spiritual and few people who saw the three television documentaries on his gradual recovery will ever forget his decency and self-effacing courage. When asked why they had chosen the Welsh Guards ahead of the other Welsh regiments, a handful of shy South Walians at the Guards Depot in 1989 admitted that Simon Weston's story had influenced their decision.

No one who experienced the death and destruction of the Falklands can outlive the grief of war. There is a part of the Welsh Guards that will always be touched by what happened in those remote South Atlantic islands in 1982 but as with all despair, there came a time when the healing process had to begin:

> As soon as we came back from the Falklands we were off on a different tack. We were sent to Germany, we had a new commanding officer and he was extremely robust in his attitude towards the battalion: he insisted that we should be looking ahead instead of behind us with the result that on a day-to-day basis we never think about the Falklands.

Oh, one sits over a pint in the Sergeants' Mess or the Officers' Mess on occasions and talks about it and sometimes you will see a sergeant with a badly burned hand and you'll think, 'Gosh, he was there with us.' But, no, we don't dwell on it at all nowadays.

The officer, now in his early thirties, was a young man when he witnessed war at the sharp end and he believes firmly that the experience provided him with a new perception of himself as a soldier. Before he went to the war in the Falklands fighting was just a glorious adventure and his mind was filled with the imagery of derring-do fostered by the Victorian paintings he had seen at Sandhurst, all flashing swords and high gallantry. 'But when I see guys still in the battalion with crinkly skin on the backs of their hands or with scar tissue on their arms when their sleeves are rolled up, they serve as a very good reminder that war isn't glorious or even terribly heroic.'

It is not within the nature of the well balanced soldier to dwell overlong on past setbacks. To do so, as every good commander knows, is to allow whole groups of men to sink into a morass of despair from which they can only be extracted with the utmost care. Here the Welsh Guards were helped both by their past traditions as a Guards regiment and by their position as a key infantry regiment in the modern British Army, neither of which gave them any time for introspection. Within a year of returning to London the Welsh Guards began training for conversion to its new role as a mechanized infantry battalion in 22 Armoured Brigade, part of the British Army of the Rhine. It was twelve years since they had been in Germany and they had just finished four years of public duties, a period that had taken them to exercises in Kenya and Cyprus, to operational tours in Northern Ireland and the Falklands and adventure training from the Appalachians in the United States to the Cairngorms in Scotland. As one senior officer noted, on the surface, it was a fair demonstration of the range and variety of life in the British Army, and, as far as he was concerned, the Welsh Guards' recruiting figures reflected that happy fact. It was what lay beneath the surface of events that gave him pause for thought, for the regiment's ability to continue attracting recruits in similar numbers is another matter. The economic position in Wales has improved dramatically in the latter years of the 1980s, young men tend not to emigrate to England in the same numbers that they did a decade earlier and the regiment will have to face the fact of the approaching demographic trough. In other words, the Welsh Guards may find that in the years to come Wales will no longer produce the rich harvest of young men that has swelled its ranks in years gone by.

To overcome that difficulty will take time, trouble and not a little imagination, as most senior members of the regimental hierarchy admit. It will not be enough to promote only the glamour of being a Welsh Guardsman in a red tunic outside one of London's Royal palaces, the image that is all too often associated with the regiments of Foot Guards. 'When you think about joining the army you imagine, well, the worst thing that can happen is that someone will shoot me,' admitted a terribly young looking guardsman who will leave the Welsh Guards to join the Metropolitan Police, even if it means forsaking Wales for the south-east of England. 'So you join with that in mind, sign on the dotted line, knowing that you could end up dead. Instead you do three years of Queen's Guards and there isn't a lot of danger there.' The men in his platoon nod their heads in agreement – we are talking in the hot afternoon sunshine of Belize, not very far away from the border they have been told they are guarding. In a few months time they know they will be back in London on the treadmill of public duties in the depths of winter, without the sustaining admiration of summertime tourists.

'It's too much like a nine to five job; you work, you get time off and at first you can't get enough of it. Then the excitement wears off and you feel more like a dressmaker's dummy than a real soldier.' The guardsmen were giving vent to a perennial problem, one that has been voiced often in the past but one which seems to be gaining a new urgency as the Welsh Guards enter the last quarter of their first hundred years, a time that will see them pass into the twenty-first century. They are a Household regiment and they are as proud of that fact as they are of their ability to do all the operational tasks carried out by the infantrymen of the line regiments. The trouble is, as some of the older NCOs admitted, they have a split personality. Their minds tell them that they are a regiment whose ceremonial duties must come first and that perfection must be their constant aim; but their hearts also say that they would rather be out in the field on exercise 'digging holes and sleeping rough'. And, being Welshmen with all their countrymen's inborn ability to swing high and hard between the two extremes, the Jekyll and Hyde existence can be an uneasy burden:

> I don't think there's a man, if he's really honest, who doesn't feel the hair rise on the back of his neck when he marches on to the Forecourt of Buckingham Palace. It's good for the old ego. But sometimes, when they reflect on the down side, they definitely go through the doldrums and say that public duties are tedious. What helps them is a great natural resilience but you have to remind them that they have it.

The company commander, a surprisingly young officer, sees the consequences of too much public duties in the numbers of men who leave the battalion after completing the minimum of three years service. 'Normally they've given it a good try but they only want to do something different before it's too late. One of my men told me that although an employer might be impressed by his appearance and bearing, what else could he offer by way of training? I fear that might be true.' One solution which the company commander and others of his age and experience would like to see adopted is a reduction in the number and frequency of public duties but, realistically, that could only be granted with Royal approval. 'No one wants to duck out of the responsibility,' he insists. 'After all, we're jealous of our status with the monarchy and mightily proud of our expertise at drill. The actual parading we don't mind at all but the end result is that we can't always run things as well as we'd like to.'

Another solution would be to spend more time in Wales: this idea is much favoured by the younger guardsmen who often feel orphaned from their past when they live in Chelsea or Pirbright. Whereas the Scots Guards feel quite at home in Scotland – the new colours of the 2nd Battalion were last presented to them in the grounds of Hopetoun House outside Edinburgh – the Welsh Guards only visit Wales infrequently. There are good historical and logistical reasons for this apparent anomaly – Scotland has an established military presence, Wales does not, apart from the large training areas – but such sophistry does not always make sense to the average guardsman. He knows that the regiment has the honour of having the freedom of seven Welsh cities, boroughs or towns (Swansea, Aberystwyth, Cardiff, Caernarfon, Carmarthen, Merthyr Tydfil, Taff-Ely), but he would like the presence to be more

visible, especially after he had heard the older men talking about
the recruiting tours and the appearances at the Cardiff Tattoo.
'Spending three weeks there was tremendous. It gave us a real fillip
appearing in front of our friends and families; it made us feel good
and it made them feel proud.' In that way, they argue, the people
of Wales come to recognize them as a proper Welsh regiment and
not as an alien Anglo-Welsh outfit whose roots and traditions have
been transplanted to London and the south-east of England.

But perhaps that, too, is only part of the antisyzygy, the zigzag of
contradictions that runs through the public perception of the Welsh
Guards. They were raised as a Welsh regiment of the Royal
Household and over the years they have proved themselves illustri-
ous members of that great institution. In time of war, during the
two world wars of this century, in Aden, Northern Ireland and the
Falklands they have emerged as doughty fighters, fierce in attack
and stalwart in defence. Modestly, they will say that while they are
no better than any one else no other regiment can surpass them.
That, said one of the younger generation of officers, was the true
meaning of being a Welsh Guardsman. A polo player with a keen
interest in field sports he could be regarded by some as an a-typical
Guards officer, were it not for his well stocked library and keen
interest in contemporary theatre. The image could have been
reinforced in Belize when at dinner in his mess the silver stood on
the table and the port was passed. Outwith the verandah's pool of
light in whatever savagery lay beyond, insects buzz-buzzed and the
night was alive with the sounds and shrieks of the tropics. The
shade of many a pre-war empire builder would have walked into
that welcoming mess and immediately felt at home. 'That would be
to miss the point, though' added the major. 'These aren't just for
show. They're a tangible reminder of the traditions that have made
us what we are today and they make us humble, I hope, when we
think of those who went before us, some of whom presented these
pieces to the regiment. Besides, any fool can be uncomfortable in
the jungle: we prefer not to be!'

It would be misleading, perhaps, to leave the last word with the
officers mess. That a sense of regimental pride pervades the Welsh
Guards is obvious, that they are willing to demonstrate it to others
is a sign of their self-confidence. One of the platoon sergeants in
Belize who had earlier poured scorn on the time-honoured notion
of the regiment as extended family cheerfully contradicted himself

when regimental pride came into the conversation. He had been posted to a Royal Artillery regiment to teach them the mysteries of drill for a Queen's Guard. The Gunners were delighted both by his soldierly bearing and mirror-like boots and by his total reliance on his pace-stick which he had set to a thirty-inch pace. 'That was what they wanted to see – this picture of a Guards sergeant pace-sticking everywhere.' And he played up to the image for all that it was worth even when the camp went on to a state of high alert. It was then that he showed his true mettle. 'Someone came over to my office and asked me to move my car from in front of the Sergeants' Mess – and to do it as soon as possible as it was a real emergency. So I just started calmly undoing my pace-stick and they started shouting, 'What are you doing?' I merely said, 'I'm setting it to a thirty-three-inch pace so that I can get there faster!' Where other people are concerned, he added, appearances can sometimes be more important than reality.

A regiment, though, is only the sum of its many parts; a battalion is only as good as the people who comprise it. Both are ever changing organisms which have to struggle to keep a sense of continuity and community in an army whose whole purpose is forward progress. Those who made up the Welsh Guards during its first seventy-five years will soon pass into history, but others will arrive to take their place. Only a percentage of their stories and experiences have been told in this account. Some have been introduced by name, others anonymously by rank. Many more have not been mentioned at all, a poor recompense, they might think, for all their endeavours. Yet they can take comfort in one simple fact: whenever the words 'Welsh Guards' or 'battalion' have been used, it is the achievement of the Welsh Guardsmen that is meant.

Index